AF540623

LIBRARY INFORMATION SERVICES AND SYSTEMS

By
Dr. Pankaj Kumar Singh
Librarian & H.O.D.
Dept. of Library & Information Science
D.S.N. (P.G.) College
Unnao - 209 801 (U.P.)
(India)

DISCOVERY PUBLISHING HOUSE PVT. LTD.
NEW DELHI-110 002

Published by:
Namit Wasan
DISCOVERY PUBLISHING HOUSE PVT. LTD.
4383/4B, Ansari Road, Darya Ganj
New Delhi-110 002 (India)
Phone : +91-11-23279245; 23253475; 43596065
E-mail : discoverybooksindia@gmail.com
discoverypublishinghouse@gmail.com
namitwasan9@gmail.com
web : www.discoverypublishinggroup.com

***Reprinted:* 2019**

***First Edition:* 2014**

ISBN: 978-93-5056-428-8

Library Information Services and Systems

Printed at:
Infinity Imaging Systems
Delhi

Preface

Libraries are part of the human environment. They represent our attempts to understand, to wonder, and to reflect on the myriad wonderfulness of our universes, local and far away, real and imagined. Libraries house riches, from books to journals to maps to globes to pictures in all sort of two- and three-dimensional formats. Libraries also provide ways of knowing and understanding a topic or place or persons through classification and naming. Libraries provide ways to access and acquire those materials that can give us a deeper understanding of all those factors that make us human and that help create societies. Libraries are also places of instruction, of learning how to find that bit of knowledge that keeps us wondering of lying awake at night trying to figure it out.

Library information services and systems have been part of college and university computing systems since the early-1980 would seem to be 'old technology' and part of text-based mainframe systems. In the past decade of this age of information, a shift in awareness of the role of monitoring and information has become apparent. Today's library information services and systems is a multi-function web-based multimedia content information management system, generally built on a standard relational database structure. While the system architecture remains grounded in bibliographic citations presented via structured indexes, the basis of these indexes is moving beyond the MARC fields designed for text information to include metadata descriptions for multiple digital file formats and content.

—Author

Contents

1

Library and Information Technology

The *'Information Technology'* revolution has brought about impact upon the society and economy activities. Information has become a significant component of world economy activity and being recognised as a major economic resource. Organisations have grown to view their information resources as a *strategic asset,* utilising these resources as an instrument in enhancing the country's competitiveness in industry and international trade.

Traditionally, major organisational assets were classified as human, financial, material, equipment and management resources. Khosrowpour view that during the decade of the 1980s, the technological advancements of information technology caused many organisations to regard their information technology resources as the *sixth major organisational asset.* Harker claimed that a tidal wave of *change* is headed towards the *telecommunication industry,* and it will ultimately transform the economic, and social and political environment for nearly every person in the world.

Researcher added that technological advancements in telecommunications allowed information users to exchange information more freely and globally. Living standards have been raised and the problems of everyday living eased considerably. Much of this change is being brought by *technological innovation* and the *information revolution*—the convergence of computing, communication and information.

Organisations that acknowledge and prepare for this revolution will emerge as winners.

THE EVOLUTION OF INFORMATION TECHNOLOGY

Researcher provide a comprehensive remarks of the evolution of IT where he claimed that during the 1950s, computer systems were used mainly for scientific applications, with scientists the primary users and custodians of these systems. Business use of computers for mainly functional applications, such as accounting, began in the 1960s. The era of the 60s is known for the birth of *Data Processing (DP)* or *Electronic Data Processing (EDP),* which created a whole new profession.

During this period:

- The computer was perceived as a number crunching tool.
- Attention was focused on the power of these modem tools to compute, with much less emphasis placed on the overall value of information as a resource.

In the 1970s, more organisations moved towards the use of computers to provide management with information. This concept soon became known as *Management Information Systems (MIS).* Although MIS concepts were considered to be a major breakthrough in the use of computer systems to process information, organisations still emphasised the computer itself rather than focusing on the data and information as major components of the systems.

Many other concepts evolved during this period, examples:

- Database Management Systems (DBMS).
- Decision Support Systerns (DSS).

The domination of mainframe computer systems gave way to the introduction of *minicomputers.* This new generation of computers became instrumental in the development of *Distributed Systems (DS).* The introduction of personal computers or microcomputers was another landmark development of this period. The technological advancements of the 1970s paved the way for a new era in the 1980s, which became known as the *Information Age.*

The significant phenomena of this era include the greater recognition of information as a major organisational asset and its importance in a competitive world economy. Another important characteristic of this era is the emphasis on the management of information and related resources utilised to maintain information resources. Furthermore, greater participation by users of information services became a major fact of this age.

The new generation of end users are more knowledgeable than their counterparts of a few decades earlier, and they created many networks of information systems sharing the vast powers of computers, data, information, and knowledge. In addition, technological advancements in telecommunications allowed information users to exchange information more freely than ever. The old dream of developing computer systems that could think intelligently, learn, and make recommendations to decision makers carne closer to reality through many new applications of *Artificial Intelligent (AI)* and its component Expert Systems (ES).

New Information Technology Resources

There are several developments which have lead to a new perception and assessment of the use and management of information technology resources.

These include:

- Recognition of information as a major organisational resource.
- Greater emphasis on utilisation of information as a major driving force in achieving effective strategies.
- New integration of telecommunications and information processing systems.
- A vast array of components comprising information technology resources.

Today, information technology resources consists of all types of information, representing various *functional entities* of organisations. Organisational information now can appear in all forms, which are processed by a conglomeration of computer machinery, examples:

- Mainframe,
- Minicomputers,
- Microcomputers,
- Reprographics, and
- Video discs.

It is communicated through the use of communication systems. The information is generated through the use of many information processing and management systems in diverse organisational structures. In addition to mechanical, procedural, and technical components of information technology resources, one must also consider the human elements.

These human elements can be divided into three categories:

1. Those individuals who are involved in different activities of generating information.
2. Those who are the primary users of information.
3. The management team responsible for the overall management planning functions of information technology resources.

One can argue that the role of the information technology resources management team has become more important to the overall success and growth of many organisations. In addition, the task of managing these resources is far more complex and sophisticated in the information age. Information technology resources are no longer viewed by many organisations as number crunching 'black boxes,' but rather as vital resources for identifying new opportunities and developing strategies.

Information Management in the 1990s

The cost of computing has dropped drastically in the past two decades. There is considerably more advanced information and communication devices available. AB a result, organisations of all sizes and types have been employing this technology to increase their competitive advantages. With the rapid evolution in information technology, the effectiveness of the traditional management techniques to the management of this technology has been the subject of much speculation by both researchers and practicing managers.

Clearly, this changing technology is in need of an evolution in its management as well:

- A management approach that is as dynamic as the technology itself,
- Keeping pace in its methods and strategies as the technology matures,
- Making drastic shifts in direction when necessary, and
- Always providing new opportunities for growth, is the essential ingredient for strategic management of information technology resources.

As information technology resources become more important to the overall success of the organisation, its management may not only be limited by technical planning and execution as was true in the past. With the current number of end users and their demands for information technology services, successful organisations will utilise the expertise of their information tecnnology personnel to provide needed support for the end user in order to obtain the necessary competitive edge.

COMPONENTS OF INFORMATION TECHNOLOGY RESOURCES

Processing Hardware:

- Mainframe-based Systems.
- Mini-based Systems.
- Micro-based Systems.
- Word Processing.
- Micrographics.
- Reprographics.
- Video Disks Processor.
- Desktop Publishing Systems.

Telecommunications:

- Private Branch Exchange (PBX).
- Broadcasting Systems.

- Local Area Networks.
- Telecommunication Access.
- Systems.
- Facsimile Systems.
- Satellite Communications.
- On-Line Processing Systems.

Information:

- Marketing.
- Production.
- Personnel.
- Financial.
- Strategic.
- Intelligent.
- Accounting.
- Legal.
- Economy.
- Government.
- Trade.
- Publication.
- Public.

Office Automation:

- Text Management Systems.
- Electronic Mail.
- Teleconferencing.
- Computer Conferencing.
- Video Conferencing.
- Intelligent Copies.
- Intelligent Printers.
- Dictating Systems.

Systems Professionals:

- Chief Information Officer (CIO).
- Systems Managers.
- Systems Security.
- Administrators.
- System Analysts.
- Database Designers.
- Programmers.
- Computer Operators.

- Data Entry Personnel.
- User Support Personnel.

Processing Software:

- Operating Systems.
- Database Management Systems.
- Procedural Programming Languages.
- Fourth Generation Languages.
- Word Processing Software.
- Electronic Spreadsheet Software.
- Communications Software.
- Graphics and Desktop Publishing Systems.
- Project Management Software.
- Miscellaneous Software.

Management Structures:

- Centralised vs. Decentralised Structures.
- Departmental Computing Structure.
- Information Center Structure.
- End-User Computing Structure.
- Chargeback Processing Structure.

Information Systems:

- Data Processing Systems.
- Management Information Systems.
- Decision Support Systems.
- Transaction Processing Systems.
- Expert and Knowledge-Based Systems.
- Database Processing Systems.
- Executive Information Systems.
- Distributed Processing Systems.

End Users:

- Strategic Planners.
- Financial Managers.
- Marketing Managers.
- Inventory Managers.
- Production Managers.
- Personnel Managers.
- General Managers.
- Accountants.
- Legal Advisors.

- Economics.
- Publication Personnel.
- Training Personnel.
- Public Relations Personnel.
- Clerical Staff.
- Technical Specialists.

NEW INFORMATION TECHNOLOGY (IT) PRODUCTS

MOST IMPORTANT PRODUCTS OF THE '90S

The 1990s was a decade of rapid technological advances. Client-server architecture evolved into a viable alternative to mainframe computing. Enterprise applications such as groupware, inventory control, supply chain, and systems management emerged as platforms for the evolution of business systems. The PC became a Ubiquitous and increasingly powerful desktop tool. And the Internet was embraced as a communication medium, consumer platform, and business conduit. Here are 10 of the most important and influential products introduced in this decade.

1. *Sun Microsystems' Java:* The brave little embedded operating system started out as a platform for write-once-run-anywhere computing and ended up as the Web's favourite tool.
2. *Nets Cape Navigator:* There's probably no greater development in the history of IT than the emergence of the Internet and World Wide Web. By the time Marc Andreessen and Jim Clark launched their graphical Web browser, Navigator 1.0, in 1994, there were more than 1 million Internet hosts. While Mosaic was the first widely distributed browser, Navigator set the standard in terms of look and functionality. And in the process, it shook Microsoft to its core—no small feat.
3. *Lotus Notes:* Lotus Development Corp. licensed Notes, the product most commonly associated with the term groupware, from Iris Associates in 1989. By the time IBM bought Lotus in 1995 for $3.5 billion—primarily

to acquire the groupware technology—Notes had an installed base of almost 2 million seats. Lotus made a successful effort to integrate Notes with the Internet when it introduced Domino in 1996.

4. *Microsoft Office:* Microsoft didn't come up with the idea to bundle a spreadsheet, word processor, and graphics package into a productivity suite, but it made the most of the concept-and created a business computing standard. Microsoft has continued to enhance the bundle, including links to the Internet.
5. *Oracle's Relational Database:* The original work on relational database technology was done by Edgar Codd when he was at IBM in the early 1970s. However, Oracle took the relational model and established it as a database standard, through both rapid technological advance and aggressive marketing. In the 1990s, Oracle continued to enhance the basic architecture to incorporate symmetric multiprocessing and object extensions.
6. *Sun Microsystems' Enterprise 10000 Server:* Sun made believers out of many of those who had been skeptical about the scalability of symmetric multiprocessing servers when it shipped the 64-node E-I0000 in May 1997.
7. *SAP Rl3:* The third version of SAP's suite of enterprise applications, introduced in 1992, integrated and automated back-office systems and convinced many companies to re-engineer their business processes to accommodate the software.
8. *Computer Associates' Unicenter:* Introduced in 1993, CA's systems management software unified a disparate set of products and processes, and provided a comprehensive view of IT systems. CA continued to strengthen the product with the introduction of the graphical, object-oriented TNG version in 1997 and the three dimensional TND version in 1998.
9. *Intel's X86 Architecture:* Intel led the PC industry on

a price/performance curve that mirrored Moore's Law-and then some. When Intel launched the 66-MHz Pentium processor in 1993, it set the stage for a quantum leap in desktop processing, making possible powerful personal productivity applications and eventually online commerce.

10. *Microsoft Windows:* In the spring of 1990, Microsoft CEO Bill Gates introduced the latest iteration of the company's graphical front end, Windows 3.1 and it was an instant hit with the public. Since then, billions of copies of the operating system have been sold, and, along with its siblings, Windows NT and Windows CE, Windows has proved to be one of the highest-impact products in IT.

WELCOME TO THE INFORMATION SUPERDORM

Malone regard that "we are now at the threshold of a new era, driven this time not by the technologies of production and transportation, but by the technologies of information, communication and coordination." An extraordinary array of information technologies is providing not only powerful new tools for dealing with these changes, but also a promising framework for creating entirely new opportunities. Advances in computers, software, telecommunications, networking, and electronic media are vastly increasing the quantity, quality, and accessibility of all forms of information.

Internet

Internet as a "bunch of communications protocols that enables millions of computers to talk with each other. It is already replacing overnight mail and faxes as a way to communicate quickly and over long distances.

Begun as a research project of the US Defence Department in the 1970s, it has become the:

- Technological trend in academic libraries of the '90s with dial up databases such as CompuServe, small corporate and university databases that are interconnected via the Internet.

- Thousands of companies have started to promote and sell products over the Net and at the same time, businesses are discovering that they can streamline operations and increased productivity by connecting their in-house networks to the Internet.

Almost overnight, the net grows from an academic resource into an ocean of capitalist dream.

World Wide Web

Subscribing to the Internet opens the door to many different types of information and communication possibilities. The World Wide Web, a *subset* of the Internet and one of the Internet's most popular and employs simpler computer applications, such as Windows, and more transparent commands then the internet.

By using browser software and fast modems, a subscriber can easily:

- View individuals' and organisations' home pages.
- Graphical tables of contents to more-detailed files contained within.
- Best of all, a user need not be a computer pro or a rocket scientist to surf the Net.

With the attributes such as multimedia, hyper linked, dispersed, dynamic, versatile and multi platform, the reason for Web popularity is the ability it affords to send and receive graphics, photographs, movies, and sound along with text. Several factors have contributed to this rapid growth, "most notably, technological advances in software, hardware, and communications that have made connections more economical".

Electronic Mail (E-Mail)

A way for computer users to exchange messages in completely different offices, locations, organisations, cities, countries, even continents using the e-mail programme available through the *Internet Service Provider* (ISP) to create, read, and manage the e-mail messages. Educationally, e-mail has continue to grow more important. It has also become easier to exchange not only textual messages but a variety of files, including graphics, software programmes, spreadsheets, and databases. Ingram believe that e-mail will become part of a total distance-education system that might include elements of videoconferencing, interactive multimedia, and other learning tools.

Lotus Notes

A complete 'environment' or 'platform' for several computer applications and can be used:

- to send electronic mail,
- As an electronic calendaring system,
- As a scheduling system.
- As a bulletin board.
- As a publishing system for the web,
- As an automated workflow system and
- As a group ware system.

Intranets

James view Intranet as a network that lets people within an organisation share the kind of information one's can experience—and create—with Netscape Communicator Professional such as:

- Pages full of text, graphics, sound, and video;
- Fill-out form;
- e-mail with pictures;
- Specialised newsgroup and interactive conferences;
- Directories full of files one's can download; and
- A broad range of custom-tailored resources for research, education, or business.

Thus by using a standardised methods, or protocols for moving information from one computer to another, an entire office, or even a corporation with many physically remote sites, can communicate without worrying about specific hardware or software.

Multimedia

Multimedia tools enable us to express ideas that are more difficult to describe with words than they are to demonstrate in some way. For those who are aural or tactile learners, for example, multimedia provides a fresh new means of comprehending something.

Videoconferencing

Ingram claim that videoconferencing is increasingly used for individual and group meetings as well as to delivêr education and training at a distance. Brown University Computing and Information Services view videoconferencing as an interactive audio/visual meeting channel to sites worldwide via high speed telephone lines. Thus, videoconferencing combines the benefits of face-to-face interaction with the power of telecommunications.

As claimed by Littman, the videoconferencing rationales are as follows:

- Enhance the quality and intensity of communications.
- Engender a sense of responsibility and involvement among individuals who could not otherwise meet with each other.
- Lead to the articulation of policy, goals, and objectives through consensual decision making.
- Enable academic librarians to hold interactive sessions regardless of location on such topics as Internet access and use, intellectual freedom and copyright.
- High school students can be introduced to resources in an academic library, thus saving field trip and liability insurance costs.

Virtual Reality

Virtual reality has captured most organisations. It benefits an organisation, by gathering information on customers/users, competitors, and potential markets.

Cavanaugh describes the creation of 'virtual offices' that has enable:

- Communications between employees and vendors.
- Advertise products and services globally.
- Deliver new products or packages of services.

CD-ROMs

Rogers view that the advent of CD-ROMs in libraries was the introduction to the world of high-tech ware for many librarians. CD-ROMs are found in every library today and are loaded on most business networks but are often simply presented to end users, from car mechanics to astronauts. This technology is revolutionising the way students and professionals can assemble and access information.

Being fixed systems:

- The *content* on CD-ROMs is finite, although the amount of information on a disc is still impressive.
- The *functionality* of CD-ROMs and the number of tricks they can perform is finite.

Amendments to the software, indexing, and content are done at the will of the developer and information provider. A number of business databases available on CD-ROMs has increased steadily over the past few years. At the same time, most major public libraries, colleges, and *university libraries* have made available at no cost numerous CD-ROM databases for user and customer use.

CD-ROMs Into the Future

Beiser stresses that the emergence of a high-density CD (HiCD) technology opens exciting new possibilities for all sectors of our society—not the least of which are *libraries.* CD-ROMs was a distribution and publishing medium, and not a competitor to hard disk drives. Meanwhile, HiCD can deliver text, graphics and multimedia content as well or better than a high-speed link. It is the stuff of memory cells, the repository of incredible amounts of otherwise evanescent data, a resource without which libraries will be unable to perform their designated role in an information intensive universe.

Online Databases

It offers full texts of journal and magazine articles. Tenopir claimed that academic librarians are actively looking for alternatives to print journal collections:

- As serials budgets stagnate,
- Print journals take up as much space.
- Patrons want to locate and access everything from a single workstation.

Some examples of online databases are EBSCO Elite Periodical Database, FirstSearch Online Databases, INFOTRAC Periodical and Newspaper Databases, etc.

Electronic Journals

Researcher claimed that electronic journals are mushrooming online, on the Web and in CD-ROM format. This phenomenon is due to the rapid advancement of information technologies including the Internet and digitising techniques. The quantity of e-journals is growing larger although no exact number is available.

In recent years, many more journals have been earmarked for digitising, a necessary process for turning a paper journal into an electronic one. In addition, a considerable number of journals are now published only electronically, which significantly enlarges the size of the e-journal pool. Among all the users of e-journals, academic libraries especially, are the major subscribers of e-journals.

ROLE OF INFORMATION TECHNOLOGY IN MANAGING ORGANISATIONAL

Researcher provide a comprehensive remark of the role of IT in managing organisational change and interdependence. He commented that the world is observing a strong trend of convergence of the technologies of computing and telecommunications. Changing technology economics, merging of formerly disparate technologies with different managerial traditions, and the problems of managing each of the phases of IT assimilation in different ways calls for a major reappraisal of the organisational structures designed for yesteryears. IT is becoming all pervasive and is having impact on all business—in service as well as in manufacturing. It is affecting workers at all levels of organisations—from the executives to assembly hands and clerks. IT is increasingly becoming an integral component of all types of technologies—craft, engineering, routine and non- routine.

IT'S ROLE IN MANAGING ORGANISATIONAL CHANGE

IT and Environment - Goals-Structure

Researcher defined environment as those factors which not only are outside the system's control but which determine in part how the system performs.

Uncertainty is the difference between the amount of information required to perform the task and the amount of information already possessed by the organisation:

- *Proposition* 1: Turbulent environment drives organisations to use IT for monitoring the preferences of the environment. System theorists have recognised the importance of 'feedback' for the survival of the system and for maintaining a 'steady state' or 'homeostasis'. Organisations are purposive systems that learn of the impending threats by scanning. Scanning is the process by which the organisation acquires information for decision making. The modes of scanning are primarily determined by the external environmental stimuli and are determined by the magnitude and by the direction of the discrepancy between the goal and its realisation. While surveillance is useful for information-gathering process, search is oriented towards finding a satisfactory solution to a specific problem. Complex systems require complex controllers. IT will provide the 'complex controller" to the increasingly complex organisation. The information systems of an organisation need to evolve to remain consistent with the changing organisational structure. Referring to the obscurity of causal laws of turbulence, Aldrich argued that scanning could provide the firm with the desired 'competitive edge.'

- *Proposition* 2: Turbulent environment drives organisations to use IT for translating the information on environmental preferences into goals. Continuously changing environment requires organisations to continuously reassess their goals. Effective structuring requires a consistency among the design parameters and contingency factors have demonstrated that organisations' goals can be generated by external forces, such as other groups seeking to use the organisation to further their own ends.
- *Proposition* 3: Turbulent environment drives organisations to use IT to align their structure with environmental preferences. The very efforts of the organisation to maintain a constant external environment produce changes in organisational structure. Scott argued that organisational structure and goals are driven by the preferences in the environment. The structure is determined by the information- processing capacity requirements of the organisation which in turn are governed by the IT being used. Aldrich, Perrow, Walker and Woodward have attributed structural differences to the organisation's technology. Mintzberg had suggested that the organisation's environment and technology are the independent variables that determine the structural variables of the organisation. Fowles, in his narrative on the history of organisational communications technologies contends that the phenomenal expansion of organisations can be largely attributed to advances in the technologies of organisational communication. Yates argued that in absence of technological communication organisations could have evolved differently. Preliminary econometric analyses of the overall U.S., economy for the period 1975-1985 further confirms that the increased use of IT is correlated with decreases in firm size and vertical integration.

IT and Organic Structure

- *Proposition* 4: Turbulent environment drives organisations to make more use of IT for increasing their 'organic' characteristics. 'Organic' firms are better equipped to sustain themselves in turbulent environment. A dynamic environment will drive the structure to an organic state despite other forces; the more complex the environment, the more decentralised the structure. Introduction of IT at the 'operating core' level transforms a bureaucratic administrative structure into an organic one. Effectively, automation of routine tasks eliminates the source of many of the social conflicts throughout the organisation. Law of requisite variety implies that the rate of change of organisational systems must correspond to the rate of change of environmental systems, *i.e.*, organisations with complex environmental interactions would develop complex structures like adhocracies or networks. Adhocracy is suitable for a dynamic and complex environment, when the firm has sophisticated technical systems and the focus is upon consistently offering differentiated products for retaining the customers. Future organisations would be 'networks' characterised by adhocracies with flexible systems of projects and teams brought together quickly to accomplish specific tasks. Some existing organisations have already 'farmed out' their operations by establishing them as separate organisations or contracting them out to other organisations.
- *Proposition 4a:* Turbulent environment drives organisations to use IT for empowering workers at all levels. Growing availability of telecommunications has offered technologies like distributed systems and client-server architecture that facilitate the process of empowerment of the lower levels. In the 'informated' organisation, workers would be 'empowered' by virtue of access to necessary information to perform

higher-level tasks. Ramstrom has argued that tactical decisions relating to 'soft' information would be delegated to the 'grass-roots' where there is easy access to relevant information concerning the immediate environment, at the same time providing these levels with the information generated within the system by means of 'cheap' internal information systems.

- *Proposition 4b:* Turbulent environment drives organisations to use IT for increasing the spans of control. Information technologies, by facilitating the standardisation of coordination would facilitate larger spans of control or work units which would be characterised by extensive lateral communication and self- contained authority structures.
- *Proposition 4c:* Turbulent environment drives organisations to use IT for increasing lateral communications. Selective use of lateral decision processes for situations involving task uncertainty increase the information processing capacity of the organisation. Bringing the points of decision down to the points of action reduces the information overload on the managers. Since specification of 'procedures' in complex situations creates inefficiencies, organisations in turbulent environments would use more IT resource for delegating the decision-making to workers. Increased use of groupware for lateral coordination will spell the demise of middle management.

IT and Differentiation - Integration

- *Proposition* 5: Turbulent environment drives organisations to reduce their 'dimensions' by focusing on core competencies by leveraging their use of IT.
- *Proposition 5a:* Turbulent environment drives organisations to use IT to reduce differentiation and integration to focus on increased specialisation. Organisations structure themselves to minimize

coordination costs and group together similar activities to achieve the benefits of process specialisation. Environmental uncertainty or 'task predictability' is the basic independent variable influencing the design of the organisation. Faced with increased uncertainty, organisations can reduce the need for information processing by decreasing the 'diversity of outputs'. Reduced differentiation and integration of activities would decrease the coordination effort involved thus reducing the information processing requirements. Reduced coordination costs with IT would result in the substitution of IT for human coordination. Greater specialisation would be achieved by focusing on few core competencies.

IT's Role in Managing Organisational Interdependencies

- *Proposition* 6: Turbulent environment drives organisations to actively seek Inter-organisational relations to leverage their core competencies. Cooperation, especially in the international context, will be necessary to gain a competitive advantage in the future. To survive in an increasingly competitive environment, firms would form alliances that would bring together their core competencies to create the 'best of all" products.
- *Proposition 6a:* Turbulent environment drives organisations to reduce environmental complexity and uncertainty by seeking interdependencies with other organisations in the environment.
- *Proposition 6b:* Turbulent environment drives organisations to use more IT - effort to establish coordinating mechanisms with other firms.

To survive in the fast-changing environment the 'adaptive organisation" would be more like a shifting 'constellation' that has 'linkages' with independent and semi- autonomous organisations. Use of inter organisational linkages such as EDI would enable new forms of organisations and reduce the coordination costs of increasingly market-driven organisations.

Increasingly, electronic linkages are becoming the necessary condition of doing businesses with larger firms. Using an analogy to the study of community chests conducted by Litwak and Hylton, we observe that in the increasingly global competition, the firms are competing for the common customers' 'fund' and the increase in one firm's revenue would come at the expense of other firm's loss. Coordination, being a function of interdependency, should grow in periods of increased competition for 'funds.'

The IT Paradox

- *Proposition* 7: Increasingly turbulent environment would feed the need for further advancements in IT which would further increase turbulence.

Business needs are incessantly driving the demands for increased capabilities of IT. In turn, increasingly advanced IT is being utilised in more and more sophisticated ways by the businesses to outdo competition. IT, which is being deployed as a solution to the increased complexity and uncertainty of the environment, has paradoxically contributed to the situation by 'compressing time and distance.' In absence of the present day advances in IT, would we be talking of globalisation or time based competition? Perhaps, not.

The pace of complexity is increasing fast. Hopefully, the advances in technology would be able to keep up with the environmental changes. Turbulence refers not to chaos in the environment, but to an increasing causal interconnection that renders environments obscure to local observers. Thus how can IT help organisations in responding to the challenges of an increasingly complex and uncertain environment? How can IT help the organisations achieve the 'flexible' organisation structure? We provide academic libraries as a living educational example that has been impacted by the strong trend of convergence of the technological advancements.

THE IMPACT OF INFORMATION TECHNOLOGY ON ACADEMIC LIBRARIES

In the 1990s, academic libraries are undergoing

unprecedented change deriving from a combination of accelerating prices of library materials and space, an enormous increase in the amount and types of materials available, and rapid development in electronic technologies. Whatever the local differences in academic librarianship in the countries today, there is no question that information technology is transforming research, scholarship, teaching and learning, and with it, the role of libraries and librarians. Day strongly believes we are already seeing a shift from measuring library services in terms of size and comprehensiveness of collections to one of measuring the quality of service delivery: delivery of documents irrespective of origin, increasingly in electronic form, with access to the electronic library from the users' desktop.

THE EMERGENCE OF DIGITAL LIBRARIES

Definition of Digital Library

A working definition of digital libraries provided by Waters are: "Organisations that provide the resources, including specialised staff, to select, structure, offer intellectual access to, distribute, preserve the integrity of, and ensure the persistence over time of collections of digital works so that they are readily and economically available for use by a defined community or set of communities."

Digital Libraries Concepts

The digital library concepts requires librarians to be information architects in order to build effective, scalable Web sites to serve the digital demands of patrons. 'Just in time", a method introduced in the early '80s to manage inventory, is now an expectation of consumers for any business providing online. 'Just in time' applied to libraries is information delivered "where you need it, when you need it, and in a format that is useful. This strategy requires libraries increasingly to adopt 24/365 service to keep up with the demands of their patrons for core services, and to offer services through what is often called the digital, electronic, or virtual library or reference desk.

Technical Requirements of a Digital Library

The United States National Information Infrastructure programme has identified a number of critical technical challenges that need to be resolved if usage of electronic networking is to be both simple and efficient.

The listing of them below illustrates that all are important for the proper running of a digital library:

- Network components that can handle voice, and text simultaneously, and can operate seamlessly
- Information appliances and services that can provide access and services in a scalable, efficient and interoperable way
- Information access techniques that can enable efficient searches of large distributed information repositories, making the myriad of information resources understandable
- Multimedia information technologies that can, for example, synchronise and integrate real-time delivery of voice, and can support search and retrieval based on image content
- Infrastructure for application development that can provide common solutions
- Technologies that are dependable and manageable
- Technologies that are easy to use and services that are accessible by users with widely varying skills, experiences, abilities and backgrounds
- Inter-operability among heterogeneous systems will be required on an unprecedented scale
- Security and privacy technologies that are easy to use and provide appropriate levels of security to suit the requirements, cost constraints and convenience of the end user
- Technologies and services that provide portability, mobility and ubiquity.

The Roles of Digital Libraries in the Academic Environment

Researcher provide a comprehensive remarks of the roles

of digital libraries in teaching and learning. A library is fundamentally an organised set of resources, which include human services as well as the entire spectrum of media. Libraries have physical components such as space, equipment, and storage media; intellectual components such as collection policies that determine what materials will be included and organisational schemes that determine how the collection is accessed; and people who manage the physical and intellectual components and interact with users to solve information problems.

Libraries serve at least four roles in learning:

1. *First, they serve a practical role in sharing expensive resources:* Physical resources such as books and periodicals, films and videos, software and electronic databases, and specialised tools such as projectors, graphics equipment and cameras are shared by a community of users. Human resources—librarians support instructional programmes by responding to the requests of academicians and students and by initiating activities for teachers and students. Responsive services include maintaining reserve materials, answering reference questions, providing bibliographic instruction, developing media packages, recommending books or films, and teaching users how to use materials. Proactive services include selective dissemination of information to faculty and students, initiating thematic events, collaborating with instructors to plan instruction, and introducing new instructional methods and tools. In these ways, libraries serve to allow instructors and students to share expensive materials and expertise.
2. *Second, libraries serve a cultural role in preserving and organising artifacts and ideas:* Great works of literature, art, and science must be preserved and made accessible to future learners. Libraries preserve objects through careful storage procedures, policies of borrowing and use, and repair and maintenance

as needed. In addition to preservation, libraries ensure access to materials through indexes, catalogs, and other finding aids that allow learners to locate items appropriate to their needs.

3. Third, libraries serve social and intellectual roles in bringing together people and ideas: This is distinct from the practical role of sharing resources in that libraries provide a physical place for academicians and learners to meet outside the structure of the classroom, thus allowing people with different perspectives to interact in a knowledge space that is both larger and more general than that shared by any single discipline or affinity group. Browsing a catalog in a library provides a global view for people engaged in specialised study and offers opportunities for serendipitous insights or alternative views. In many respects, libraries serve as centers of inter-disciplinarily—places shared by learners from all disciplines. Digital libraries extend such inter-disciplinarity by making diverse information resources available beyond the physical space shared by groups of learners. One of the greatest benefits of digital libraries is bringing together people with formal, informal, and professional learning missions.

- Formal learning is systematic and guided by instruction. Formal learning takes place in courses offered at schools of various kinds and in training courses or programmes on the job. The important roles that libraries serve in formal learning are illustrated by their physical prominence on university campuses and the number of courses that make direct use of library services and materials. By making the broad range of information resources, digital libraries open new learning opportunities for global rather than strictly local communities.

Much learning in life is informal—opportunistic and strictly under the control of the learner. Learners take advantage of other people, mass media, and the immediate environment during informal learning. The public library system that developed in the U.S., in the late nineteenth century has been called the 'free university', since public libraries were created to provide free access to the world's knowledge.

Public libraries provide classic non-fiction books, a wide range of periodicals, reference sources, and audio and video tapes so that patrons can learn about topics of their own choosing at their own pace and style. Just as computing technology and world-wide telecommunications networks are beginning to change what is possible in formal classrooms, they are changing how individuals pursue personal learning missions. Professional learning refers to the on going learning adults engage in to do their work and to improve their work-related knowledge and skills. In fact, for many professionals, learning is the central aspect of their work. Like informal learning, it is mainly self-directed, but unlike formal or informal learning, it is focused on a specific field closely linked to job performance, aims to be comprehensive, and is acquired and applied longitudinally. Since professional learning affects job performance, corporations and government agencies support libraries with information resources specific to the goals of the organisation.

The main information resources for professional learning, however, are personal collections of books, reports, and files; subscriptions to journals; and the human networks of colleagues nurtured through professional meetings and various communications. Many of the data sets and computational tools of digital libraries were originally developed to enhance professional learning. The information resources—both physical and human—that support these types of learning are customised for specific missions and have traditionally been physically separated, although common technologies such as printing, photography, and computing are found across all settings. This situation, is depicted in fig. 1.1.

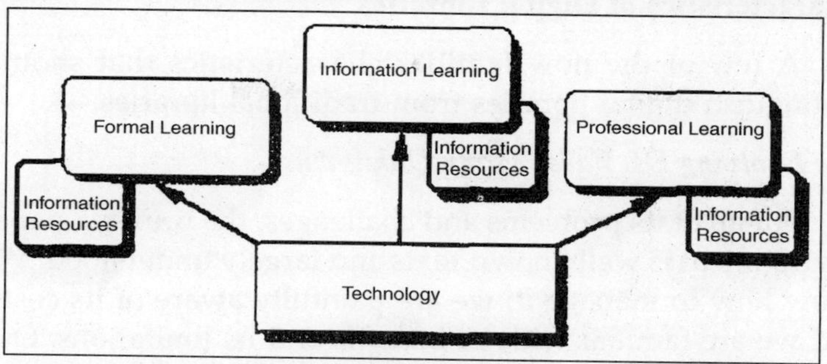

Fig 1.1 Current Models of Technological Support for Types of Learning

Digital libraries combine technology and information resources to allow remote access, breaking down the physical barriers between resources. Although these resources will remain specialised to meet the needs of specific communities of learners, digital libraries will allow teachers and students to take advantage of wider ranges of materials and communicate with people outside the formal learning environment. This will allow more integration of the different types of learning, as depicted in fig. 1.2.

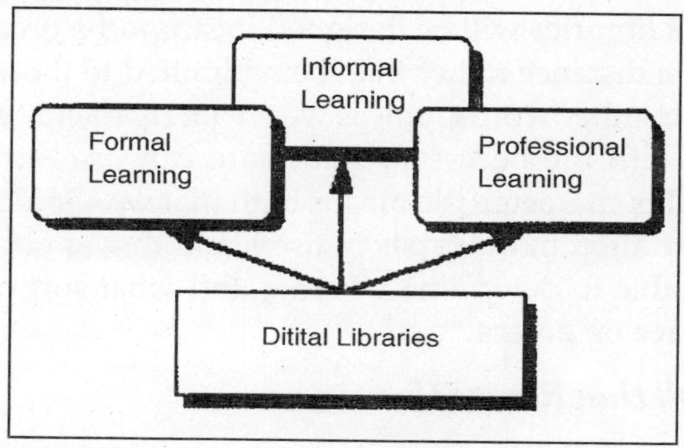

Fig 1.2 Digital Libraries Lead to Integrated Resources and Type of Learning

Although not all students or academicians in formal learning settings will use information resources beyond their circumscribed curriculum and not all professionals will want to interact even occasionally with novices, digital libraries will allow learners of all types to share resources, time and energy, and expertise to their mutual benefits.

Characteristics of Digital Libraries

A few of the now familiar characteristics that should distinguish digital libraries from traditional libraries.

The Evolving DL Faces Many Unknowns

For all of its problems and challenges, the print-on-paper environment is well known to us and largely understood. We know how to manage it; we are painfully aware of its costs; and we are familiar with its benefits and its limitations. Our digital library future, by contrast, is full of unknowns and unsolved problems. The list of these is too long and too well rehearsed to need reciting. In addition, the underlying digital technology continues to change. So, even if we could discover the unknowns and solve the problems today, we could not freeze our solutions. Consequently, we are faced with the prospect of creating organisations that are flexible and that accommodate changes, including large changes, easily and regularly.

The DL will Offer Ubiquitous Access

Digital libraries will be designed to support a great range of users at a distance rather than being limited to those on the premises. In other words, unless we create restraints, any and everyone with the necessary hardware can use our digital libraries. This characteristic means both that we should expect a larger variation in the types of users and that as suggested, be responsible to determine whether and what sort of limits will we place on access.

The DL will Host Remote Users

Since digital library users will ordinarily be off the premises, anew, entirely different set of challenges will arise with regard to what we have known as reference and other help services. Our experience with help services has largely been face to face and interpersonal, and efforts to create sophisticated, remote help services are still rudimentary today.

The DL will be more Fully Technology Based

From the creation of metadata to the provision of information services and training, digital libraries will be predominantly technology based. This stands in stark contrast to the essential character of traditional, residential libraries. This is problematical not only because librarians are reluctant to design systems that are technology as opposed to people based but also because often librarians do not possess the necessary expertise to do so. Yet we are not eager to let the process out of our hands. On the positive side, much of the cost of traditional libraries has resided in the manual processes and procedures. While no one supposes that digital libraries will be inexpensive, we should design them in so far as possible to avoid many of these costly manual procedures.

The DL will be open and Customisable and a Part of a Much Larger Information Smorgasbord

Though the qualifications of a digital library can be conveniently limited by definition, they cannot be so conveniently limited by practice. There is a debate over whether or not the Internet is a library. An approach to this question is rather more pragmatic: if growing millions of individuals use the Internet regularly as the source for information on all subjects, it is a library. For all its limitations, it may be a very poor library but it is one nevertheless. For this reason, it is unlikely that our digital libraries will monopolise the library activities of our constituencies in the same way that our traditional libraries have. Digital users today have already sampled the smorgasbord information world of the Internet and have correspondingly broadened their appetites. In addition, it is increasingly common for information users to desire to customise information retrieval, a desire that reduces patience with our more inflexible information systems.

The DL will Offer Distinctive Functions

As surely as digital libraries will discard functions

common in traditional libraries, they will necessarily concern themselves with new functions. Commonly named among these are such activities as intellectual property management and database creation and management, the latter being normally associated with administrative computing and data processing. In terms of functionality, therefore, digital libraries will differ markedly from traditional libraries.

Radically Altered Job Descriptions for Information Professionals Will Evolve

To the degree that digital libraries are the business of librarians, this means the incorporation of radically changed or new functions in the librarians portfolios. Digital libraries ignore old boundaries and fall across lines currently marking divisions between libraries, computing organisations, and telephony/networking departments. Therefore, that digital libraries are not solely the province of librarians and that the new constellation of functions inherent in digital libraries will require the evolution of new information professionals with job descriptions that are as yet unspecified.

Such new job descriptions will reflect new combinations of skills represented in these currently distinct agencies along with those from other areas, such as intellectual property law and business.

As Suggested, See New Focuson Original Materials

In the rapidly passing era of traditional libraries, most of our resources and energies were expended on acquiring, organising, managing, and explaining commercially published materials. Because of the slow but steady movement of commercial publishing into the Internet environment, it is likely in the future that access to commercially published digital resources will increasingly be provided directly by publishers.

The role of libraries as gateways to commercial academic materials, therefore, will diminish. At the same time, however, because of the capabilities of technology, digital libraries will increasingly focus on providing access to original materials, both those born digitally and those converted from analog formats. The effect of this will be to enrich vastly the research potential of our resources and to provide new opportunities for our institutions to benefit from the potential commercial value of such holdings. The new content paradigm for digital libraries will be raw, source materials.

The DL will have Commercial Characteristics

As a result of the shift in digital libraries to original materials, as suggested, find the means to exploit the commercial value of such materials to a degree never before possible. Digital libraries, therefore, must from the outset be designed to support commercial activities. Correspondingly, support for digital libraries will likely include business plans, replete with market assessments, commercial partnerships, and new concerns for cost-effectiveness and year-end financial performance. In other words, because of the value of their data, digital libraries will have an imperative to function in a more business-like, for-profit manner.

As Suggested, Experience New Competition

We must be increasingly aware that, as representatives of primarily traditional, not-for-profit institutions, we do not enjoy sole ownership of the future of digital libraries. Even as we gather here, a host of new competitors for the business of education and the distribution of knowledge and information resources is assembling.

For this reason, we must not presume that the digital library world will evolve to our specifications, especially if we work on digital libraries as a closed community of librarians. Just as the world-wide-web swept over us and, with unbelievable swiftness, changed the nature of our communication environment, so too may we be over-washed by some new inescapable digital library model from unanticipated sources.

Custom, User-Built Digital Libraries

Apart from large commercial interests, some user-built,

highly focused information storage and retrieval services, such as the NASA Astrophysics Data System or the on-line journal of high energy physics, suggest that elements of the digital library may best be developed by the users. Creating these technically customised data and information retrieval systems requires intimate familiarity with the subject matter, jargon, and academic habits of the user communities and likely could not be accomplished by librarians. Clearly we must ponder the implications of these examples for our assumptions and methodologies.

WORKPLACE ENVIRONMENT IN THE DIGITAL ERA

What might we expect of the workplace environment in the new millennium academic library?

Libraries will take Over Campus Computer Centers

Academic libraries will pursue bolder organisational experimentation. This will include focusing on the information and services needs of users. There will be wider distribution of administrative responsibility and authority, as hierarchical structures are broken down and key activities and operations are integrated.

We can expect more fluid and flexible structures, enhancement of team and small group processes, and more collegial and collaborative working relationships. Continuing a trend that is already taking root, the academic library will assume administrative control of campus academic computing services. With the expanding mandate for accountability, there will be a greater focus on data collection and analysis. This will entail a rethinking of standards and benchmarks for assessment and more creative approaches to defining output measures and quality impact.

Academic Library Funding will Remain Stable

Responsibility-center budget models will expand across higher education, embracing the library. This relatively new system of distributed financial authority places libraries into a more rigourous fiscal relationship with academic programmes. Units will be taxed to support library operations, requiting intensified communication and accountability. Library funding will remain stable. The greatest growth will continue to be in collection and information access programmes.

The library budget as a percentage of total campus budget will not change substantially. Library development and fundraising activities will accelerate, as more colleges and universities pursue external funding from private, corporate, and foundation sources.

This will involve a greater focus on endowments rather than on raisin funds for specified capital projects. Library budgets will increasingly fund research and development, infrastructure upgrade and replacement capabilities, and risk capital for innovation and advancement. The trend towards outsourcing of library operations and services will accelerate. We have already seen substantial success with serials jobbers, approval plans, binding, photocopy services, building maintenance, and security. This will lead to further experimentation in cataloging, collection maintenance, document delivery, and preservation.

Digital Acquisitions Budgets will Quadruple, and more, Eating up 40-50 Per cent of Acquisition Budgets

Print-based collections will remain dominant over the next decade. However, substantial resources will be allocated to the acquisition of electronic information, as reference sources and scholarly journals become computer-based and the economic feasibility of the scholarly monograph is increasingly questioned.

The percentage of investment in digital information will grow from the current 5-10 percent of acquisitions budgets to 40-50 percent. There will be an ongoing need for investment in local collection building, however, because what has not been acquired and preserved cannot be made available to users and other libraries. Even as collections continue to expand, the gap between what is being published and what we can afford to acquire will continue to grow. As a result, there will be a dramatic decline in ownership: new information accessible through libraries will plunge dramatically.

Nevertheless, the role of the academic library as a depository and gateway for government information will expand, as traditional print-based distribution models are eliminated.

The academic library will expand its role in scholarly publishing and communication. Project Muse at Johns Hopkins and High wire at Stanford, and the Journal Storage Project spawned by Mellon are examples of the library's central involvement in the management of current and retrospective electronic publications. More than 50 percent of reference transactions will take place over campus networks

Patron-initiated and Controlled Services will Expand Rapidly

Libraries are already beginning to employ self-circulation, computer renewals and recalls, direct interlibrary loan, and document delivery. Full-text databases are becoming commonplace. The role of library staff as interpreters and mediators of user information transactions outside of local collections and services will decrease. Inside the university, the librarians' role as instructor will be formalised in a separate college department focusing on information and network literacy.

The technology of the World Wide Web that is evolving rapidly and unpredictable with the World Wide Web Consortium co-ordinates many activities in the areas of user interface, technology and society. The World Wide Web which was first announced by CERN in 1991, 2-3 years ago most people had not heard of it but by the end of 1996, there were 300,000 Web sites. Libraries are creating Web sites to help students to distinguish between relevant and irrelevant information. The Web is likely to have a profound impact on education, communication and research activities of the universities.

Examples:

- *The Web empowers individuals:* They can easily reach a worldwide audience. Anyone can publish material that would never have been published in the past, and it is instantly available to millions of people.
- *The Web offers us the best of both worlds. Anyone can publish:* Their views cannot easily be suppressed, for good or ill. And anyone can comment, validate and offer judgement or advice.

The E-mail for example is extremely valuable for communication between the library and its users. Users Borrowers are expected to return their books within about two weeks. Very many do without reminders, but for those who need reminding, for some reason e-mail is a more effective spur than other methods. Online catalogs will increasingly define accessibility and not just local ownership. Thus the links between the local collection, the bibliography of a discipline, and the text of the publications/sources will become blurred. Remote use of online catalogs and databases is increasing rapidly at most colleges and universities.

An example, at Carnegie Mellon, already 75 per cent of catalog use is remote. Remote access to information necessitates new instructional efforts. Levels of all traditional collection circulation activity - general and reserve borrowing and interlibrary loan - will decline significantly. They will fall prey to the rapid growth in options for electronic document delivery and the implementation of electronic reserve systems. The new electronic journals already offer facilities unavailable to users of paper.

These include:

- The ability to search for particular content within a paper or a complete journal;
- The ability to move easily between the table of contents of a journal and the abstract.
- Facilities to annotate articles to create a personal virtual filing cabinet and
- The ability to move quickly from the article you are reading to one which it cites in its references, and

that includes forward citing, example the ability to go to articles that cited the one you have just been reading but which were published later.

An example, the American Astronomical Society has digitised into electronic form all the articles in the last 20 years of its journal which can now be accessed. Academic libraries will house and manage campus usability laboratories focusing on the needs of the user and will involve users as part of the design team.

Reference assistance to users will be electronic-based, with more than 50 per cent of transactions taking place over campus networks in batched or real-time communication, up from the current neglible levels. User profiles linked to SDI-type services will ensure delivery of relevant, cur-rent information to faculty and students on a scheduled basis. Academic librarians will increasingly pursue service goals as part of multiple consortia-based relationships. There will be joint investment in commercial services and acquisition of materials, in the purchase and use of technology, and in the hiring and development of staff.

Librarians will be Key Players in Developing Technological Innovations

Technology is currently poised to transform the fundamental nature of operations and services. From the early days of automation in the 1970s, academic libraries have moved to the cur-rent distribution and individualisation of technology and digital conversion and production. The challenge of the next decade will be the application of intelligence to the searching and retrieval capabilities of library systems.

The library will play a central role in the future development of the campus information environment. Rather than reacting to campus technology decisions, library staff will be integrally involved in determining what the next innovations will be. In the new world of the desktop workstation, academic libraries have a mandate to integrate high-speed access both to scholarly and institutional information. They need to provide tools for filtering, analysing, and manipulating information.

The predominant mainframe-based library management systems will be completely replaced by client-server technologies and applications that include robust full-text content and intelligent links to network-based sources. Automatic language translation software will be introduced, contributing to the development of a renewed global acquisitions programme for both based and digital sources. Campus network infrastructures will extend to all student, faculty, and staff work and living areas.

This will provide dependable connectivity for a growing array of applications, including distance learning. Wireless technology will be introduced and will receive its initial testing in library services. The retrospective digitising of library collections, particularly unique materials, will evolve as a central activity in academic libraries. Newly formed digital knowledge centers will manage the operations and partner with academic departments, publishers, and other libraries.

The Number of Librarians Working in Academic Libraries will Decrease

Libraries will increasingly view staff development as an integral and essential component of organisational success. With retooling of skills emerging as a three-to-five year cycle, participation in training courses will be mandated for all employee groups. As technology programmes advance and dominate library collection and service activities, technical staff as a percentage of total staff will increase significantly. This will produce a net reduction in the number of librarians employed in academic libraries.

It will also promote more effective working relationships between librarians and technologists, improving current conditions marred by distrust, inadequate communication, and lack of shared investment in planning. Academic libraries have not responded effectively to demographic cultural, racial, and ethnic shifts. They will collectively enter the next century still recognising the important trends producing a more pluralistic society but without well-developed and well-coordinated strategic directions for the role and contributions of the library. Telecommuting, which is increasingly commonplace in commercial settings, will become a viable and acceptable option for *academic* library employees.

An expanding array of library operations and services will be performed from home, enabling improved competitiveness for the recruitment and retention of talented staff. Academic libraries and library education programmes will collaborate on the development of internship and certification programmes for new professionals. This will be necessitated by the anticipated rapid increase in retirements in the next 15 years, as well as by the need to develop new approaches to the preparation and orientation of the next generation of academic librarians. An example of a university library, De Montfort University in the UK that has been developing a digital library environment for some years past.

The lessons they claim to have learnt might be summarised under the following headings:

- The digital library will develop more quickly than people think;
- The digital library is still a complex, unstable entity for which little theoretical structure exists.
- Because of this inherent instability, investment and implementation are still high risk.
- Digital libraries operate in a global environment: new products and services can become *de facto* standards very quickly.
- Co-operation is therefore a key factor for maintaining competitiveness.
- The content of the digital library will become the dominant factor.
- Copyright issues will be resolved or side-stepped because the market will demand it.
- The economics of the digital library are not yet well understood.
- Library jobs and roles will change very rapidly.

IMPACT OF INFORMATION TECHNOLOGY ON INFORMATION PROFESSIONALS

As quoted by Matson, new technology is, of course, very powerful and brings in 'an imperialistic thrust' not only into librarianship, but into everyday life. Not surprisingly, the new roles created by the changing technology have commanded attention and have made up a large part of recent literature about librarians. He added the resulting proliferation of online catalogs, librarian have been spurred by technological developments to become more efficient organisers and planners. They have, in short, brought their traditional skills to the service of the new technologies. As claimed by Hyams, the role of the New Information Professionals (NIP) in the learning environments is likely to be much more global. It is a call for librarians to rethink their job functions and the future of the academic library as center of technology. The change that's happening isn't at all like the automation change the librarian went through. It is a fundamental kind of change: 'To Who We Are and What We Do."

NEW ROLES, NEW SKILLS AND NEW PEOPLE

Researcher argue that library jobs and jobs for information professionals are changing at the same—or even greater as experienced in other parts of our economy and society. Are librarians, new and old, keeping pace with these changes? Are they stuck in a traditional mind-set about their jobs and the settings for those jobs? What are some of the new horizons available to librarians willing to 'think outside the box" as far as their careers are concerned? What prepares the librarian for these emerging jobs? The struggle of librarians in academic libraries to cope with the dynamic changes brought by technology is real. The new roles and skills include:

As Library Webmaster

The single most significant factor in the changing information jobs has been the Internet. It has changed everyone's job, some people's job descriptions', and the job market itself, example as Webmaster.

Definition of Webmaster

The essential assignment of the Webmaster as defined by Richmond is:

- "... a person who manages a Web; a mediator between Web authors and system administrator—ensures that applicable standards such as HTML validity and link liveliness are met; optimises the Web architecture for navigability; takes editorial responsibility for the content, quality and styles of the site; finds, creates and installs tools to create Web content and check consistency; develops and enforces the house style; liaises with graphic artist; provides first level user support..."

From this definition, it is clear that Webmasters must be responsible for several roles in their day to day activities.

Task Analysis of the Webmaster

Van der Walt strongly believe that Webmasters were originally depicted as members of an organisation who were early adopters of Internet and Web technologies and who saw the need to educate the rest of the library users in using those technologies. His statement is strongly supported by the researchers who claimed that an area where early Web expertise could be found was the *academic,* and specifically *university,* environment.

Vander Walt listed several responsibilities of the Webmaster such as:

- Administration and daily management of a Web site such as home page design, Web-based online searching, searching Web sites, Intranets and Internal database publishing
- Understand the broad purpose and potential of a Web site—that is, what the site can accomplish and what it may be able to do in future
- Possess a thorough understanding of the organisation and have a background in marketing, familiarity with the Internet

- A solid understanding of programming languages and technology
- Keep up with and also recognise the significance of emerging technologies and business models, and be able to inform and educate the rest of the organisation
- Experiment with unproven technology to develop WWW sites and the Webmaster is a solo space explorer, often looking at way-out-in-front technology'
- A person with the necessary technical talent in user interfaces and a good knowledge of operating systems, as well as creative skills in graphic design, marketing, advertising, copy writing and event planning

The Growing Importance of the Webmaster

These basic responsibilities are slowly being enhanced. Today the Webmaster has become an integral part of an education venture vital to the entire strategic planning of the library. As a newcomer in the information retrieval field, the Webmaster forms an essential part of the online presence of any organisation, as it is he or she who leads the Web site development team in managing an effective and efficient Web site.

The value of librarians as webmasters in the university as claimed by Stover is for a number of reasons:

- First, to support the scholarly communication process because disseminating information is a function that traditionally been associated with librarians
- Second, librarians have a certain measure of expertise in the area of organising and providing access to information. What better way to share their skills with the academic community than by turning Web documents into one-stop-shopping malls that offer the end user subject access to a document along with the full-text of the document itself?
- Third, Web publishing gives us a higher profile on campus, which is an important asset these days because of the changing nature of higher education and changing role of librarians
- Fourth, the Web provides unique access to scholarly

information because of its serendipitous nature, its immediacy, its hypertext structure, and its universal appeal. Why wouldn't librarians want to be involved with this exciting technology at the publishing level?

- Fifth, it provides our parent institutions a positive reputation in the national and international academic communities. This is more important ever given the current climate of declining enrollments that many colleges and universities face today.
- Sixth, Web publishing allows us to bypass the profit-based system of print publishing that has tormented librarians for years by gouging out huge chunks of money from their budget.

As claimed by Van der Walt, many Web sites are now becoming mission critical in the sense that they are seen as a marketing tool for the university and also as a support tool for the end-user or library customers. The Internet and World Wide Web are both essential elements in the IT infrastructure of any organisation. Thus the Webmaster can play an important role in managing the library assets according to the information center's strategic planning.

As Systems Librarian

Shearer describes the term Systems librarians as:

- "Individuals who are responsible of designing, supporting and developing systems to enhance access to and management of the library's collection. Ensuring that the computer-based systems are essential to the library's work at all times."

Responsibilities

- Evaluation, planning, implementation and maintenance of library automation and Internet access, network maintenance as well as web page design and maintenance.
- Evaluation and selection of databases and software and staff training.
- Maintains computer security and hardware.

Skills

- Knowledge of networking, Internet and software applications.
- Ability to master new computer hardware and software.
- Ability to diagnose and solve hardware, software and networking problems.
- Ability to communicate technology to the uninitiated.
- Ability to work in a dynamic and changing environment.

Electronic Access to What and by Whom

Selecting academic information resources requires a broader view. For any library, the determination of which databases to provide and who will access them has become an ever more complex due to the number of databases that are now available has grown by leaps and bounds over the past few years. Today's systems librarian is often involved in the decision of which database service to supply to end-user desktops. There are myriad choices of general topic and specialty products available online, on the Intranet, on CD-ROM, and via the Web, at all price points. In today's academic setting, the librarian not only has to take into account the resource for the library's own collection but has to weigh offering the database to a wider user base against what end users within the university are already accessing by way of their own desktops.

Thus the systems librarian must weigh the type of access to provide against questions of:

- Timeliness,
- System capabilities, and
- Client expectations of good service.

Access Policies

Schuhnan quote that once the library decides which databases to select, it must determine how to deploy them and who will have access to them. As electronic access to external databases becomes more prevalent throughout all academic areas, the systems librarian's budget and equipment come under greater pressure. Whenever contemplating the addition of a new database resource it's also a good opportunity to review internal corporate access policies. As quickly as events dictate change in resource selections, policy revisions will naturally be carefully thought about more frequently. Decisions such as supplying access to information for those with a 'need to know' are undergoing modification.

Increasingly, those with a 'need to know' occupy expanding outward circles within organisations. Schulman added, smart organisations are extending information resources access to more employees as competitors become more aggressive and move more quickly. They are finding that providing more employees with timely access to competitive information allows an organisation to respond to competitive threats more quickly.

As the system librarian continuously evaluate databases and the provision of access to them, here is a series of questions to ask each time considering a new source:

- Is this source unique or does it duplicate an existing resource.
- If it's a close duplicate, is it less expensive, easier to use, or unique in another beneficial way.
- How does this database fit in with the corporate mission.
- Who within the university will benefit from this database—all users, faculty members and university community.
- What is the cost-benefit ratio.
- What critical element does this database supply that overcomes a poor cost-benefit ratio.
- Does this resource fit within our existing budget.
- Does another resource have to be eliminated to bring on this resource, and, if so, what impact will that have to the budget and to those who depend on the resource under consideration for elimination.
- Will this resource improve service to our clients/ customers? How?

- In what format will we purchase the database.
- How will this database be integrated into our other resources.
- What changes have to be made to the hardware/ software configuration to accept this new database and how will this impact our budget? How will it impact access to other resources?
- How will we provide access to this resource?
- Who in which departments and at which levels within the university will have access to this resource? Directly? Indirectly.
- Will end-user training have to be provided?
- Will additional staff be required?
- What other departments should be involved in this decision?
- How much time and effort is involved in implementing access to this resource?
- When will the corporation see a return on investment?

Thus by using this list as a guideline and foundation for decision making should help the system librarian to revise the questions as the mission, budget, environmental influences changes and stay ahead of the game.

As In-House Content Providers

The meaning of In-house Content Provider refers to:

- "one who was interested in exploring the balance between making its content freely available on the Internet while protecting its print-based revenue stream."

Funke provide a comprehensive comment on the new role of the Information Professionals as an In-House Content Providers. He claimed that along with the new technologies comes interacting with different groups within an organisation such as the MIS people, an information professional must have the ability to effectively 'bring content to the table" and work effectively with MIS as a team to make this content readily available. In order for information professionals to effectively do this, they must keep up with the latest technologies related to text retrieval, content organisation, search technologies, and knowledge management.

Bringing Content to the Table

Making MIS people understand the importance and expertise of people who know content and how clients will use it can be a constant uphill battle. Many programmers in this situation view another 'player' either as a threat or someone who doesn't have their background. Unfortunately, the onus lies on the information professional to make programmers understand what we can contribute, the value we can provide.

For starters, before you can integrate content into a Web site, you must understand:

- The overall requirements of the current Web site, including servers,
- Their ability to handle various indexes; search engine capability; and
- How the parser is set up to integrate content.

The Information Professional can provide expertise on how to organise content on a site; how users might search for the content; and the search requirements needed to access the content.

Metadata

Many information professionals have taken courses such as cataloging and indexing. These courses can serve as a foundation for the resource-organising activities on the Internet involving metadata. Metadata provides document information on and from Web sites, producing an index or directory to the resource. With the tremendous growth of content on the Web, there is a need to standardise the organisation of the information.

As metadata standards are further defined and organisations embrace these new standards, many questions will need answering such as:

- What will be worth cataloging?
- How detailed should the descriptions of various resources be?

Information Professionals can play a major role in helping answer these questions.

Search Engines

Researcher added, the evaluation and use of search engines is a 'product' that Information Professionals should manage within their organisations because they:

- Understand and know how to use Boolean logic.
- Can evaluate search engines from the user perspective?
- Know how to implement effective user searching of content.

Some of the major Intranet search engines available these days include Fulcrum Surfboard, Verity, Microsoft Index Server, and Excalibur. Thus, when implementing the Boolean logic features of these search engines, most programmers, will say that users cannot grasp Boolean logic or that such control is unnecessary as long as the search engines do relevancy rankings of documents retrieved. Users can go beyond basic Boolean operators such as AND, OR, NOT, which programmers usually dictate for them, and take advantage of proximity operators such as NEAR and NEARIN.

From experience, when one explains the differences in search results to users, e.g., the effect of using the Boolean operators and NEAR, end-user searchers understand and respond positively right away. Programmers may support their positions by doing a query to see how many searches were performed using each Boolean operator. Information Professionals should try search queries for this type of data, too. Request the tools to perform this kind of query. What some programmers find difficult to understand is that you just can't implement a feature without some user education. Information Professionals can play an important role by providing this guidance within their organisations.

Information Retrieval Agents

Making sense of the overwhelming amount of indexed information constitutes one of the biggest challenges of the

Web. To help, we see a rising use of Web robots, called information retrieval agents. These agents know where to look for relevant information based on user direction, advanced search algorithms, and learned behaviour. Major players in this area include NewsBot, Agent ware, and Wise Wire. As organisations move towards managing knowledge, intelligent information retrieval agent software tools will playa major role and will require people with the ability to manage and evaluate these tools. Search agents work when a user sets up search queries to 'train the documents,' whereby the agents learn from human behaviour and use pattern recognition to find relevant information to automate the retrieval process.

Information Professionals with expertise in searching and content analysis can help manage and evaluate these tools. Note that several of the traditional electronic publishers have already begun exploring this technology, e.g., LEXIS-NEXIS and UMI with WiseWire Professional, an agent technology that evaluates user's viewing habits. Like it or not, new technologies are changing the information professional's role and the opportunities to enhance one's role have become boundless. To take advantage of the opportunities, Information Professionals must keep up with the emerging technologies, recognise the opportunities to utilise our skill sets, and work with MIS to effectively implement change. At times it can be frustrating and overwhelming, but the opportunities to grow and learn outweigh any negatives.

AS KNOWLEDGE MANAGER

Peter Drucker has predicted that the most important profession in the next century will be knowledge worker, and knowledge workers are not the same as computer systems specialists. He claimed that the most competent ones are likely to be reference librarians using sophisticated hardware and software, tools which the end user does not know how to use. Certainly, those who have exploited the almost unlimited opportunity to provide more information have taken advantage of this development.

Still, Drucker assumed that this deluge of knowledge would drown us and force us to seek people to manage that knowledge. Knowledge workers would assess knowledge on behalf of those who had neither the time nor the inclination to do so. The concept of knowledge management embraces the need to organise large data files, and to link and integrate different but related files and databases to one another so that users can move between and among related resources efficiently.

Thus, Church believe the transformation from librarian to knowledge manager is clearly underway; however, a deeper look at the direction that the Internet is taking business reveals the possibility of more far-reaching changes. As many library services processes move to the Internet, the use of information will become integrated with these processes. In this environment, information as a distinct function or resource may no longer exist.

Changing Roles and Responsibilities

The information transfer cycle is directly affected by Internet use. They should "embrace the entire new information transfer cycle, from the creation, restructuring and representation of information to its dissemination and use." They have an important and valuable role to tell users what users ought to see and read. It is to protect library clients from drowning in the information overflow and help them work smarter.

How their role as knowledge managers would evolve within the next few years, Church outline five key functions:

1. *Consultant:* Their role would involve less 'doing' and more consultation. This role would require remote support to endusers within the organisation. In effect, 'foot traffic' would be replaced by remote consultation for complex search strategies.
2. *Analyst:* Some information professional felt that their role would require increased value-added in the form of analysing and interpreting information that is presented to end-users.
3. *Intranet content manager:* With the integration of

external data into corporate Intranets, a key function of the information services professional will be to source and manage the content which is accessible through the system.

4. *Product planner and marketer:* Data integration also forces information professionals to become product developers and planners, with responsibility for packaging information and marketing products, services and delivery strategies to internal audiences.
5. *Corporate knowledge manager:* Increased recognition of knowledge as a valuable strategic resource could heighten the importance of the information professional. It foresee a merger of all information functions into a single department or function. Being the Knowledge Manager just means that they create value to my organisation by facilitating access to high quality information and by networking people and their ideas together using the technological infrastructure.

These new responsibilities imply a totally different skill set. The emphasis will shift from:

- Technical skills in the library to communication,
- Facilitation, training and management skills.
- Interact with IT staff and managers beyond Knowledge Management (KM).

To adjust to these more far-reaching changes, information professionals must search beyond current bounds and think in terms of benefits to their organisations. Right now, information can be used to enhance competitiveness and productivity. These same benefits will remain in the future, no matter what the role involves.

If information is to be seamlessly integrated with transaction processes, then someone must scope out work-related behaviours to ensure that it is done in the most efficient and effective manner. And, if equal information and technology is available to everyone, then competition rests on the ability to interpret and apply these tools. Clearly the impending shift to knowledge management represents an exciting change for academic librarians. However, it's an opportunity that requires a great deal of preparation, and a new way of thinking.

AS COLLABORATORS/PARTNERSHIPS

All organisations are in the period of transformation including academic libraries and librarians should use this period of change to establish, refocus and strengthen partnerships with other professionals groups within their institutions.

There are two significant groups with which library professionals should establish strong collaborative relationships:

1. Faculty and
2. Technologists.

Creth suggest in order for a real partnership to succeed, librarians need to see themselves as part of the teaching and research endeavor, and participate as an active and integral member of the education team. He added, for some librarians this idea of a partnership with faculty may require incorporating a different concept of their importance in relation to the faculty and developing new expectations and different behaviour. In the most general sense, librarians need to be certain that their commitment to service does not display itself through behaviour that is like of a servant.

Library professionals also need to reshape and strengthen their relationships with the computer specialists in the university with reasons such as:

- To eliminate much of the waste that occurs in most organisations where computer and information technology remains untapped or barely utilised because the learning curve is too steep for so many people and because the design of the equipment and software is so often far from intuitive.
- The New Information Professionals can provide constant feedback to designers and programmers about what works, what does not work, what new functions are needed.
- They can become the voice of the inexpert user, the

typical person who is not technically inclined but strongly needs the service that the technology promises to deliver.

- They are both dealing with changing and chaotic times, and their activities are centered around information technology, so they should naturally consider themselves partners in addressing the many challenges that exist.
- They need to be willing, to share the act of discovery, to be able to identify shared goals, and to work together as peers.

If, librarians are to be prepared to absorb and even help shape the magnitude of predicted change into this 21st century, then it will be important for librarians to realign their relationships within the university so that strong partnerships exist to provide us with necessary support as well as knowledge for meeting the challenges ahead.

AS EDUCATOR

Anderson emphasised that librarians have always played a key role in education. They have formed relationships with subject specialists to build library collections to support instruction in the classroom and provided instruction in the form of classes on library skills and have conducted library instructional orientations sessions to assist students doing research in their classes. Today, in the digital age, librarians can no longer be simply information providers or the 'keepers of knowledge'.

The changes in technology using electronically stored and retrieved information has changed the way patrons and students are able to access, retrieve and use information. The instantaneous access of information through the Internet has made vast amounts of information and data available to anyone with a computer, a modem and a provider. Digital information is changing the role of librarians from "a person who students ask for assistance in finding information to someone who needs to provide services and instruction regardless of place, time or format." But how do we make important and valid information available to our faculty and students that may appear on the Web tomorrow?

Big Six Information Skills

As educators, Eisenberg have suggested that librarians must acquire these skills; the ability to:

- Define the task,
- Information seeking strategies,
- Location and access,
- Use of information,
- Synthesis,
- Evaluation.

The librarian's role too has:

- Expanded with a much broader instructional and participatory role in the instructional process. This role can be one of actively participating in the building of on-line courses by providing assistance in finding current and valid information for instructors delivering instruction on the Internet.
- Extend into the area of providing instruction and librarians must be involved in creating independent thinkers.
- Enhanced their roles to knowledge navigators and instructors teaching the discipline called information literacy.
- Be one of teaching critical thinking and resource-based learning.

New vocabulary in education such as: living curriculum, critical literacy, information power, information literacy, and information problem solving mandate that we re-examine our roles as professional information providers and educators. Students need to acquire the skills of evaluating information. This new vocabulary is bringing new challenges in library instruction. Changes in education such as the infusion of instructional technology and the use the Internet to deliver instruction has also changed how libraries and librarians can provide and assist instructors in teaching in the digital age.

New Trends in Instruction—Web Based Course Delivery

The trend in education towards distance learning and web-based courses is providing new challenges for information professionals as service providers as well as instructors. We are required to provide access to quality and valid information to support on-line instruction as well as provide on-line instruction both indirectly in the form of guides and on-line tutorials as well as directly in the form on courses to teach information literacy. Universities are recognising the necessity of requiring an information literacy course as part of the curriculum in the digital age.

As educators, the librarians are using a variety of tools and teaching techniques to assist students such as:

- *Provide instruction through learning guides and on-line tutorials:* Finding quality information is the biggest challenge our faculty and students are faced in the research and instructional process. With the advent of distance delivery of instruction and web-based pages for libraries using the vast amounts of information available on the Internet, it is essential that independent learners are skilled in locating information. Students can access these tutorials and guides from home or from the computers in the library and walk through self-paced instruction on any topic from "What is the Internet? To How do I do research?"
- *Provide access to guides to recommended search engines for the Internet:* Using search engines effectively and choosing the best search engines for your specific needs may be the most challenging skill that learners need to master. Guides to recommend search engines that introduce and compare search engines in a standard format are an invaluable tool for independent learners. Students can readily compare the different features of several search engines and access the search engines directly from your library's page.

- *Provide instruction in the area of Information Literacy:* Teaching Information Literacy in the electronic environment is a new and exciting role for librarians. Creating courses and formal instruction in the discipline of information literacy with the purpose of encouraging independent learners and critical thinkers to meet the challenges of the new information age is the role of the future for librarians. In today's workplace, employees are not only expected to work well with others, communicate well, find creative solutions to problems; they will also be expected to use the Internet and electronic information effectively to solve problems and conduct business. More and more businesses are moving towards conducting business on the Web for advertising, delivering services and products as well as using the Internet as a communication tool. Librarians must be involved in creating valuable employees with the current skills required to be successful on the job.

Librarians are the most appropriate professionals to lead the team of people in finding the answers to the challenges we are facing in the digital environments of electronic information and the Internet. They have always been the experts at teaching people how to use the tools to locate that information regardless of format. They are the most effective searchers and researchers and their basic role of teaching those skills has not changed. Thus, in this fast and ever-changing information environment, librarians need to make full use of information and multimedia technology to support a greatly expanded teaching venture. The technology and varied format of information is changing and making new demands on their profession. In this fast-paced world it is important that they change with the changing roles and challenges.

AS MANAGERS

Researcher address how change has affect everyone in the

organisations from leaders to employees and clients—the needs to shift his or her mind-sets, seeing the organisation and their established and new roles sometimes highly threatening and unfamiliar activities. Thus he added, employees need emotional support to adapt to change; support in learning new ways of working and relating. Linda claimed that information technology has changed a librarian's jobs; they have to readjust to new situation and develop new skills of managing the investments of an organisation—in people, technologies, and collections. As managers, they need to look for outcomes rather than just thinking about managing a resource at the resource level. The human resource in any organisation is the key to its success or failure.

Changes in Library Management

We have seen that the major external force that is technology had affected libraries; that means the library managers must use new structures in their management. *Strategic planning—strategic thinking*—should be a fundamental concept that librarians incorporate into their daily activities. Overall they need to give greater attention to strategic planning at the organisation and departmental level, and then integrating these strategic plans into the goals and activities of individual professionals. With a shifting organisational environment and culture, managers should shift their responsibilities and approach to one that is more consultative and supportive rather than one of authority and control.

The role of the manager should focus on:

- Coaching and mentoring staff.
- Development of staff.
- Developing shared values and vision among staff.
- Providing resources within framework of cost-benefit assessment.
- Taking pride in the accomplishments of others,
- Providing incentives to team work.

Library staff who are struggling to keep up with the demands in today's work environment require, indeed deserve, new ways for accomplishing their work. The redesign of the library organisation is imperative if we are to move rapidly and with an entrepreneurial spirit in the delivery of services in the current interactive high- speed communication environment.

Thus to be successful, libraries must reshape the prevailing corporate culture and build into their organisational structures and their approaches to work.

As managers, researcher stress that they must possess:

- The ability to identify, anticipate, and quickly respond to constantly changing customer needs.
- Capable of leaps forward and breakthrough performance.
- Must be ready to abandon formerly successful approaches to work, strategies, processing systems and services.
- Good communication at all levels, staff participation and training.

The librarians in transition that want to consciously manage their change efforts need to help their staff understand the change process and how they can positively participate. Creating an overall framework that shows the considered changes are a natural evolution from current practices, assessing that the organisation has the expertise and climate to implement the proposed changes.

Instead of organising personnel around how librarians do their work, librarians must:

- Organise around customers and how they do their work.
- Reduce hierarchy, flatten the organisation, and eliminate redundancy in order to be more responsive to changing needs and new opportunities and developments.
- Give up their need for control and their desire to create stability.

We Live in a Time of Change

The information has change our profession and library

managers today have to pick up new skills to adjust to changes and to be able to survive in the future.

AS INFORMATION RESOURCE MANAGER

The term Information Resource Manager refers to:

- "Individuals who are responsible for the provision of information resources—be they print or electronic or technical infrastructure—and the power of digital technology, which grows everyday. To provide the leadership to conceptualise and manage the broad array of information resources that are necessary to support its mission".

As an Information Resource Manager, the librarian would continually go through a ten-step process:

- *Step 1. Define the Customers:* Who are the library's primary customers?
- *Step 2. Understand the Customers Needs:* One of the best ways to help you analyse the needs of the workforce and effectiveness of your current information strategy, is to arrange an information audit examples:
  - Implementation of custom survey designed to take an inventory of products, services and personnel related to information activities
  - Interviews with key personnel
  - Understand the users needs
  - Analysis of surveys and interviews
  - Creation of 'information strategy' designed to help maximize investment in users and services
  - Recommendations
- *Step 3. Map Needs against Decisions and Sources:* This will list information originators and users; sources required and decision supported. It will also identify high pay-off opportunities, for example where certain information has multiple uses.
- *Step 4. Implement a Sourcing Strategy:* The source/ needs map from step 3 will point to clusters of

information needs that can give economies in purchasing. For example, purchasing a networked CD-ROM may be more cost-effective than doing multiple ad-hoc online searches.

- *Step 5. Define Information Policies and Standards:* Steps 1-4 will reveal, often to many people for the first time, the sheer wealth of information that is available. This step therefore involves:
  - Classification standards,
  - Ownership,
  - Life-cycle management standards
  - Agreed 'protocols and procedures' between owners and users.
- *Step 6. Select a Pilot Project:* Select a key decision process that involves people across several departments as a pilot.
- *Step 7. Select and Adapt Appropriate Technology:* With the selected pilot project acting as a focal point, now is the time to start detailed consideration example of the computer solution. The choices are bewildering, and are proliferating daily.
- Step 8. *Nurture the Intelligence Processes:* This requires encouraging interaction across departmental boundaries and subcultures. Therefore, the creation of events and forums to encourage this interchange is often a useful starting point.
- *Step 9. Focus Dissemination:* Issue weekly or monthly bulletins of key developments; it should be short and focused. They give organisation relevant and specific information that no external newsletter, with its generic coverage, can provide.
- *Step 10. Market the Capability:* Create two way interactions with library clients. Use all the techniques of marketing to reach the library's internal audience and consider carefully the incentives the library can offer to encourage the regular inflow of useful information.

AS TRAINER

Ben regard managing technological change is somewhat akin to the Queen's concept of progress in Through the Looking Glass. He claimed *"It takes all the running you can do, to keep in the same place. If you want to get somewhere else, you must run at least twice as that."* Thus to 'manage' this frenetic running pace, training is critically important. Trainers have to be very philosophical people, very adaptable, too. MacKellar claimed that two million anecdotes of unhappy and unavoidable crisis situations, however, do not replace the necessity of thorough preparation and competent training coverage, especially with basic tools such as Internet, CD-ROMs and other electronic sources.

He added, in the documentation manual for Folio VIEWS, the following four statements are listed, emphasising the fact that trainers have to train users to do more than simply be able to push the right buttons:

- *Information* does not equal knowledge.
- Use of *information* can lead to knowledge.
- If you can't find the *information* you need, gaining knowledge can be difficult.
- If you can't use the *information* once you find it, gaining knowledge can be impossible.

So, what can trainers do to move users from button pushing to knowledge gathering? They can be patient, teach some underlying technology, and explain some basic search rules. Erlendsdottir consider training in libraries as in other organisations, is divided into two main categories:

1. *Maintenance training*—that enables the library to maintain its existing procedures and include induction training for new entrants to the library system or particular parts.
2. *Basic updating and improvement training in identified areas*—whereby training should be concerned with the whole person, concepts, skills and behaviour patterns.

As suggested, the technological training needs of the librarians in libraries depend on the IT level of the particular level.

Thus, the librarian must:

- know the Art of the Search.
- know what the systems contain example how the shopping streets of information are laid out.
- know the back alleys as well as the main routes to the information example on the CD-ROMs.
- bargain with the system to get the 'best answers' in the cheapest, quickest way.
- consider using a greater range of visual and auditory challenges in the presentation.
- keep abreast of the ongoing and latest technological advancements.
- able to identify the body of core knowledge and skills required by them to run information and communication technology applications.
- improve and promote the existing and new library services to reach their clients.

Training library users to use these technological resources, and to understand the cultural rules and the new environment such as functional setup, linking, split screens, exporting, cutting and pasting) are the challenges. Trainers are similar in a way to personal shoppers for Westerners who land in Hong Kong and don't know the environment or culture. Thus the trainer's end goal is to see these clients finally doing their own shopping in the information marketplace, hopefully with enough expertise to be able to pick up a few bargains.

Why the Need for Training

The three major benefits are:

1. Appreciate the gaps that may exist between what is currently being done and what needs to be done.
2. Opportunity to make corrections in their systems within a safe environment.
3. Develop 'ownership' and reduce or eliminate staff

and users resistance to change, thereby adding longevity to the system.

Training for trainers is regard a necessity in academic libraries and it is the library's responsibility to structure training so as to help librarians clarify both their own expectations and the expectations of their clients and the organisation itself.

AS RESEARCHER

In a complex and rapidly changing environment, higher education must help students to become information literate. Information literacy enables students to recognise the value of information and use it to make informed choices in their personal, professional and academic lives. An information literate student effectively accesses, evaluates, organises, synthesises and applies information from a variety of sources and formats in a variety of contexts. Information literacy requires an ongoing involvement in learning and in evaluating information so that life long learning is possible."

As research and teaching increasingly rely on global networks for the creation, storage and dissemination of knowledge, the need to educate information-literate students has become more widely recognised. Students often lack the skills necessary to succeed in this rapidly changing environment, and faculty need training and support to make use of new technologies for effective teaching and learning. The current environment provides an opportunity for librarians to playa key role in the evolution of an integrated information literacy curriculum, in contrast to past efforts which were sporadic and rarely programmatically based. Librarians have always played a key role in research activities in the academic environment.

They have conducted library instructional orientations sessions to assist students doing research. Thus, to assist clients in their research activities, the librarian must acquire the information skills to manage the overload of information available in many formats propelled by technological advancements.

The Search Strategy

The best strategy involves identifying "what type of information need and which library resources will best provide that information." The time spent developing a well-organised search strategy will reduce the overall time and effort required to assist and conduct research. Following the steps in the *flowchart* below will lead to a well organised research report:

Follow chart

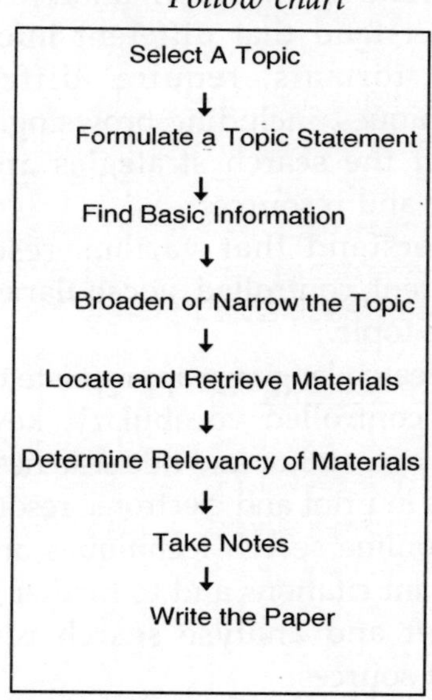

Information Literacy Competencies

The impact on student who is information literate is able to:

- Identify and articulate needs which require information solutions:
  - Recognise a specific information need.
  - Focus and articulate the information need into a researchable question.
  - Understand that the type and amount of information selected is determined in part by the parameters of the need, as well as by the information available.

- Identify and select appropriate information sources:
  - Recognise the availability of a variety of sources and of assistance with using them.
  - Identify types of information resources in a variety of formats and understand their characteristics.
  - Select types of information resources appropriate to a specific information need.
- Formulate and efficiently execute search queries appropriate for the information resource:
  - Understand that different information sources and formats require different searching techniques, including browsing.
  - Select the search strategies appropriate to the topic and resource.
  - Understand that various resources may use different controlled vocabularies to refer to the same topic.
  - Use search language appropriate to the source, such as a controlled vocabulary, key words, natural language, author and title searches to locate relevant items in print and electronic resources.
  - Use online search techniques and tools to locate relevant citations and to further refine the search.
- Interpret and analyse search results and select relevant sources:
  - Understand that search results may be presented according to various ordering principles.
  - Assess the number and relevance of sources cited to determine whether the search strategy must be refined.
  - Recognise the components of a citation and differentiate between types of resources cited, such as a book, periodical, or government document, as well as the format.
  - Use the components of a citation to choose those most suitable for the information need.
  - Perceive gaps in information retrieved and

determine whether the search should be refined.

- Locate and retrieve relevant sources in a variety of formats from the global information environment:
  - Understand the organisation of materials in libraries and use locally produced location guides.
  - Understand how to use classification systems and their rationale.
  - Use location information in the bibliographic record to retrieve locally owned resources.
  - Use local resources to locate information sources in the global information environment.
  - Understand that libraries have developed methods for locating and sharing resources not owned locally and use the appropriate resource sharing system, such as interlibrary loan or document delivery, to retrieve information.
  - Understand that the Internet may be a useful resource for locating, retrieving and transferring information electronically.
- Critically evaluate the information retrieved:
  - Use a variety of criteria, such as author's credentials, peer review, and reputation of the publisher, to assess the authority of the source.
  - Assess the relevancy of a source to an information need by examining publication date, purpose, and intended audience.
  - Recognise omission in the coverage of a topic.
  - Recognise and evaluate documentation for the information source, such as research methodology, bibliography or footnotes.
  - Distinguish between primary and secondary sources in different disciplines and evaluate their appropriateness to the information need.
  - Apply evaluation criteria to all information formats.
- Organise, synthesise, integrate and apply the information:

- Use appropriate documentation style to cite sources used.
- Summarise the information retrieved.
- Recognise and accept the ambiguity of multiple points of view.
- Organise the information in a logical and useful manner.
- Synthesise the ideas and concepts from the information sources collected.
- Determine the extent to which the information can be applied to the information need.
- Integrate the new information into existing body of knowledge.
- Create a logical argument based on information retrieved.

• Self-assess the information-seeking processes used:
  - Understand that information-seeking consists of evolving, non-linear processes that include making multiple decisions and choices.
  - Describe the criteria used to make decisions and choices at each step of the particular process used.
  - Assess effectiveness of each step of the process and refine the search process in order to make it more effective.
  - Understand that many of the components of an information seeking process are transferable and, therefore, are applicable to a variety of information needs.

• Understand the structure of the information environment and the process by which both scholarly and popular information is produced, organised and disseminated:
  - Understand that information structure, *e.g.*, how information is produced, organised, and disseminated, can vary from discipline to discipline.
  - Understand that the value of a particular type of information resource may vary from discipline to discipline.

   – Understand that the information structure in a particular discipline can change and modify search strategies to accommodate these changes.

- Understand public policy and the ethical issues affecting the access and use of information:
   – Understand the ethics of information use, such as knowing how and when to give credit to information and ideas gleaned from others by appropriately citing sources in order to avoid plagiarism.
   – Respect intellectual property rights by respecting copyright.
   – Understand concepts and issues relating to censorship, intellectual freedom, and respect for differing points of view.
   – Understand the social/political issues affecting information, such as:
      – Privacy.
      – Privatisation and access to government information.
      – Electronic access to information.
      – The exponential growth of information.
      – Equal access to information.

CYBRARIANS

The word 'Cybrarian' was coined by Michel Bauwens, Information Officer at BP Nutrition in Antwerp, Belgium, to describe the staff in a virtual library. We may expand this definition to an Information Professional/Librarian who utilises digital and networked communications technologies to the fullest to retrieve, evaluate and disseminate information. While it is not currently possible to obtain a degree in 'cybrarianship', there are possibilities for advancing your knowledge of these technologies.

Characteristics of Cybrarians

So, what then are the characteristics of cybrarians. Keller commented:

- They remember the fundamental functions

librarians perform: selection, description and intellectual access, interpretation, distribution, and preservation.

- They remember that they are present to serve the current, local population of readers first, but also perhaps remote readers as well, thanks to the networks.
- They remember also that they perform a vital role as custodians of culture, assuring that the records of man's investigations and creative works survive for those not yet born.
- Many of them are subject specialists, expert and educated in a discipline as well as prepared to 'teach' in structured and unstructured settings.
- Many of them are technical specialists, catalogers, circulation librarians, conservationists.
- Some of them were either subject specialists or technical specialists or both and then became managers or leaders.
- All of them are comfortable with the constant on-rush of LT. and realise their fundamental functions must be performed regardless of the media or format of the information carrier.
- All of them are acutely aware of the need to be as responsive as possible to individuals even while translating a cacophony of individual needs and requests to systems and services intended to serve whole populations, whole communities.
- All of them will be ready to work with their colleagues in the next building, the next city or town, the next country or continent by using the communications potential of the networks.
- None of them will need a lot of sleep, for there will be more and more for them to do.
- Many of them will have strong entrepreneurial spirit.

The IP is knowledge-based and service-oriented. In some form, the role of the IP has always been to assist others with a quest for knowledge. Information and the knowledge to which it leads have evolved through many forms-speech, writing, print, broadcast media and computer-based electronic media. Access to a high speed, national or international computer network will significantly alter the way in which professionals will work in the coming decade. He added tomorrow's cybrarian who is familiar with this multitude of information databases and services which can be searched, will possess a role that will emphasise on information-hunting strategy and provide a strategic advice for users with technologically literate background

ISSUES AND CHALLENGES

The impact of high technological development of digital libraries implies changes from the traditional role of the library as a service provider for printed publications, to a role as supplier of digital information. In comparison to conventional libraries, digital libraries provide efficient and qualitative services by collecting, organising, storing, disseminating, retrieving and preserving information.

TECHNICAL ISSUES

Cataloging and Capture of Images

The quantity/quality of information to be provided with each document must be decided. Most access to images will begin with text-based queries, so recording and representing this textual information in a usable form is critical. This would include information about the original work as well as about the technical characteristics of the digital image, and for WWW access all text must be annotated in HTML. If multiple copies of an image are maintained, careful documentation must distinguish between the same image in different formats or resolutions.

This will also relate to capabilities for image manipulation, such as zooming, changing colours, etc. The library materials should be scanned with much care. Some of them are very old and fragile materials. Capturing and preserving them is an issue to scanning, image processing and display technologies. The illumination of scanning must be held to a minimum in order to avoid damaging the original source. Qualitative scanners with accurate colour and high resolution are required. Scanning into the binding requires scanning cameras because the pages are not flat. Putting and pressing them into the scanner bed will lead to their deterioration.

The high resolution CCD camera allows any specific detail of the writing and painting to be reproduced. Extending library services to Internet resources is obvious. Because many institutions and private authors are nowadays publishing their works on the Internet. The integration of Internet resources into OP ACs presents fundamental challenges to a library catalog. Technical and semantic difficulties should be addressed in order to ensure the availability, actuality and quality of the Internet resources.

Access

User will want information easily accessible. The need of access tools will be more evident. The information needs to be immediately available on the net. A web user interface will be developed to provide unlimited and platform-independent access to the holdings. Each user who has access to Internet can via Web browser retrieve in the built digital library. This is the issue of access control.

The license agreements can influence the means of access. Can the service be accessed via passwords or can only be provided for organisation members? The access control should be implemented for different types of information and for various types of users. Libraries will provide access to *very* different types of information and to heterogeneous repositories. Z39.S0 allows simultaneous searches in different databases on different hosts and the presentation can be done using the facilities of WWW.

It simplifies the search process by making it possible for a searcher to use the familiar user interface and search the local library catalogs as well as any other remote databases that support the standard. So users do not need to learn new retrieval methods for each database and each library. Z39.S0 can be implemented on any platform. It enables different computer systems—with different operating systems, hardware, search engines, database management systems—to work together providing the end users with nearly transparent access to other systems. Thus, it will be desirable to establish the standardisation of Z39.S0 which will playa key role in information retrieval and in the Web.

Encoding Formats

In traditional libraries, the information is printed in books, journals, manuscripts, microfilms, etc. In contrast, in the digital era the information is stored in digital media, such as hard discs, CDs, etc. The storage formats differs from medium to medium, software to software and from generation to generation. Therefore, the digital materials should be stored in suitable formats which allow possible conversion from one to the other.

There are many digital projects which started to save their images in TIFF because TIFF is very suitable for black-and-white images reaching best compression rate and loss free. However, the well known web browsers, such as Netscape or Internet Explorer still do not support TIFF-Format. To display TIFF images you need to purchase a separate suitable viewer. Some plug-ins and shareware viewers are still unsatisfied. To increase the acceptance of end-users many libraries have converted those images to other suitable formats, *e.g.* GIF (Graphics Interchange Format), PDF (Portable Document Format), etc. Several big publishers like Kluwer, Elsevier, etc., supply electronic articles to libraries as PDF files. PDF viewer, called Acrobat Reader, is provided by Adobe for free.

Technological Obsolescence

OP AC was the first computerised application which stores document description about books, journals, etc. However, the size of these catalogs is very small. Now the information itself will be stored on computers and disclosed for the worldwide community. The libraries should be aware of the difficulties in preserving digital information for the future generations. The longevity of digital information should be ensured over generations. Users need assurance that digital archives remain readable and useful for a long time. Digital media have limited life.

Software and hardware is becoming from generation by generation obsolete. Therefore, a strategic plan is required according to data migration, integration of news media, new formats, etc. Data must be migrated from computer technology generation to the following generation in order to preserve the information and to ensure its use and exploitation in the far future.

Thus, building deep infrastructure is necessary. Furthermore, a work plan is also very important to set-up the framework and strategies for digital preservation, such as analysis of infrastructure, studying stakeholder interests.

System Capabilities

The system librarian must overweight the type of access to provide against questions of timeliness, system capabilities, and client expectations of good service. Pressure has been coming from library patrons and information system vendors to acquire systems and capabilities that provide access to a wider range of information resources.

Questions such as:

- Should the library select a 'free' screen-saver information product or a low-cost news-alert service for its collection?
- Should the library accept that these services are easily and inexpensively available to their end users from their own desktops, and that the library would better serve its corporate mission by choosing databases that provide more in-depth information?
- Will the library provide entry-level services for the users?

While the pressures of reduced budgets call for responsible management, the vision of the digital library raises the expectations of both library staff and patrons.

HUMAN RESOURCES

Constantly Changing Technology

Change is an opportunity but it does have its negative side as well. Librarians are being overwhelmed by the constantly ongoing and advancing technology.

The major drawbacks are:

- Mostly *'psychological'*, librarians find it nearly impossible to master all the tools. As claimed by one librarian, " Keeping up with the changes is like being in a huge race—you can't always see where you're going but you're going very fast and learning the wrong way could be a costly mistake.'
- Learning to cope with an increasingly frenetic pace of life brought about by the pressures of rapidly changing technology.
- Coming to terms with a sudden, significant expansion of the definition of what it means to be literate in an information-based and high technology-driven society.
- In addition, handling the *'human consultations'* again require greater demand and attention to:
  - Help users cope with problems involving net-working software, Web browsers, printing and downloading.
  - Dealing with library users which lack of information and library skills.
- *Clientele background*—knowledge of the user is the foundation on which decisions have to be based on how best the user can be served. How do librarians serve a clientele they know little about and coping their needs is the most tasks.

The technological empowerment isn't achieved by simply pushing a button on a machine. Putting information technology to work effectively requires a tremendous investment of time, effort, and resources.

Leadership for Managing Technology

The questions that academic libraries face today are finally about leadership:

- Will there be leaders who are able to recognise the historical moment and the choices it presents.
- Will they find ways to create the organisational conditions in which new visions, new concept, and a new language of workplace relations can emerge?
- Will they be able to create organisational innovations that can exploit the unique capacities of the new technology and thus mobilise their organisation's productive potential to meet the heightened rigours of global competition.
- Will there be leaders who understand the crucial role that human beings from each organisational stratum can play in adding value to the production of services.

If not, libraries will be stranded in a new world with old solutions. Librarians will suffer through the unintended consequences of change, because they have failed to understand this technology and how it differs from what came before.

Restructuring Job Manual and Library Activities

Changes in the nature of the job, the gap and psychological stress between the traditional roles and new roles. Change is scary especially if you've got staff who confused their worth with their job title/description. A great deal of work is needed on the restructuring of staff duties, physical structure and training for both staff and patrons. In terms of library activities such as marketing, it's not always easy for librarians to think of programmes and services as if they were consumer products. Limited time and cost often push marketing to the bottom of the priority list.

Core Competencies

A number of questions regarding core competencies for librarians: knowledge of sources, collection management skills, conducting a reference interview, communicating effectively in writing, and the ability to apply critical thinking skills to library patrons.

This raises issues such as:

- Is it possible to define minimal core competencies within the information disciplines.
- Are there common fundamental theories that librarians as information professionals should understand.
- What practical experiences should librarians possess.

Refashioning' Library Patrons

The changing IT opportunities create ever changing needs and expectations; thus underscore the need for academic libraries and librarians on:

- How to cope with an ongoing changing environment—one very different from the past and present?
- How to facilitate the networking needs of the users that will dominate the next ten years? This is the most toughest challenge.

AUTHORITATIVE AND VALIDATED INFORMATION

The growing demand from users for authoritative and validated information to be delivered in any format—print, e-mail or on disk at any agreed time and price. Users are overwhelmed with the vast array of information because of job pressure, and need to be able to contact the most reliable information services and resources.

COLLECTION DEVELOPMENT

There are significant increases in the quantity, range, and variety of globally published resources available for acquisition. Especially in the academic, research, and scholarly arena, tremendous and explosive growth in the volume and kind of material produced challenges the collection development objectives and resources of the university's library. This growth is fueled both by the drive towards specialisation creating sub disciplines, inter disciplines, and cross or multi disciplines or 'twig subjects'—and by technology's ability to create greater volumes of research data.

PUBLISHER/LIBRARIES

Researcher comment that in the Gutenberg era, publishers supply libraries with journals and other information products. Based on license agreements, libraries distribute these materials to their users. But now in the Post Gutenberg Galaxy, publishers distribute their products in digital forms. Therefore, a special issue has been raised by license agreement on digital information. The libraries should be aware and care about the future role of publishers. Will they still continue to distribute those materials via the library? or will they provide this service to the user directly? If the libraries continue providing these services, do the publisher allow them to store the materials on the library site? It is obvious that license agreements on digital materials with publishers are necessary in order to deliver these materials to the users to make print-outs and to download them. Publishers will not accept that libraries store digital archives at least at beginning of the publication because they worry about the control access. However, the long-term digital archiving will remain the task of the libraries.

To this end, profound expertise and qualified infrastructure are necessary to ensure the usability and preservation of this digital archive in the far future. Furthermore, a major issue is whether institutions could publish their own materials over the network instead of employing official publishers. There are some libraries and other institutions which collect in-house published materials and make them accessible via the Web.

DEALINGS WITH COPYRIGHT ASPECTS

Copyright protects 'literacy and artistic' works, such as scientific papers, stories, movies, music, software, etc. In libraries, very large part of the information is available in digital form and will be accessible to remote users. This lead to problems with the copyright owners regarding the exploitation of the work. The digital era has changed the content of the normal work exploitation.

So, on the one hand agreements between libraries and publishers should be negotiated, and on the other hand copyright regulations should be adapted to the new challenges. Current copyright legislation with regard to photocopies is very ambiguous and different from one country to another. On the other hand, it is quite clear that electronic copying is strictly forbidden without the explicit agreement of the copyright holders. It requires the understanding of what users actually want to do with information: 'how it will be used, by whom, for how long?" It is for this reason that many working groups and commissions are discussing what the legislation on electronic delivery should be.

COST AND MAINTENANCE

Financial pressure is driving much of the change taken place in academic library. Rapidly increasingly costs of IT materials, human resources, and facilities maintenance resulting in a gradual shift in library expenditure patterns. Expenditures required on IT for academic libraries will approximately increase.

VISION AND BUREAUCRACY

Problems of 'vision' and people not understanding the direction in which the top management of the libraries intend to take the organisation. Bureaucratic issues and culture are barriers to a more effective in delivering the best services to library patrons. The need to address quality issues/targets/ standard as we move into a global arena.

FEE FOR SERVICE

Charging for educational and intellectual reasons are also confronted with the issues of pricing. Charging direct fees to patrons for printed documents is an economic, practical, and managerial necessity if librarians are to provide users/patrons with the fullest possible range of service options. Librarians must choose to impose charges to users of specific services or be forced to eliminate and reduce services altogether.

THE LIBRARIANS' IMAGE

As in other countries, librarians for example in Southeast Asia have been facing the same crisis of low image. This problem consists of several factors including low salaries, lack of excitement, passive role as information resource custodians in providing services. Their work and capabilities have not been highly recognised by the society at large. And now with the future evolution in the world of the digital and virtual libraries, librarians fear that their profession as intermediary for the users will disappear when there are no longer any printed documents, but only computer terminals. Do digital libraries need librarians for future service and operations?

CONCLUSION

The scope and magnitude of change that are occurring in libraries today are both exciting and daunting, particularly when Information Professional contemplate how they will manage the many streams of technological innovations pouring into the libraries and the networked information world. And as the continuing evolution of IT will soon enable, and indeed require changes both in the design of information systems and in the way Information Professional define their roles.

The coming years may be difficult and to avoid becoming 'obsolete', librarians will need not only to accept, but embrace the emerging information technologies. The challenge for librarians is to rethink and recreate their place in this process, and to move the focus away from the library as a physical space to a new reality of the library providing knowledgeable people who offer a variety of essential and timely services. Therefore, like it or not, librarians must change, for failure to do so would mean lost of opportunities and career to individual in other disciplines.

2

Change Management Process

CHANGE MANAGEMENT STANDARDS

- All substantive changes to the IT Environment must adhere to the XX change Management process. A substantive change has the potential to affect the ability of users and systems to interact with each other.
- All changes must conform to the published guidelines that dictate the 'look and feel' of the XX web environment.
- All web page content changes must have the approval of the web page owner prior to change implementation.
- All changes to the production systems within IT will have a corresponding set of documentation that describes the change, the business reason for the change and the disposition of the change. This includes emergency and exception changes.
- The risk and/or impact ratings of the requested change will determine which of the four phases of the change workflow will be required to promote the change into production. For 'minor' changes only Analysis and Implementation will be required.
- Anyone with a valid XX Notes access will be able to enter a change into the Change Request process. Only authorised approvers will be able to accept a change request into the Change Management process.

STATUS OF CHANGES

The following status codes are used to reflect the status of a change request:

- *Open* – The change has been received and accepted but has not been assigned
- *In-Progress* – The change has been received, acknowledged and assigned. Work is in progress to fulfill the change request.
- *Approved* – The business and technical assessments have been completed and the change has been approved and committed to the change scheduler.
- *Rejected* – The change has been rejected and will be routed back to the Request for Service process and sent back to the customer with an explanation and a recommended course of action.
- *Closed* – The change request has been closed.
- *Canceled* – The change request has been canceled.

TYPES OF CHANGES

The Change Management Procedure applies to all types of changes related to the XX IT environment.

The following is a description of each of the types of changes that can take place and the rules that apply to each:

- *Application Changes:* Changes to any application code that is running on or linked to by any hardware or software in the XX IT environment. These changes are typically made to enhance the function or performance of or to fix a known error in the IT application environment. These changes cannot be implemented without approval of the owner of the application and cannot be requested by any programmer other than the one assigned to the programme. Assignment of Risk Category Level of the change is to be a joint effort of both the owner and the Change Implementer.
- *Hardware Changes:* All XX IT and IT support equipment installations, discontinuances and

relocations are controlled by the Change Management Procedure. This activity can be requested by anyone but must have the approval of the Operations Manager.

- *Visual Image Changes:* Changes to the 'artistic' presentation of web pages are not required to make entries into the Change Management system. Changes to 'Active' areas of the web page are required to use the XX Change Management procedure.
- *Software Changes:* The criteria for entering a software change into the Change process are based upon the effect that the changes may have on the IT support resources. If the changes affect the system, users or the support staff there is a requirement to enter it into the Change process. If the change is made for the exclusive benefit of the requester and if failure could not affect anyone else, that change would be exempt from the Change Process. For example, a change made by a programmer affecting a procedure or a programme under development on a test application requires no entry. However, when stand-alone test time is required on a production system, a change request form is required.
  - Typically, software changes would include changes to the Operating System, Vendor supplied Programme Products, e.g., Visual Studio, Java, etc., or common application support modules. However, during the last two and first five workdays of each month changes are restricted to emergency and critical necessities as determined by the Director of Information Technology.
- *Network Changes:* All installations, discontin-uances and all relocations of equipment used for IT teleprocessing communications are entered into the change process. This includes all routers, switches

and telephone lines as well as Personal Computers if they are connected to the network.

- *Environmental Changes:* Environmental changes normally involve the facilities associated with the IT Installation. These facility changes include items such as air conditioning, chilled water, raised flooring, security, motor generators, electricity, plumbing and the telephony system for voice and data. For example, when there is a planned weekend power outage initiated by the local power company this information is submitted to the Change Management Process a minimum of two weeks prior to the scheduled outage and communicated to management, staff and the user community.
- *Documentation Changes:* All procedural changes to the standard operating procedures will be implemented through the Change process. Also, all permanent deviations from the published schedule time for running of production applications will be communicated through the Change Management system.

CHANGE LEVELS

The following guidelines for definition of Change risk levels are provided for consideration during the planning cycle. It must be clearly understood that these requirements are the minimum for each of the defined levels. The Requester may wish to plan additional lead times, documentation or reviews to insure that targets can be met and planned implementation schedules can be achieved. All changes are tracked, correlated and used for management reporting, statistics, trending, etc., to identify when and where additional resources should be provided.

For any change that fails, the Change Requester must enter an explanation in the comments section of the Change Record for that change and notify the Change Coordinator. The Change Coordinator will then close the change with the appropriate close status. If the change is to be attempted at a later time, the Change Requester should re-enter the change with the new date. Changes that cause a Platform outage will be reviewed at a Quality Measurement Meeting.

LEVEL E CHANGES

Emergency changes are those changes that are vital in order to ensure that IT's committed service levels are maintained. An Emergency change should not be used in order to bypass the appropriate lead-time for a change that has been entered into the system.

Exception changes are those changes that are a result of a business need and must be installed prior to the required lead-time. These types of changes proceed to the implementation phase when the requester's manager and the Director of Information Technology acknowledge that an Emergency or an Exception situation exists and authorise the modification planned. These changes will be post-reviewed to assure successful implementation, along with identification of any external impacts or new requirements. Post-review will also evaluate the reason for the Level E change request and try to determine a way of eliminating this requirement in the future. The post-review will also evaluate if, in fact, the change addressed a real or a perceived emergency condition. In all cases, the review must determine if additional action is required, what that action should be and who will be responsible for the action. Documentation requirements for Emergency changes are the same as any change. The Requester is responsible for meeting all requirements for the change documentation within one week of the implementation.

For non-application changes:

- Is the change needed to restore immediate service to the end user.
- Is the change necessary to fix an existing problem immediately.
- Is this a change that must be installed immediately but the need for it was not recognised early enough to be approved through the regular process.

For application changes:

- Must this change be done immediately to fix problems for jobs that ABENDed during the previous night or are required to run in order to bring up on-line systems.

What Types of Management Approval is Required for Level E Changes

Approval required by:

- Director of Information Technology or her designee.
- Change Management Process Owner or his designee.
- Manager of the user department requesting the change.

Depending on the scope and impact of the proposed change, approval by one or more of the following individuals may be required.

- Operations Manager.
- Application Development Manager.
- Network and Technical Services Manager.

LEVEL 4 CHANGES

A Level 4 Change would have a major impact on IT services if a problem occurs during install. The install time is lengthy and the backout is very difficult or impossible. Level 4 Change Requests are to be entered into the Change Management Data Base at least thirty business days prior to the planned implementation date. The Requester or representative for a Level 1 change is required to attend the Change Communication meeting immediately prior to implementation so that any questions or concerns may be addressed.

Whenever a Level 4 change must be expedited to address a critical timing situation, a special meeting must be held. To expedite a Level 4 change, all parties that may be affected by this change must be present or represented at the special meeting. It is the responsibility of the change requester to arrange the meeting and assure attendance by the required groups or individuals. If the required groups or individuals cannot be assembled, the change cannot be expedited and an escalation will be required.

How do you know that the Change Falls Under Level 4

For non-application changes:

- From the end user's eyes, is it possible for the change to have a major impact on services if problems occur.
- Is the change visible to all end users.
- Is this a high-risk change.
- Is this the first time this change has been done.
- Is the change difficult or impossible to backout.
- Is it extremely difficult to install the change.
- Does the change involve a lengthy install time.

For application changes:

- Would failure of the job being changed stop the flow of all jobs for critical files or an application system.

What Types of Management Approval is Required for Level 4 Changes

Approval required by:

- Change Review Board.
- Manager of user department requesting change.

Depending on the scope and impact of the proposed change, approval by one or more of the following individuals may be required.

- Operations Manager.
- Application Development Manager.
- Network and Technical Services Manager.

LEVEL 3 CHANGES

A Level 3 Change may impact a large number of end users. It is a high-risk change that requires a significant effort to backout. Level 3 Change Requests must be entered into the Change Management database fifteen business days prior to implementation. All Level 3 changes will be communicated via the Change Management reporting system. The requester or representative for a Level 3 change is required to attend the Change Communication Meeting immediately prior to implementation so that any questions or concerns may be addressed.

How do you know that the Change Falls Under Level 3

For non-application changes:

- Will the change be visible to a large number of end users.
- Is this a high-risk change.
- Has the change been done only infrequently?
- Will a significant effort be required to backout the change.
- Is it difficult to install the change.

For application changes:

- Would failure of the job being changed stop the flow of jobs for non-critical files or applications.

What Types of Management Approval is Required for Level 3 Changes

Approval required by:

- Manager of user department requesting change.
- Network and Technical Services Manager.
- Change Review Board.

LEVEL 2 CHANGES

A Level 2 Change is not transparent, but is minimal in risk and impact. It is the responsibility of the Requester to notify any areas of a potential impact. The change is a Level 2 if it requires an IPL of a system, subsystem or the restart of a critical component on a production system. Level 2 Change Requests must be entered into the Change Management database prior to the Scheduled Change Window being requested. The Requester or representative for a Level 2 change is required to attend the Change Communication meeting immediately prior to planned implementation so that any questions or concerns may be addressed. All Level 2 changes will be communicated via the Change Management reporting system and will be tracked and reported by the Change/ Problem Coordinator.

Examples of Level 2 changes:

- Single fixes—APAR, PTF, etc.
- Low usage programme product upgrades, installations.
- PARMLIB updates which require an IPL to implement.
- Regular maintenance updates to system or application libraries.
- Hardware Preventative Maintenance.
- Data management to critical volumes.

How do you Know that the Change Falls Under Level 2

For non-application changes:

- Will the change have only minor impact on services provided to the end users if problems occur
- Will the change be visible only to a small group of end users.
- Is this a moderate risk change.
- Is the change relatively simple to install.
- Has the change been implemented successfully a number of times before.
- Does it require only a moderate effort to backout the change quickly.
- Will it require only an IPL, recycle of major application or reloading of an NCP to implement or backout.

For application changes:

- Is this the first time the job has been installed.
- Must this job be fixed to run tonight.

What Types of Management Approval is Required for Level 2 Changes

Approval required by:

- Manager of user department requesting change.
- Change Review Board.

LEVEL 1 CHANGES

A Level 1 Change has little or no external visibility, no

external dependencies or no operator intervention. There is no associated risk or impact with the change, either to the system if the change is incompatible or to the Requester if the change implementation is delayed. The change does not require an IPL or recycle of an application to implement or backout. Level 1 changes are entered into the Change data base and will be communicated daily to any affected areas where impact or interest can be identified outside of the Requester's own area.

How do you Know that the Change Falls Under Level 1

For non-application changes:

- Will the change have only minimal or no impact on services provided to the end users if a problem occurs.
- Is the change familiar or common to those who will implement it.
- Is the change reliable and low risk.
- Is the change easy to backout if a problem occurs.
- Can it be backed out without an IPL, recycle of a major application, or reloading of an NCP.

For application changes:

- Would failure of the job stop just this job.
- Is this a low priority job.

What Types of Management Approval is Required for Level 1 Changes

Approval required by:

- Manager of user department requesting change.
- Change Review Board.

CHANGE REQUEST FLOWS

ASSIGN CHANGE IMPLEMENTER FLOW

Description:

- The Assign Change Implementer flow begins once a change request has been documented and selected for the change management process. During this workflow, a change record is assigned to an appropriate owner, the change record is updated with this assignee information, and the change is sent to the assignee.

Scope Inclusion:

- All changes reviewed by the Change Review Board.

Scope Exclusion:

- Changes not accepted by the Change Management process or Changes not reviewed by the Change Review Board.

Goal:

- To ensure that change requests are assigned to appropriate implementers.
- To ensure that the change management workload is allocated by area of expertise.
- To balance workload within an area of expertise.

Start Trigger:

- Initial change record.

Stop Trigger:

- Initial change record is assigned to an owner.

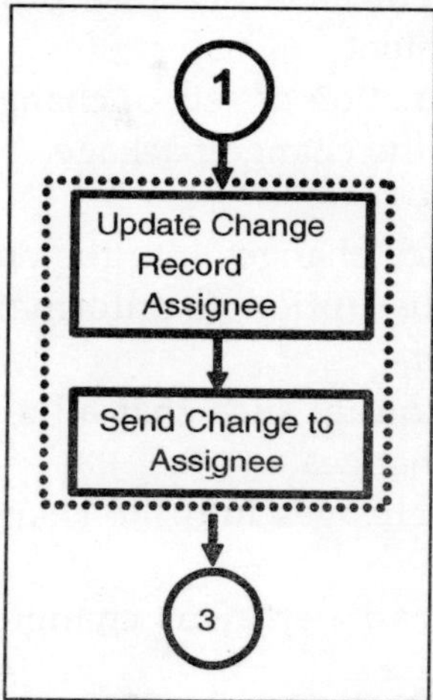

Fig 2.1 Workflow Diagram for Assign Change Implementer

Workflow Details for Assign Change Implementer (fig. 2.1):

- *Update Change Record Assignee:* Assign the change an owner based on the classification of the change.

- *Send Change to Assignee:* Place the assignee information into the change record and send an e-mail notification to the assignee.

ENTER CHANGE REQUEST FLOW

- *Description:* The Enter Change Request flow begins when a change request is submitted. In this activity, all required information about the change and supporting documentation is entered into the Change Management system. The change request should be submitted in accordance with the time frame required by the initial impact assessment.
- *Scope Inclusion:* All changes, including software, hardware, control mechanisms, configurations, environments, facilities, databases, business applications, processes, and procedures.
- *Scope Exclusion:*
  - Development activities that produce the actual change content.
  - The coordination of sets of changes.
  - Testing of the change package.
- *Goal:*
  - To introduce changes into the environment with minimal disruption to information technology and its users.
  - To communicate such that all affected users are aware of changes.
  - To log all changes into the change management system.
  - To ensure all pertinent change information is collected.
  - To ensure all changes meet lead time criteria.
- *Start Trigger:*
  - Change Request.
- *Stop Trigger:*
  - Fully documented and approved change request.

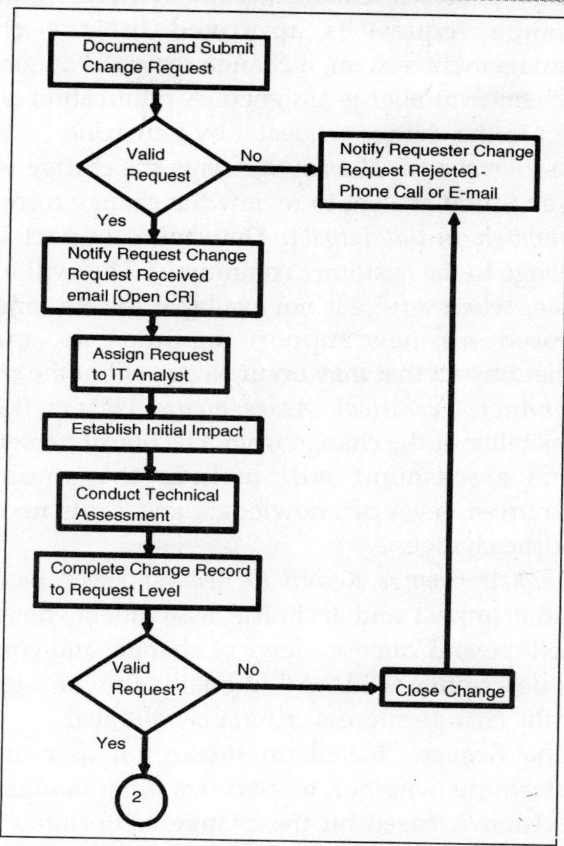

Fig 2.2 Workflow Diagram for Enter Change Request

Workflow details for enter change request (see fig. 2.2):

- *Document and Submit Change Request:* Collect system change request and begin preliminary review of the change.
- *Valid Request:* Determine whether or not to submit change request into change management system based on whether the request form has a managers signature, it is within IT responsibility, and filled in correctly.
- *Notify Requester Change Request rejected – phone call or e-mail:* If change request is rejected, provide a form of notification.

- *Notify Requester Change Request received – e-mail:* If change request is approved for the change management system, a change record is opened and a change number is assigned. A notification is auto-sent to the change requester by Peregrine.
- *Assign request to IT analyst:* Assign the change request to an initial analyst to review the change record.
- *Establish Initial Impact:* Determine impact of the change to the customer community. This will include times when service is not available, testing time, new procedures, new support requirements, and any other impact that may occur as a result of the change.
- *Conduct Technical Assessment:* Determine the feasibility of the change from a technical perspective. This assessment will include the amount of resources, level of knowledge, and skills necessary for the change.
- *Complete Change Record to Request Level:* Based on initial impact and technical assessment, determine the type and category level of change, and complete all descriptive fields. Additionally, the completeness of the change success criteria is validated.
- *Valid Request:* Based on the initial assessments, determine whether to perform this change. This decision is based on the change conforming to the strategy, resources being available, and whether or not it is already being worked on.
- *Close Change:* Mark change record as closed when it doesn't pass validation requirements.

MONITOR CHANGE CALENDAR FLOW

Description:

- The Monitor Change Calendar flow determines the scheduling for changes to be deployed. During this workflow, changes are penciled into a calendar, and the schedule is monitored for changes that are completed or have run out of time in their scheduled change deployment window. If time has expired for a change then it can be escalated and rescheduled based on escalation standards.

Scope Inclusion:

- Changes that are formally put into the change calendar.

Scope Exclusion:

- Changes that are not formally put into the change calendar.

Goal:

- Monitor the change calendar for changes that have not been completed and have run out of time for the purpose of change escalation.
- Allow for changes to be rescheduled.
- Allow for changes to be removed from the change calendar upon completion.

Start Trigger:

- A change request has been assigned an owner and has been sent to that assignee.

Stop Trigger:

- A change is complete and removed from the calendar.

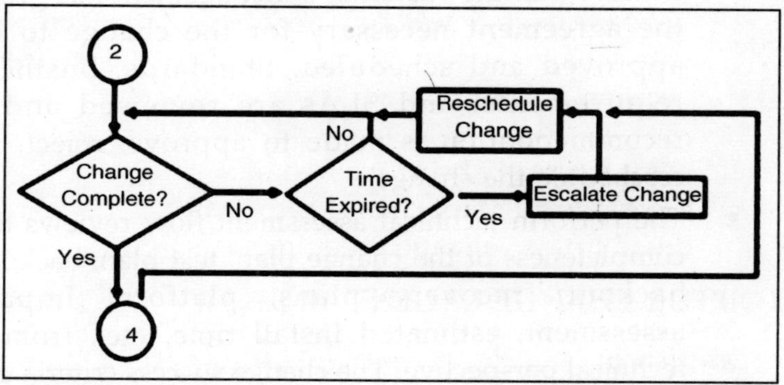

Fig 2.3 Workflow Diagram for Monitor Change Calendar

Workflow Details for Monitor Change Calendar (fig. 2.3):

- *Change Complete:* Monitor the change calendar for change work that has been completed.
- *Time Expired:* Determine whether a change record

that is incomplete has run out of time.

- *Escalate Change:* Reclassify the change to a higher change category level if time has expired.
- *Reschedule Change:* Update the calendar with a schedule for the change after it has been escalated or if the change package is incomplete.

PERFORM ASSESSMENTS FLOW

Description:

- The Perform Assessments flow involves conducting both a business and technical review of the change package. The assessments determine if the change package is complete and can therefore continue through the change management process.
- Specifically, the perform business assessment flow involves validating the impact of the proposed change on XX from a business perspective, evaluating the completeness of the success criteria and communication plan and reviewing the backup/ backout/ recovery plans. The assessment looks at the proposed timing of the change and ensures that the customer's management has given the agreement necessary for the change to be approved and scheduled. Standards, business requirements, and SLAs are reviewed and a recommendation is made to approve, reject, or reschedule the change.
- The perform technical assessment flow reviews the completeness of the change plan, test plan, backup/ backout/ recovery plans, platform impact assessment, estimated install time, etc., from a technical perspective. The change success criteria are validated and the impact of the change to the environment is reviewed to ensure it has been accurately evaluated. Technical standards are enforced and a decision is made to approve, reject, or reschedule the change.

Scope Inclusion:

- All documented changes with a change category that requires a formal business or technical assessment.

Scope Exclusion:

- Changes with change categories that specifically do not require formal business or technical assessments.

Goal:

- To ensure that all factors have been taken into consideration in terms of the business aspects of the change.
- To ensure that all factors have been taken into consideration in terms of the technical aspects of the change.
- To ensure that everything required to deploy the change and to maintain service is included in the change request.

Start Trigger:

- Fully documented change record.

Stop Trigger:

- Assessed change.

Workflow Details for Perform Assessments (fig. 2.6):

- *Business Review of Change Package:* Review the change package for the following points:
  - Ensure that the business requirements will be met.
  - Verify existence and completeness of backup/ backout recovery plans.
  - Verify existence of test plans, including the testers names and expected results.
  - Ensure that the change conforms to business standards and policies.
  - Determine whether the change conforms to service level agreements.
  - Review communication plan for change.

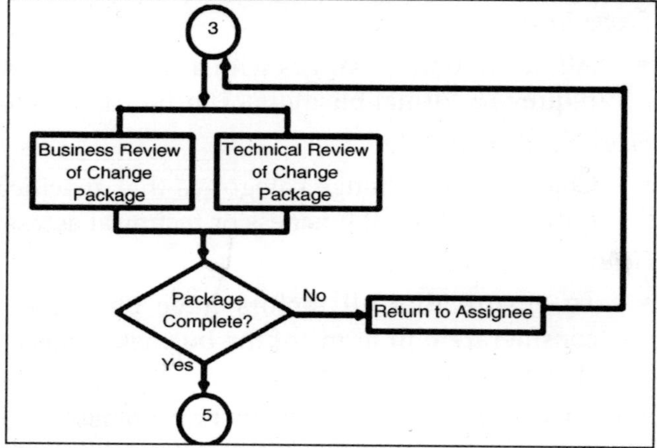

Fig 2.4 Workflow Diagram for Perform Assessments

- *Technical Review of Change Package:* Review the change package for the following points:
  - Determine the impact on the technical environment.
  - Ensure that the change conforms to technical standards.
  - Verify the completeness of the change plan.
- *Package Complete?:* Make a decision on whether the package is complete based on the results of the business and technical reviews.
- *Return to Assignee:* If the package is determined not complete than the change is returned to the assignee and can be rescheduled.

APPROVE CHANGE FLOW

Description:

- The Approve Change flow is initiated as soon as both the business and technical assessments have been completed. If the change is approved, it is passed on to the next sub-process to finalise scheduling. If the change is rejected or determined to be rescheduled, it may be sent back to the business or technical assessment subprocesses once the necessary actions are taken. All parties that have been involved to this point in the process should be notified of the approval, rejection or rescheduling.

Scope Inclusion:

- All changes that have been forwarded for approval from a business and technical perspective and whose change categories indicate the requirement for formal approval.

Scope Exclusion:

- Changes with change categories that specifically so not require formal approval.

Goal:

- To ensure that appropriate approval is obtained for change requests.
- To ensure that the change record is properly updated.
- To minimize service interruption.

Start Trigger:

- Completed change record with business and technical review including recommendation.

Stop Trigger:

- Approval for change deployment.

Workflow Details for Approve Change:

- *Final Change Review:* Final review of change prior to acceptance and scheduling.
- *Accept Change:* Based on the result of the final change review, determine whether to go ahead with or close the change.
- *Close Change:* If it is decided not to continue with change, then change record is closed by change coordinator.
- *Notify Requester Change Request rejected – phone call or e-mail*

IMPACT OF INFORMATION AND COMMUNICATIONS TECHNOLOGY

Information and Communications Technology (ICT) have transformed Library and Information services globally. The Internet has provided universal access to information.

Technological innovation has dramatically increased the rate of conversion of knowledge, information and data into electronic format. Developments in the software arena has generated powerful knowledge management software which has transformed the way knowledge is organised, stored, accessed and retrieved.

The digital revolution driven by ICT innovation has transformed academic libraries fundamentally. It has impacted on every sphere of academic library activity, e.g., the form of the library, collection development strategies, library buildings and consortia. Information and communications technology have changed the academic library in a profound way. Computers and networked electronic resources had become an integral part of the academic library the past decade. This has been underscored by the phenomenon of knowledge or information commons in academic libraries, which refer to a specific environment in the library where a designated number of PC workstations, networked to databases and other e-resources, are made available to students. Every sphere of the academic library is being affected by ICT quite radically.

No longer is the library the untouchable custodian of information. It is being shaken to its very foundation, in fact its existence is being threatened. The academic libraries' traditional role of information custodian had been reduced to that of being one of many information providers. Of all the information and communication technologies the Internet and particularly the World Wide Web with its graphical user interface, has had the greatest impact on the information revolution. The number of electronic resources available on the Internet is growing at a phenomenal rate.

One of the major search engines Alta Vista has reported in 1996 that it has indexed 30 million Web pages. By 1998 the number of Web pages indexed by this search engine has leaped to 90 million. According to Farrow wide spread publicity has lead to assumptions that the Internet will meet all user information needs and that there will be no need for professional librarian intervention in future between user and information resources. Moyo states that student expectations that all their research needs will be met online are on the increase. Not only do students expect to find the information they need online, they also expect it to be available in full text. According to Tam and Robertson these assumptions have lead to a reluctance to use the physical library materials and to a decrease of visits to the library.

This phenomenon has fuelled fears of potential future job losses amongst librarians. Cheng explores the impact of information technology from an information ecological perspective. In information ecology the focus is not on information technology but on the human activities that are served. Cheng cites Nardi and O'day who draw a parallel between the explosive growth of information technology and the consequential Information explosion and a volcanic eruption. This eruption is impacting on everyone existing with the information ecosystem. Cheng emphasise the importance that we as academic librarians are clear about the challenges posed by this situation and also the opportunities offered.

Cheng highlights some of the changes that took place within the information ecology:

- The way we gather information, organise it, disseminate and use information has changed.
- The evolution of the Web has lead to availability of masses of information, electronic journals and databases.
- The way information is being published is evolving rapidly, e.g., it is threatening current practices.
- New problems have come to the fore, e.g., the issue of intellectual property rights of e-resources.
- User expectations have changed. Users expect full text delivery to the desktop.

Researchers are of the opinion that the changes that library and information services face are of an unknown and unpredictable nature. He states that it is impossible for library managers to predict future trends accurately. He feels traditional change management techniques are inadequate to deal with the changing environment that libraries are facing. For him it is a scenario where one has to brace oneself for whatever occurs. Under these conditions it is crucial that libraries make optimal use of the entire workforce.

It is of fundamental importance that customer service be given top priority. It is also essential that flexible organisational structures be created where workloads and responsibilities are shared and trust and responsibility are the norm rather than control. For library and information services in academic libraries to prevail under these conditions real leadership and real changes in management styles and organisational structures are necessary.

CONCEPTS DEFINED

Change

Robbins and Coulter defines change as any alterations in people, structure or technology. Change involves moving from the current state of things, the status quo, to a new state of things. It is therefore a process of moving from what is known to the unknown.

Information and Communications Technology (ICT)

Adeyoyin cites Bayode who defines ICT as "the acquisition, processing, storage, and dissemination of information by means of computers and other telecommunication equipment." The Wikipedia free Internet encyclopaedia defines "information technology (IT) or information and communication(s) technology (ICT)" as the "technology required for information processing. In particular the use of electronic computers and computer software to convert, store, protect, process, transmit, and retrieve information".

From the definitions it is clear that the terms IT and ICT are used interchangeably and has the same meaning. According to Jimba information technology is rooted in three sectors namely information technology, telecommunications and the media and these sectors are converging on one another.

TYPES OF CHANGE

Researcher define change along a continuum ranging from low-scope to high-scope change.

Evolutionary Change

Evolutionary change is incremental by nature. Incremental change is smooth and happens gradually in an organised and predictable way. Incremental change tends to be small changes that lead to improvement but does not alter the operational structure of the academic library.

Strategic Change

Strategic, revolutionary or transformational change leads to radical transformation and often changes the general organisational structure. Transformational change tends to be very traumatic by nature. It can be generated as a response to a major crisis or a complete change in organisational strategy or purpose. The outcome of this type of change can lead to organisational transformation to the effect that the organisation might look completely different from what it used to be.

Discontinuous Change

The academic library is confronted with change that is unlike anything it has been exposed to before. Management theorists use the term discontinuous change. Pugh notes that discontinuous change is different from revolutionary change that is change undertaken to generate rapid results. Discontinuous change is unique in the sense that established management practices are inadequate to deal with it, in fact there is no model, paradigm or pool of experience that managers can fall back onto.

Researcher describes discontinuous change as turbulent, complex, traumatic, uncertain and of a revolutionary nature which requires different management skills to survive, supported by highly trained, motivated, flexible and multi-skilled staff that can be redeployed quickly and effectively if necessary. There is a stark contrast between the clearly defined boundaries of businesses in the 1960's and 1970's and the postindustrial era that is characterised by volatility, complexity and uncertainty. "This type of random, discontinuous change—which, by definition, is fast, traumatic, and revolutionary – requires very different management and leadership skills if the challenges it presents are to be handled innovatively and opportunistically." What organisations need in order to survive is highly committed, skilled, informed and trained staff which is willing to give their all.

Until 15 years ago change was incremental. One could build on lessons learned before. Since then change had become discontinuous. In this climate old management behaviours are inadequate. New ways of doing things are imperative which questions the practices that worked in the past. Information services in the academic library are driven by ICT with all its uncertainties and instability. Change is occurring at a greater dimension than ever before. The volume, pace and complexity of change is increasing at an unprecedented rate. A comparison between 1970 and to-day reveals that in 1970 only 5 per cent of change within organisations was of a continuous nature. Currently 75 per cent of all organisational change is of a continuous nature.

IMPACT OF ICT DEVELOPMENTS ON STAFF

Managers often introduce drastic change without considering its impact on people. People respond to change in a myriad of ways. Any significant change will impact on people's self-esteem, their motivation to do well, their status or the stress they experience be it positive or negative. It is of vital importance that managers do not overlook people when dealing with an ever-changing environment.

According to Morgan research suggests that 90 per cent of change initiatives fail because people are not taken into consideration. Change is good for academic libraries but its adoption requires tremendous input of physical, mental and emotional energy. After having to make intense inputs to accomplish change people expect to reach a plateau, a period for review and restoration of energy. The problem is that in the academic library this plateau had become non-existent because one peak follows after the other.

Phases People go through when Exposed to Radical Change

Elizabeth Kubler-Ross has identified 5 stages that patients

experience when confronted with personal loss or death. These stages are denial, anger, bargaining, depression and acceptance.

Conner has used Kubler-Ross's 5 stages as a basis and extended it to 8 stages:

1. *Stability:* This is the phase just prior to change where everything is still normal.
2. *Immobilised:* When confronted with radical change people initially experience shock, confusion and become disoriented. During this phase people are out of touch with reality.
3. *Denial:* Conner defines denial as a refusal to accept reality. According to Fossum denial is a psychological defence mechanism that kicks in when individuals are confronted with radical change. It is a refusal to accept reality while the person's internal resources are being mobilised to eventually face a situation. To help staff to deal with this phase managers should use techniques designed to promote awareness that change has occurred or is in the process of occurring. The denial phase is a critical stage in the change process and people experience it differently. While some people are still dazed and out of touch with reality others may be ready to move on. Spending time on an individual bases with people struggling with this phase can be very useful.
4. *Anger:* During this phase people experience anger and outrage. They become emotional, irritated, frustrated and hurt and may often lash out at those supporting them.
5. *Bargaining:* This is a negotiation phase with a view to avoid the negative aspects of change. A typical example would be negotiating an extension of a deadline one is facing. This phase indicates the person is reaching a position where he or she can no longer avoid reality. This phase also demarcates the beginning of acceptance.

6. *Depression:* It is normal for people to become depressed when confronted with major change that affects them negatively. This is a very unpleasant phase but is an indication that the individual has come to complete realisation of the negative change being faced. It is an unpleasant phase but indicates another step towards acceptance.
7. *Testing:* At this point a sense of control is regained. A person might explore how to set new goals.
8. *Acceptance:* At this point people accept change. To go with an employee through the negative response model can be a costly exercise because people need support at every step of the way. However the cost of an employee failing to go through the process can be more costly to an organisation.

Resistance

Managing change within the academic library is essentially about managing people since it is people that effect change. People who are such a critical factor in change implementation can also be a stumbling block to the change process by resisting change. Change initiatives are often shipwrecked because of resistance. Resistance leading to escalation in costs often delays change processes.

Resistance is such a central element in change management that it deserves serious attention in the change implementation process. Researcher states that one must neither fear resistance nor make efforts to avoid it. The inertia of systems which have relied on doing things as they have always been done and achieving objectives through well-tried methods is not to be underestimated. It is part of the organisational instinct for survival and as well as comfort and complacency and it breeds resistance.

The successful implementation of change in the academic library is by and large dependent on the attitudes of people to the change process. People respond in different ways to change. Whereas some people will experience change as an exiting and stimulating event others may find it frightening and intimidating and consequently resist change.

Causes of Resistance

Pendlebury identified the following causes of resistance:

- Lack of realisation of a problem.
- Not grasping the implementation of a solution.
- Outright rejection of a solution as it is seen as the incorrect option.
- Fear of the outcome of change.
- Lack of interest.

This kind of behaviour is often the result of a vision not clearly communicated or staff's unwillingness to face up to the demands of change.

Researcher identifies the following additional reasons why people resist change:

- *Security:* Fear of potential job losses.
- *Financial:* Fear of loss of income.
- *Pride and satisfaction:* Technological innovation might make jobs and skills redundant.
- *Freedom:* Structural changes might impact on freedom of decision-making.
- *Authority, responsibility and status:* Restructuring might lead to a loss of authority and responsibilities.

Resistance tends to manifest itself in many different ways. Conner distinguishes between overt and covert resistance. Overt resistance is open and can be constructive. Covert resistance is submerged and can gain momentum unobtrusively and ruin a project. Fossum describes covert resistance as a passive-aggressive form of resistance. It is difficult to manage because on the surface a person appears to do nothing but is often busy sabotaging a project through negative statements. In major change there will always be resistance. Creating an environment where people can openly express their fears will go a long way to minimize resistance. Managers need to be aware that resistance often manifests itself in an increase in absenteeism, reductions in quality, decreased productivity, strikes or slowdowns and increase in grievances.

STRATEGIES TO FACILITATE CHANGE WITHIN THE ACADEMIC LIBRARY

The prevailing organisational culture will determine how easy or complex it will be to communicate the need for change, share the vision and get people's opinions and participation. In an open culture communication is easiest. The leadership style, the trust people have in top management and the extent to which people are able to openly express themselves is of cardinal importance. Managers who have successfully implemented change understand that resistance is a natural reaction and would encourage it rather than suppress it. They would even reward people for open resistance in a constructive manner.

Fossum states that clear and open communication about pending change is crucial. Managers must not allow people to hear via rumours or the grapevine or the media about pending change. They should be open and upfront about pending change. Hearing from a third party will undermine trust and credibility. When communicating change it is important to send out positive and optimistic messages. Conner is of the opinion that effective leaders can change people's mindsets to a realisation that meaningful change is not only essential but also possible.

Morgan argues that buy-in is crucial in change management. If staff can take ownership of change, it will bolster commitment and assist in overcoming any obstacles. It is also crucial to involve staff in the decision making process. Participation will break the management versus staff syndrome. Instead of letting management do the problem solving it is useful to involve staff at all levels in this process. Managers must be careful not to make assumptions about the acceptance of change. It is better to get accurate feedback through interviews or surveys.

Techniques to Make Change Positive

Change creates conflict but the negative energy generated can be turned in constructive energy. Managers should realise that conflict in itself is not necessarily negative. It creates an opportunity to do creative problem solving with the staff. Conflict must never be taken personally. If people disagree managers should see it as an opportunity to find a more elegant solution that more staff members will find acceptable. People should be encouraged to be honest about how they feel and support one another. Managers should maintain their sense of humor. It is essential to cultivate an atmosphere that will transform negative issues of conflict into positive constructive energy.

Celebrate Success

It is important to sign-off change to ensure closure and enable people to move on. It need not be a celebration in the real sense. It could be a scenario where the team is thanked for their contribution. In that way they will see smaller change events as temporary unpleasant things to deal with and move on. If change events are seen as individual unrelated events it can lead to resistance.

ACADEMIC LIBRARY STRUCTURES

Organisational structure can be defined as "one of the interrelated components that define any organisation referring to the definition of individual jobs and their relationship to each other as depicted in organisational charts and job descriptions." It clarifies how information is distributed, and jobs are organised. For decades the hierarchical structure of management was regarded as the most efficient way of managing an organisation. This system worked well in and environment where the future was predictable and librarians were in the driving seat. Hierarchies were not designed to foster creativity and lead workers to self-fulfilment.

It is therefore very difficult to introduce fundamental change within hierarchical structures which are naturally resistant to change. In an effort to bring about reorganisation within organisations institutions try to either modify the existing hierarchical structure or replace it with something else. Deming as cited by Mullins states that management systems still prevalent today have had a destructive impact on people. According to Deming "people are born with intrinsic motivation, self-esteem, dignity, curiosity to learn... " Qualities such as these are undermined by a management style that reward top achievers and punish those that do worse. Managers that exhibit such management styles use disapproval as a negative control measure. This approach leads to a climate where staff performance is primarily directed at pleasing their superiors and that inevitably lead to average performance.

According to researcher managers have a natural tendency to maintain the status quo. They would instinctively fall back on models and practices that worked in the past. The volatile nature and unpredictability of information services is forcing managers to adopt new management styles. It is beginning to dawn on people that the bureaucratic way of management is becoming outdated and that change will be more effectively achieved through education, sharing, motivation, teamwork and coaching.

Moran states that unprecedented change has forced managers to re-evaluate structures. Customary practices designed to maintain organisational stability are being questioned. To cope with change, organisations have started flattening structures to induce more flexibility within those organisations. These new structures being adopted have decreased levels of hierarchy, increased flexibility and resulted in diminishing boundaries between departments.

Issues to Consider when Introducing New Structures

Management theorists are very reluctant to prescribe to a particular structural model but advise that structure should rather be designed to meet organisational needs and goals. Organisations should try and learn as much as possible from others who have implemented organisational change. They should never introduce a structure simply because it is being used elsewhere but always to meet specific organisational needs. Of cardinal importance is to determine how people within the organisation will adopt the new structure. Researcher shares the following points learnt from a process of restructuring:

Before implementing a process of restructuring it is important to have clear vision, goals and objectives with the focus on service delivery. It is useful to establish a core team to lead the restructuring process. It is vitally important that senior management support the process, e.g., a deputy vice-chancellor. It is important to involve the entire staff component, listen to their inputs and concerns since ownership by the staff is vital for successful change implementation. Staff development programmes should be part of the process to prepare staff for new functions or roles they may be involved in.

After implementation it is important to critically analise the performance of the academic library within the new structure. Managers often do not adapt easily to the flatter less bureaucratic structures that are generally being adopted. Even staff members at lower levels experience this problem. Generally it is very difficult to introduce change that goes against prevailing organisational culture. Proper planning is needed to take the organisation from the existing structure to the new one.

Employee input in developing such a strategy is crucial. Research indicates that organisational transformation had been most successful in scenarios where employees had maximum input. Finally evaluation is necessary after change implementation to determine its success. In reorganised libraries structures are always flatter resulting in manager's roles reverting from directing to coordinating. The prime purpose of reorganisation is to create a more effective organisation. Reorganisation results in academic libraries becoming learning organisations.

The learning organisation is characterised by staff empowerment, is team based, decentralised, practices participative management and information sharing. In the learning organisation the person closest to a problem has the responsibility and authority to deal with it. Tom Wilson as cited by Moran states that the academic library is in bad need of reconstruction. To Wilson academic libraries were essentially designed to manage physical artifacts. The rise of the Internet has completely transformed the way information is created, distributed and accessed.

The e-journal is a typical example. Johansen and Swigart as cited by Moran states "we had outlived the usefulness of models from the Industrial era but don't yet have robust organisational models for the information era". It is therefore of paramount importance that academic librarians continuously re-evaluate current structures and through an experimental process adopt new models. Moran states that for people who advocate restructuring there is good and bad news. The good news is that people understand that technological change will compel fundamental organisational change. The bad news is that there is a lack of urgency. Generally organisational change appears to be incremental rather than radical.

IMPACT OF ICT CHANGE ON ACADEMIC IBRARIES

The Internet has made information access and retrieval both simplistic and complex. Information retrieval systems are being designed to suit the needs of end users and therefore try to simplify the process. Simultaneously however the user is overwhelmed with so much information resources and choices that the process becomes complex. This creates a situation where the users need skills and knowledge in terms of search strategies and conceptualisation. Herrington is of the opinion that information literacy instruction at the point of need can be very effective. Wood and Walther is of the opinion that unlike popular believe the Internet will not completely replace the skills of professional librarians but rather make them indispensable.

Changes in the Job Description of Academic Librarians

An overview of the core competencies required by academic library and information workers gives one an idea of how dramatically information and communications technology has changed the library profession.

Cheng identifies the following core competencies needed by the future librarian:

- Good communication skills.
- Should be more than just computer literate and should have a good understanding of ICT and its relation to information resources.
- Should have an in-depth understanding of organisational and user needs that is research based and should organise library resources to satisfy those needs.
- Competent in Web publishing techniques.
- Skilled in manipulating metadata to organise digital information.
- Skilled in training users in the use of e-resources.
- Skilled in filtering, evaluating and appraising Internet information.

Researchers identifies another quality required, an in-depth understanding of what information resources are available on the Internet, as well as insight in terms of its reliability and scope.

The Changing Nature of the Academic Library

ICT is busy transforming the nature of academic libraries. A variety of terms such as hybrid, digital and virtual library are used to refer to the academic library. A digital library can be defined as "a managed collection of information, with associated services, where the information is stored in digital formats and accessible over a network".

The virtual library has been defined as "remote access to the contents and services of libraries and other information resources, combining an on-site collection of current and heavily used materials in both print and electronic form, with an electronic network which provides access to, and delivery from, external worldwide library and commercial information and knowledge sources". Hybrid libraries are libraries that provide access to both electronic resources and paper-based resources.

From the definitions it is clear that most of today's academic libraries fall in either the hybrid or virtual category.

The library of the future is unlikely to be a physical entity as we know it but would probably be a Web portal providing access to information.

The emphasis will be on access to information rather than physical ownership. Akeroyd supports this view and states that as a physical space entity the library, as we know it is unlikely to prevail in a digital environment. One reason for this is that because of Web access the digital library is accessible from anywhere.

Changes in the Information Seeking Behaviour of Users

Academic librarians have a good understanding of the tremendous value of printed and electronic resources available to students at academic libraries. Academic library users do not necessarily share this insight. New generation academic library users have a preference for Web resources rather than visiting the library.

Research done on undergraduate engineering students in 2004 revealed that they would turn to the Internet as the primary resource for information for their projects. Moyo refers to a scenario where users were asked what they expect from an academic library service.

They responded as follows:

- All resources should be available in full text and be printable.
- The library service should be fast and easily accessible.
- 24/7 availability of a virtual reference service.
- Wish to do all library transactions online.
- Web resources that is easy to use and Web search engines that meet information needs.

What is clear is that new generation academic library users prefer the convenience of digital access above reliance on assistance from librarians. This preference for the Internet poses a serious challenge to the academic library which has to move from a paradigm of the library as a physical entity to a library where the users do not have to come to physically to make use of it's services.

Electronic access to information resources does have many advantages, e.g.:

- Multiple access which implies more that one user can access a resource simultaneously.
- Lots of resources are available in full text.
- 24/7 access which means users can access resources remotely, e.g., from off campus or from dormitories.

One of the disadvantages of remote access from an academic library point of view is that users are not always aware of the fact that they are using library resources. One user stated: "No, I don't need to use the library, I use Internet resources".

Despite the apparent preference for digital content the need for access to high quality digital content remains constant. Greater cooperation between library and faculty is necessary to develop ways to connect users and high quality digital materials.

IMPACT OF ICT ON COLLECTION MANAGEMENT

Collection development can be defined as the selection and acquisition of library materials based on current and potential user needs. Collection management goes beyond this. It is concerned with managing the utilisation, storage and accessibility of a collection. Collection development can thus be seen as a subdivision of collection management. Academic librarians find themselves in an era of unparalleled access to information.

The latest edition of Uhlrich's has indicated the availability of more than 1,72,000 journal titles. Although this appears to be a most ideal situation it is not because the financial resources available in acquisitions departments have not necessarily increased. The sheer volume of information available also makes selection of the most suitable information a complex task. The impact of electronic resources has made collection management a very complex and challenging task. There are budgetary constraints, numerous formats, ever changing user needs. Collection management implies involvement in tasks such as analysis of needs, negotiation of contracts and evaluation of resources. There was a time when the size of an academic library collection determined its stature. At that time the library's resources were generally adequate to meet most of its users needs. Since then the academic library has exchanged the ownership model for an access model where physical location becomes completely irrelevant.

Access versus Ownership

Information and communications technology has had a fundamental impact on library collection development policies. Academic libraries had traditionally applied an ownership or just-in-case approach to collection development. The premise was that users would need the material and make use of it. Having the material available in the library would also provide immediate access to it than having to borrow it from a third party. The cost of maintaining collections and increased demands for more information had forced academic libraries to reconsider the ownership model and adopt another model. Unparalleled price increases and shrinking budgets had ushered in a new model called access or just in time where the focus is to give the user the information that they need when they want it.

Cost

Technically it is more cost effective to produce an e-resource, for example an electronic journal, because the first copy costs are reduced. There is also savings in terms of packaging, delivery and storage. In practice these savings have not lead to reductions in the cost of e-journals. It has been suggested that the academic library adopts a pay-as-you-use approach. This make sense according to research done in 1997 that indicated that 22 per cent of science articles published in 1984 were never cited for the next 10 years. In the social sciences this figure goes up to 48 per cent.

Storage Space

With the access model there is no need for storage space, *e.g.*, back copies. Moahi cites Cooper who states that the storage cost per single copy is between $25 and $40. Calculations to determine JStor pricing lead to the conclusion that the cost per single volume was between $24 and $41. When costs for re-shelving and maintenance were included, the estimated cost rose to $45 per title per year for a core journal and $180 per title per year for a large research library.

Enhanced Access to Information

One of the benefits of ICT is enhanced access to library services and resources. The academic library can expose its users to a much larger collection than it can house physically because users can access information remotely. With online access it is possible to accurately measure utilisation of e-resources and that is invaluable in determining which resources to purchase. It is easier to search e-resources and access speed is greatly enhanced. Other advantages are that users can simultaneously access the same resource, and there are no incidences of lost copies or mutilated issues. Singh is of the opinion that a paradigm shift is taking place within the academic library as more academic librarians are doing collection management rather that collection development. The focus is rather on interpretation of information rather than selection. Librarians are becoming knowledge managers rather than collection managers.

Digital Preservation of Data

One of the major costs facing the academic library is the cost related to the conversion and preservation of information in digital format. The cost of this process amounts to $1 per page. This does not include the cost relating to the annotation for indexing purposes and the cost of conversion of audio-visual material. One of the problems with converting records into digital image is the fact that the technology used to store these pages as a digital photograph results in large files which have storage implications and place demands on band-with. Funding allocated to preservation of digital material is generally inadequate. This has to do with expectations that the costs of digital preservation over length of time might be very high. It is also difficult to forecast cost in terms of how long to retain digital material in an archive and computer architectures needed to access material. Preservation of digital materials poses many challenges. It is further complicated by the fact that computer technology changes at an unprecedented rate.

There are concerns that changing interfaces, standards, formats and operating systems will render it impossible to read today's computer discs at some point in future. The implication of this is that one needs migration strategies to move data to new operating systems and structures or have scenarios where computers can simulate data structures and operating systems of previous eras. This scenario will make digital preservation prohibitively expensive. A great deal of current research into digital preservation is based on overcoming the technical issues to ensure long-term preservation of digital content. The issue of digital preservation initially came to the fore as an impending crisis. Fears were expressed that large portions of our cultural heritage were in danger of disappearing forever. Examples were cited of Web sites available today that might be gone to-morrow.

Although digital materials are more fragile by nature than analog materials the risk varies within different categories of digital materials. Although it is true that a Web site currently available may disappear overnight, the same does not apply to electronic journals. This realisation has transferred the focus from the immediate rescue notion to an approach that sees digital preservation as part of a carefully planned digital access management process. One way academic libraries can deal with digital preservation is through cooperation. Through cooperation various institutions can share costs. Another advantage would be that it would reduce redundancy. Because of the fragile nature of digital materials libraries cannot put off decisions to preserve digital information *ad infinitum*. Time is of the essence.

Unlike a book that can be repaired or rebound, once a digital file becomes corrupt it may be impossible or prohibitively expensive to restore the data. Another problem facing the academic library is the long-term preservation of digital information. There are questions concerning the long-term stability of digital information stored on disks and tapes. There is the potential of these media deteriorating over a period of time. Another way digital preservation is approached is by letting the vendors do the preservation. These days there are also escrow repositories, e.g. Elsevier has agreed to provide the National Library of Netherlands with a copy of Science Direct which the National Library will maintain and make available should Elsevier be unable to do so.

ELECTRONIC RESOURCES

ICT has fundamentally changed academic library collections. Forever gone is the era when an academic library's physical collection determined its stature. In the modern networked technological era the emphasis has shifted from ownership of physical resources to access to electronic resources that are globally accessible.

Internet Information

There are huge amounts of unedited information on the Internet. There are countless Web sites and no single listing of them all. There is also the phenomenon of Web sites disappearing overnight that create problems in terms of access.

The Invisible Web

Academic library users make use of search engines such as Google and Altavista to find information on the Web. As a result they are only exposed to a small portion of the Web called the 'Publicly Indexable Web' These students are only exposed to Web pages accessible via hyperlinks. Search engines do not index Web pages that requires authentication or Web pages behind search forms. The Web consists of two components namely the 'Publicly Indexable Web' also referred to as the visible Web and the invisible Web. The invisible Web refers to all those information resources available yet not indexed by conventional search engines yet accessible via the Web.

Masses of information available via the invisible Web are found in subject databases. Most of the databases that academic libraries make available to their users resort under the invisible Web, e.g. EbscoHost and Eric. Conventional search engines can find databases such as EbscoHost but cannot access them. Search engines can only find content that was indexed by their software called spiders or crawlers. The problem is that they only index Web content available in formats such as HTML and PDF. Michael K. Bergman in year 2000 in a paper on the invisible Web for an Internet Search Company called Bright Planet suggests that the invisible Web is 500 times larger that the visible Web with approximately 550 billion documents.

The Issue of Quality of Resources Available on the Visible Web

The Internet had become a very important research tool for academic endeauvour. Slaouti as cited by Stapleton notes that the relevance and importance of the Web as a research tool should not be underestimated. There is a stark contrast in the way resources are published on the Web versus traditional publishing. In the traditional print environment publishing generally was done by a publisher hence a controlled environment that impacted on quality as well as the scope of the audience being reached. The open nature of the Web, the development of sophisticated search engines, browsers, Web creation and publishing software and easy access to networks via low cost connectivity has developed the Web into a tool that can be easily utilised by the masses for publishing purposes, people who were formally shut out of the publishing process.

This has lead to a flood of Web publications of variable quality. During the 1990's library scholars recognised this dilemma and suggested criteria to evaluate Internet resources, *e.g.*, authority, purpose, coverage and objectivity and accessibility. These days a single search can yield hundreds of thousands of items. The unfiltered nature of Web resources has made evaluation of these resources essential. One often finds that unlike in traditional printed media, e-resources found on the Web often lack important criteria such as author or date. Web pages because of its non-linear textual nature has added new effects to the search process such as sound, videos and access to thousands of items by clicking a mouse. These new elements imply that new sets of skills are required on the part of the researcher.

Reference Works

According to Moyo reference statistics in academic libraries are plunging. At the same time electronic access of these resources are increasing. This tendency can be ascribed to the fact that users can access these resources remotely via the Internet. Internet connectivity and e-resources had become absolutely essential for the new reference service paradigm. One of the key elements of e-reference service success is that the service is available at the point of need. The tremendous growth in the use of online reference works has created a need within the academic library to develop services to support this type of service.

Academic libraries are turning to on-line real time reference tools also referred to as ORR to support students remotely. The Pen State University library has more than 300 databases that students may access. On-line real time reference support is used to assist students at the point of need. E-reference works share all the benefits of e-resources, e.g., 24/7 remote accessibility, concurrent access for multiple users and the potential for online updating to keep content up to date. Electronic communication had become the primary mode of communication in e-reference services. Online chat had become the method of choice. Some e-reference application providers have added *Voice over IP* (VOIP) to their products which enable voice dialogue with the library user.

E-reference services have many advantages, e.g.:

- Availability via the Internet.
- Service at the point of need.
- Easy for people who are unable to come to the academic library, e.g., the physically disabled.
- 24/7 availability.

Moyo cites Stormont who states that online real time reference support is very labour intensive. In order to cope academic libraries have adopted a distributed staffing model where the load of the service is shared among various libraries.

E-Journals

The e-journal can be defined as "a version of the traditional print or paper-based journal which is disseminated electronically in some form or other directly to the end user." Although e-journals had been in existence since 1976 it became prominent during the 1990's. Since it's inception in 1665 the printed journal remained the primary vehicle for communication among academics and researchers. The advent of the Internet transformed publishing radically as it made it possible to publish cheaply. Internet also made access universally available. Because of the Internet academics and researchers became more creative and productive.

Cost Factors

There had been major increases in the cost of journal subscriptions during the last two decades. According to researcher between 1986 and 1996 the average increase per journal subscription had been a whopping 147 per cent. This state of affairs had been laid at the door of the commercial publishers. Moahi states that simultaneously there had been a significant increase in the number of science and engineering journals published. Because of ever decreasing budgets academic libraries are unable to purchase the titles they deem necessary. Falk cites McCabe of Georgia Institute of Technology stating that publishers offer libraries bundled packages of e-journals under the pretense that it is cheaper but these deals actually inflate prices.

Moahi is of the opinion that a consequence of these bundled deals is that academic libraries end up with titles they do not want or need. Despite the fact that publishers have substantial cost savings on first copy production of e-journals and also save on distribution costs, these savings are not passed onto their customers. Cost of e-journals tend to be similar or higher that their printed counterparts. What further complicate matters are the fact that provision has to be made for connectivity and desktops, which means additional costs. Aggregate publishers also tend to drop titles without prior consultation with academic librarians.

Academic Library's Response to Publishers

Despite general expectations that e-journals should be cheaper than printed versions publishers maintain the status quo by maximizing profits. Publisher's attitudes have forced academic institutions to take a tougher stance against them. Recently the Senate of the University of California instructed the library to sever all ties with Elsevier, *e.g.*, cancel subscriptions and cease submission of research papers if negotiations with them fail to obtain a reduction in the price of subscriptions. Harvard University has cancelled their Elsevier subscriptions of bundled journals. The Senate of North Carolina State University urged that excessive prices from publishers be resisted.

Four North Carolina universities had signed a deal for a bundle of 1300 journals in 2003 with the proviso that no titles are dropped. When these institutions wanted to renew subscription for 2004 the price was so exorbitant that they all cancelled the deal. Cornell University and the University of Missouri also cancelled subscription with Elsevier for the same reasons. Three North Carolina universities have drafted policies to only forward research to publishers whose journals are reasonably priced and widely accessible.

In the event of this not being possible they will include an "authorisation to publish' clause in contracts that empower the author to retain copyright to reproduce research for academic and research purposes. Kansas University includes a clause in their contracts that give them permission to use their research for teaching and research purposes and retain the right to make it available on public accessible Web sites.

Open Access Journals

The open access initiative is aimed at making scholarly

research freely available via the Internet. Open access journals are journals available on the Internet for academics, researchers and the general public. The open access journal philosophy received a tremendous stimulus with the birth of the *Public Library of Science* (PLoS). At its conception 30,000 scientists promised their support in terms of submitting research. The first open access journal to emerge was PLoS Biology in the year 2003 which was received with great enthusiasm. In the publishing arena the Biomed Central publishing house embarked on free access to peer-reviewed journals. Recently the *Directory of Open Access Journals* (DOAJ) made open access journals available covering different languages and subjects.

Open Access Archives

Many leading universities are setting up electronic archives as depositories for their research output and are granting access to it. There are plans in progress to use theses archives as a platform to provide open access journals. The *Massachusetts Institute of Technology* (MIT) has made software freely available for managing electronic archives. Currently there are approximately 140 universities that have established open access archives. The number of journals held in these archives have increased from 20,000 in 2001 to 1.3 million in 2003. Although this is still fairly insignificant compared to the 2 million peer reviewed journals printed annually it nevertheless sends out a clear warning signal to commercial publishers of what is to come. In Europe the Open Archives Forum was established. The goal of this forum is to establish electronic archives and make it globally available.

e-Books

There are various definitions for e-books but e-books are essentially published books and reference materials that were digitised and are distributed electronically. In the year 2000 e-books were heralded as the new publishing revolution. One market research company predicted that by 2005 there would be 1.9 million users. Forrester Research predicted that income generated from e-book sales would increase from $9 million in 2000 to $414 million in 2004.

Unfortunately e-book popularity never rose to expected heights. Despite the negativity surrounding e-books it had not demised completely. There are still some companies dealing with e-books that are profitable and experiencing growth. One of the first commercial e-book services, NetLibrary, was established by OCLC in 1998. The NetLibrary collection has since grown to over 400 000 titles. The shortcoming in the NetLibrary system is the fact that an e-book can only be used by one user at a time. Questia, another commercial e-book service went live in 2001. Their target market was students and they employed librarians to manage collection development. By 2003 Questia had more than 400 000 titles from more than 200 publishers.

Advantages of e-Books

E-books have numerous advantages. There are no printing, storage, warehousing and shipping costs. Consequently e-books can be published at costs much lower than conventional books. Additional advantages are online availability, keyword-searching capability, cross-referencing, adjustable fonts, electronic bookmarks and imbedded audio. Updating e-books will be easier than re-editing conventional books. From an academic library point of view benefits would include cost savings in terms of shelving, binding, circulation, overdue notices and management of fines. All needed would be a person to maintain the collection and a person to manage user accounts. Print collections in academic libraries are very expensive to acquire and maintain. E-books are also environmentally friendly in the sense that no tree pulping is necessary to for its production. The flaws in current e-book technology will be overcome. When that day dawns e-books being much cheaper to produce and publish than printed books as well as economies of scale will tip the balance in favour of e-books.

Disadvantages

The devices needed to read e-books are relatively expensive, *e.g.*, hand held devices, PC's and laptops. In order to minimize piracy publishers use proprietary hardware devices and software platforms. This lack of universal standards is a problem. The question many ask is whether e-books pose a threat to libraries. Can it eventually put libraries out of business. Although e-books did not take off as well as expected within the public domain, the use of e-books at schools, colleges and universities are rapidly increasing.

Use of e-Books

Falk refers to research done by Forrester that indicated that 4 million e-books were sold at campus stores in year 2000. Forrester forecasted that by year 2005 e-book sales should have increased to 140 million. Research indicates that students are developing a preference for e-books above printed books. At the University of Rochester Rush Rhees Library course reserve section students were exposed to printed books and their e-book equivalents. Statistics compiled on a weekly base indicated a three to one preference in favour of the e-books.

SOME OF THE PROBLEMS RELATING TO ELECTRONIC RESOURCES

Online full text implies availability of articles rather that the entire content of a particular journal. The complete contents of a publication are seldom put into a full text database. This implies that an author one might have seen in a physical publication may not be traceable in electronic format. This predicament also applies to archiving where there is uncertainty about the percentage of a journals content that is archived in digital format.

Another concern is that the academic library in a sense has lost control over the resources it make available to its users. When academic libraries subscribe to aggregator databases, *e.g.* EbscoHost or ProQuest they subscribe to a service, a list of titles bundled together of which many are useful and many not so useful. One of the problems is that aggregators sometimes drop titles. Typically this would happen when publishers withdraw all their titles.

The Chronicle of Higher Education has reported in 2003 that Elsevier has been removing articles from aggregator files because of various reasons, *e.g.*, scientific misconduct, plagiarism and errors. On the Web there are masses of information available. With search engines, *e.g.* Google or Yahoo one may find useful information and record the URL or title. There is however no guarantee when one wants to revisit the site that it may still be available. Sites on the Web sometimes disappear overnight. An organisation may have merged with another one or the host server might have become dysfunctional.

The quality of information available on the Web is also sometimes questionable. Any individual with access to the Web and basic hardware and software can publish on the Web regardless of whether the person's views are factually correct. On the Web are more than an estimated billion Web pages and this create problems for users of the academic library to distinguish between what is useful or not. Another problem is that search engines cover only a small portion of what is what is available on the Web. There are lots of information behind firewalls and thus inaccessible. Many crawlers of search engines only focus on html and ignore graphics. Generally ASCII files will not be found. To assist users academic library services should try and inform users when sites have relocated or are no longer available.

CHANGES IN THE EDUCATIONAL ENVIRONMENT

ICT have changed every fibre of society including education. Lifelong learning has become essential. A very competitive working environment has influenced this. Even educational methodologies have changed. Greater interaction between learner, educator and material is becoming the norm. Learners have greater choices in terms of curricula. The 24 hour networked classroom became reality leading to the birth of the virtual library.

Network technologies and new educational methodologies have empowered learners, given them a greater measure of control and participation in the learning process and enabled network interaction with both fellow students and lecturers. Change in institutions of higher education will compel academic libraries to change accordingly. The most dramatic change according to visionaries will take place in distance education. This was a direct influence of the Internet. When the day dawns when distance education becomes the norm, universities the way we know them may vanish and virtual libraries may become a reality. Recently an author warned that the railroad managers overlooked the fact that they were in the transport business. He noted that universities must remember they are in the education business and not the campus business. If campuses disappear libraries will disappear.

There are already examples of cyberspace universities, e.g. Phoenix. If academics should fail to restructure their institutions' external forces will do it. Of cardinal importance is to focus on what education wants to achieve and how one can fulfill it. Survival of the academic library will depend on its ability to continuously reshape and reorganise.

Distance Education

New technologies driven by ICT innovation have enhanced the virtual delivery of academic programmes and stimulated unparalleled growth of distance education at institutions of higher learning. The phenomenal growth in distance education technologies has lead to an escalation in the availability of online academic programmes and a tremendous increase in remote users. In order to support these programmes academic librarians have developed excellent portfolios and programmes for remote students. One aspect that is neglected is evaluation of these programmes.

What is of critical importance is to establish how these programmes are used, which ones are used more frequently than others and why. Monash University library in Australia provides online curriculum content to their students all over the world. The university library provides online access to more than 440 online databases, 140,000 e-books and 20,000 e-journal subscriptions. Apart from full text databases and e-books the university library also provides digital audio recordings of lectures that become available minutes after conclusion of lectures.

According to Ho Monash University library has made a paradigm shift to a complete new service module that utilises e-commerce technologies. Moyo is of the opinion that the transformation in distance education has created a need for distance librarianship.

Changes in Scholarly Communication

The rising of the Internet and subsequent Web during the 1990's has resulted in the decline of the printed journal as the principal medium of scholarly publication. The costs of journals have increased dramatically driven by commercial publishers trying to control research content. This resulted in depriving many researchers of access to needed resources. The Web has also made fast and easy electronic publication possible and has increased direct communication between researchers.

Publishers immediately started making electronic versions of printed journals available on the Web. This was however seen as perpetuating the status quo in a new medium. Scholars started seeing in the new technology the potential to develop a new model for publishing research and an opportunity to return ownership of scholarly output to the rightful owners of the research.

These sentiments were driven by shortcomings in existing scholarly journal publishing which were:

- The time to publish an article was to too long.
- The existing model demanded transfer of copyright to the publishers.
- A too rigid peer review system that tends to favour publication of authors from the more prestigious institutions.
- Journal prices had become unaffordable.

One of the outcomes of this dissatisfaction was the birth of the e-print which is essentially an electronic version of a research paper. E-prints lead to the development of e-print repositories that are an archive of e-prints accessible to the public. Some of the advantages of e-print repositories are the reduction of publishing barriers, increased visibility of research and rapid dissemination of research results to a wide audience.

Consortia Collaboration

Initially libraries got involved in consortia in order to reduce costs particularly with regard to the acquisition of e-resources. Consortia development is thus an attempt to maximize limited resources through co-operation and resource sharing. In the consortia scenario the emphasis is on access to information rather than ownership. Consortia collaboration provides more power when it comes to negotiating contracts. It also provides a platform for libraries to co-operate in terms of services. Nowadays libraries also turn to consortia to provide advice and guidance in complex decision-making. The input of consortia is also valuable in terms of evaluating e-resources in terms of quality, different options, e.g., whether to subscribe to journals or pay article-by-article.

The South African Scenario

In terms of network infrastructure South Africa is not on par with first world countries where consortia cooperation is very effective. For the establishment of an information society in South Africa proper connectivity infrastructure is an absolute prerequisite. There is an uneven distribution of telecommunications infrastructure across South Africa stemming from the political ideologies of the apartheid government. This inequity is also prevalent in South African academic libraries. Institutions for the privileged white people were well financed and resourced under the apartheid regime. Institutions for blacks were under funded and thus under resourced; hence the distinction between advantaged and historically disadvantaged institutions. Because of this there are great differences in wealth and the collections of academic libraries.

In South Africa there are five academic library consortia.:

1. CALICO (Cape Library Cooperative) based in Cape Town.
2. ESAL (Eastern Seaboard Association of Libraries based in Kwazulu-Natal.
3. FRELICO (Free State Libraries and Information Consortium) based in Free State.
4. Gaelic (Gauteng and Environs Library Consortium) based in Gauteng.
5. SEALS (South Eastern Academic Libraries System in the Eastern Cape.

Essential for the development of successful consortia is low cost tariffs coupled with high bandwith connectivity. Academic institutions constantly engaged with government agencies to achieve this ideal. Library consortia can also be invaluable in assisting member libraries with change management because "An organisation needs external coaches to catalyse, guide and facilitate a change process", the reason being that people within the academic library are sometimes to closely involved with daily activities to see things objectively. An outside view often helps to see things in the right perspective.

ICT MANAGEMENT ISSUES

Libraries are caught midstream between print versus a digital setup. To navigate the transition from print to digital remains enormously challenging. Rapid ICT development had resulted in lots of incompatible systems being used within libraries. To manage ICT is a complex and daunting task. To select the right ICT technologies is a major management issue. It is very difficult in a world where hardware and software changes at a phenomenal rate.

The shift in the academic library from printed resources to electronic resources that are accessible via campus networks or remotely and the fact that users can even request services via the network has lead to a decline in users visiting the library. The growing electronic nature of the academic library is resulting in it becoming less visible as a physical entity to its users.

What is also disturbing is the fact that users are often oblivious to the fact that they are using library resources because of the seamlessness of access. Users are not aware of the fact that to make those resources available are costly in terms of subscriptions, infrastructure and staff. Academic libraries need to find a way to reverse this scenario of the library loosing its visibility. Hooper suggests that the academic library should use ICT to stimulate interaction between user and the library. It should be done in such a way that the user could identify with the academic library providing the service and experience a sense of ownership.

As a starting point the academic library can interact with the user relating to loans, database searches and other services available. It is also important to create an environment where the user can provide feedback relating to service shortcomings and suggestions that could lead to improvement. Stakeholder relationships are also very important. It is of vital importance for the academic library to ensure that their operations dovetail with the strategic goals of the university it supports. In these days where accountability is becoming the norm it is essential to run operations in such a way that the academic library at any point is in a position to provide proof of the value of its services as a return on investment made by the university authority.

MANAGERIAL CHANGE FOR THE SURVIVAL OF LIBRARY

DIGITAL LIBRARY AND ITS IMPACT

The origin of ICT has changed the performance and service pattern of every institution and organisation, library is not excluded from it. Impact of ICT has transformed the 'traditional library' into 'automated library'. 'Digital library' and 'virtual library' are also the gift of ICT. Many libraries have been serving as hybrid libraries. A library digital is an organised collection of electronic resources. Digital library is a very complex and dynamic entity.

It has brought phenomenal change in the information collection, preservation and dissemination scene of the world. It is a complex entity because it is completely based on ICT systems and the concept is of recent origin. Its main aim is to provide ready access to the required information at a right time to the right user with right information. The collection of digital library are not limited to document surrogates they extend to digital artifacts which cannot be represented or distributed in printed formats. Therefore, digital library is not a single unit, but a complex of multiple units that provide instant access to all information, for all sectors of society, from anywhere in the world.

Therefore, in this context, the digital library must cope up with the changing technology, information seeking behaviour of its user, user needs, etc. The day has come to adopt change management at par with information management in the library.

CHANGES IN LIBRARY AND INFORMATION CENTRE MANAGEMENT

Due to fast-paced technological change and new skill requirements, information professionals are increasingly required to renew their skills and practice in order to gain an awareness of technological advances. As a result, the profession itself exists in a state of flux alongside these emerging technologies, with traditional roles being increasingly subsumed by new skills and working environments, and, therefore, job descriptions. Thus, information professionals are now expected to be aware of and capable of using and demonstrating emerging ICTs. There is a need for additional training to augment the traditional skill and knowledge base with a competency in ICT use. Information professionals must be flexible, and adopt traditional skills to incorporate the requirements of technological advances.

Given the current situation, wherein ICTs are being continuously updated or introduced and traditional formats are being replaced or supplemented by digital formats, it seems likely that there will continue to be a need for regular training for information professionals. There is also an increased focus on communication skills, with more people involved in the electronic information environment. Information professionals are being called upon to work closely with ICT users and providers - including IT staff - and to work in collaboration with others in the profession. Some groups of users lack the necessary IT skills to obtain quality information and information professionals will therefore be called upon to act as both educators and intermediaries.

Given these circumstances, information professionals are required to have additional teaching and communication skills. Thus, it is vital for those in management positions to recognise the imperative of *continuing professional development* (CPD) and ensure that the staff is proactive in maintaining up-to-date levels of expertise. The significance of CPD in this milieu has been acknowledged by both the United Kingdom's *Chartered Institute of Library and Information Professionals* (CILIP) and the United States' *American Library Association* (ALA).

Certain active roles are necessary for change management to:

- *Establish the quality goals of the library:* Library and Information Centres (LICs) should aim to establish the quality goals for qualitative service to its user community.
- *Provide the resources to their library:* LICs should provide all necessary resources suitable in the ICT era to manage the LICs in a better way.
- *Provide the quality-oriented training to the library staff:* New generation library staff are almost trained with ICT applications to LICs but old staff and others who

are novices in such applications need quality training because without quality training library staff are unable to provide automated services.

- *Stimulate quality improvement in the day to day activities of library:* This is the age of competition. Like other organisations, to survive the LICs, top management should stimulate the staff for quality improvement in the day to day activities of LICs.
- *Review progress of the library activities:* Higher management should review the progress of library activities to maintain the quality and quantity of assigned job to the staff.
- *Give recognition to library staff:* Top level management should recognise the operational level library staff for quality performance, without which they will be demoralised to perform the job in a better way.

With the change in environment the objectives need to be revised to face the challenges of future. Over a period of time, due to the impact of technological advances, research and development, economic, social and political factors, the objectives also tend to change. To adopt these changes, it is essential to state objectives and functions of information system in changing context. For this purpose the following steps should be followed.

Structure Related Changes

The structure related changes in libraries and information centres may include:

- *Change in the work design:* The work design of a traditional library is not similar to modern automated library, so a change in the work design is compulsory for the success of automated library.
- *Change in the basis of departmentalisation:* There are various departments in university and research libraries. In case of automated library, book acquisition, classification and cataloguing, circulation, serial control assignments are being done

through computer with specific software instead of doing manually. Besides these departments, modern library has other departments like barcoding, RFID tagging, OPAC/web-OPAC, e-journals, e-books, CD-ROM, digital library, touch screen kiosk, server maintenance etc.

- *Change in the number of operation levels to perform various activities, routine work of library staff:* As there is a major change in the processing and service departments a change in the number of staff in the lower level or operational level management has become essential.
- *Change in the plans, programmes, policies and procedures to and improving integration among various sections:* Due to changse in the pattern of service; plans, programmes, policies and procedures and integration within various departments it is very essential to cater to the service in a better way.
- *Change in the span of management and levels of management for effective co-ordination mechanism and flow of task:* Since the nature of job of modern automated library is more complex than traditional library, it is very difficult to manage large number of operational level staff under one middle level manager. In view of this span of management should be narrow and levels of management should be changed because top and middle level management have to be directly linked with every department to perform each department's functions in a better way as well as for effective co-ordination mechanism with every department.
- *Change in line-staff and functional authority, work group relations between people and functions to improve their ability:* Line positions are responsible for accomplishing the organisation's primary objectives; they have final authority to make decisions. Staff positions, on the other hand, provide suggestions and advice for the line positions but cannot,

theoretically make decisions for the line positions. An organisation seeks to keep authority for decision making in the positions accountable for results and to preserve a clear chain of command from the top to the bottom of the organisation. But in the automated library system there should be no hurdle between line and staff position because anyone who is aware about a particular system can give his advice. It helps to improve the work group relation as well as the ability of the all levels of management.

Structural changes affect relationships among the organisational positions and in the interactions among internal departments, the reporting mechanism, interactions of all sections in the library and the functional relationships.

Changes for Technological Advancement

The technology refers to the sum total of human knowledge providing ways to do the things in a better way with the help of techniques. It may include inventions and techniques affecting the ways of doing things.

Thus, technology related changes may include:

- *Use of new machines and equipments for developing new services or modifying existing services:* Many new machines and equipments, *e.g.*, computer, server, barcoding equipments, RFID tools are necessary for developing new services or modifying existing manual services. So the awareness about the use of new machines, equipments and tools is very essential.
- *The procedure of doing things which may result in change of work process:* The methods and procedures of doing new tasks should be changed in context of old library system. So that the work process is not disrupted.
- *Introduction of technological devices like computers and computer related technologies:* Introduction of technological devices like computers and computer

related technologies is necessary for automated library. Without computers and related technologies, we are unable to cater to services in automated library system.

- *Change in the existing techniques for making or doing the things in effective way or adoption of new techniques for creative work:* Automated library is ICT oriented and some technique is involved in every work. So existing techniques of traditional library management should be changed and adoption of new techniques is very essential to carry out every task and service in automated library environment.
- *Change in the methods of using new tools equipments and products:* In the traditional library system, there are only a few equipments like fumigation chamber, catalogue cabinet, book rack, cardex, journal display rack, etc. But now computer terminals, server, barcoding equipments, RFID tools, etc., equipments and products are being used, so it is very natural to change the methods of using new tools, equipments and products.

The change in the technology affects the nature of work and activities, organisational structure, the processes and the people's behaviour.

Task-related Changes

Technology related changes determine the ways to complete the task effectively and efficiently. Task related changes helps to achieve major gains in terms of cost, service and time.

Task related changes may include:

- *Identifying the steps involved in performing tasks:* It is very necessary to organise meeting with library staff at all levels to identify the steps to perform the tasks effectively.
- *Task identification:* Every task should be identified to depute the staff who is efficient in that work. So,

proper task identification is the key factor to perform the task properly and to serve the user community in a better way.

- *Significance of task related changes in attaining the organisational and institutional objectives:* As the nature of library has been changed so it is very significant to change the task which is relevant in changed atmosphere to attain the organisational and institutional objectives.
- *Identifying the skills and abilities required for the changed task:* It is very natural to identify the skills and abilities required for the changed task and to assign the specific job to the specific staff that is suitable for that particular job.
- *Improving both quality and quantity of work/ service:* For the satisfaction of our customer we should improve our quality as well as quantum of day to day work/ service.
- *Bringing cost-effective solutions through maximum use of available resources:* Cost-effectiveness is concerned with the value. It asks, "This is what the service costs. Is it worth it?" So effectiveness of the resources is the key to maximum use of available resources.
- *Improving the work performance:* Quality training of staff is very essential to aware the task of each and every personnel effectively which improves the work performance.

People-related Changes

Change in any factor has an impact on human resources and human behaviour.

In the context of Library and Information Science, the people-related categories include:

- *The library staff:* In case of library staff, it requires the corresponding changes to be made in the skills, abilities and the performance of the employees.
- *New investment in training and development activities*

so that employees acquire new skills and activities: New skills and activities are required in automated library system so new investment in training and development is essential. Library can get the fund from UGC for this purpose by making a systematic and comprehensive proposal

- *Socialising employees into the organisational structure so that they learn the new routines on which organisational performance depends....':* Top management should meet with middle and operational level management to become aware about the every bit of work with theory and practical and to assign the job to every personnel as well as time required for this purpose. Through socialising the employees organisational efficiency can also be increased.

Accordingly the change may also include –

- *Change in skill levels of the workforce:* Skill levels of each and every employee should be changed to cope up with new task.
- *Change in the training programmes to improve performance levels:* Training programme should be organised in a scientific way to sensitise the employee about every practical aspect of work and service. So change in training programmes is essential to improve performance levels of the staff.
- *Change in attitude and values:* Change in attitude and values is a must for better performance in work and service in the changed library environment.
- *Change in behaviour and interaction pattern:* As the library scenario has changed from traditional to automated one, behavioural and interaction pattern regarding work and service should also be changed.
- *Change in technology requires different skills of the operator:* Presently, library is technology controlled. To cope up with this change, the library personnel requires different skills to carry out their own task because it is very difficult to work properly for a unskilled staff.

- *Change in the structure requires change in their position, their authority, responsibility, etc.:* Due to shift from traditional to automated library, structural change is required. For this purpose positional, authoritative and responsibility change is necessary for better performance.
- *The readers:* Readers/users/customers are our prime focus. To serve the right user to the right information at the right time, we have to organise our resources systematically through which they can collect their information himself/herself. Such a systematic arrangement helps us to work and serve the users with less human resources.

Any change in the processes demands that it should be communicated to the readers to enable them to adjust to these changes. Readers are ultimately getting the benefits of all the technological advances, procedures, services, activities as well as other resources for their satisfaction in the libraries and information centres.

Changes in Library Policies

Change in the objectives and functions of the library and information system by the planning body would directly impact the existing plans and policies of the library. Accordingly, change in plans and policies become essential. The developmental plans and policies should be in conformity with the objectives and functions of library and information system as well as the institution it serves.

Changes in Objectives and Functions of Information System

The information system in the changed environment shall aim at:

- *Ensuring maximum use of all available resources:* Top management should ensure maximum use of all available resources through cost-effective solutions.
- *Promotion and development of all units in the library:* In the automated library, to cater the service to the

users in a right way, it is very essential to develop all units in a proper way.

- *Better communication of ideas to achieve the objectives in an ever changing environment:* To communicate every new ideas to all levels of management is essential to achieve the objectives in constantly changing environment of library work and service.
- *Minimising the time, cost and efforts involved in all the activities, processes and functions:* Top level management should plan with with staff at middle and operational level for proper coordination of every function with minimum time, cost and efforts because duplicity of activities, processes and functions increases the time, cost and efforts.

In order to achieve the newly stated objectives as per the requirement of changing circumstances, certain functions are to be carried out. These functions may relate to adoption of latest technologies, use of modern tools and techniques, updating professional skill, ability and knowledge through education and training, future prospects of change in goals, objectives and functions, etc.

Librarians will need to be ready for competition and prepared to find new ways to make their skills and services distinct from those offered by the competition from media companies, publishers, internet companies, intermediary service providers and also from technologists parking on traditional library territory with technical names for old fashioned library ideas.

PROCESS OF MANAGERIAL CHANGE IN LIBRARIES AND INFORMATION CENTRES

The various steps involved in a planned change are:

- *Identifying need for change:* In the changing scenario of library, it is very essential to identify every need of users for effective planning and execution.
- *Elements to be changed:* It is very natural that the elements in traditional library and automated library are different. So top level management should foster

awareness about every element of change and communicate the relevant elements to every unit.

- *Planning for change:* Every organisation/institution plans the total work procedures for proper execution. So, for the sake of efficiency all the steps for success in the changing scenario.
- *Assessing change forces:* It is very essential to assess the change forces for success of the new project/ assignment.
- *Change actions:* Each and every action should be changed for proper functioning of every unit for better work and service.
- *Feedback:* This is very important aspect of every organisation/institution. Without feedback system, an organisation/institution cannot assess their customer needs and information seeking behaviour as well as their satisfaction level.

Above steps in a planned change can be applied for managing the changes in libraries and information centres.

Identifying Need for Change

Various external and internal factors necessitate change in libraries and information centres. This change may be made in staff, library building or internal layouts with infrastructural facilities, the hardware and software requirements, activities and services, etc.

While identifying the need for change, the following should be considered:

- How the change will have an effect on the system, space, staff, services, activities, etc.
- What will be the frequency and nature of change.
- How it will impact use of information sources for study, research and development.
- How it will impact users information requirements.
- How it will have an effect on the procedures, policies and programmes.

Identification of need for change depends on:

- Readers' expectations;

- Changing objectives of libraries and information centres according to changing environment;
- Policies and programmes to be implemented to achieve these objectives; and
- New challenges created by change in technology.

These steps will determine the rationale why change is essential and if change will be made, whether it will create problems or not?

Elements to be Changed

What elements of the libraries and information centres should be changed is to be decided for managing the change. It will be decided on the basis of the need for the change as well as the objectives of the change. The identification of need for change will determine the base for why change is essential whereas this step will specify what elements in the system are to be changed.

Generally change is required in the structure, technology, hardware and software requirements, database design, IT infrastructure, skills of the staff, and nature of library services, etc. The nature and extent of change in the elements will further depend upon the nature of problems being faced by the libraries. Sometimes a change in one element may require change in another element, e.g., a change in any activity from manual to machine may require change in staff and their skills but at the same time change in the structure of the libraries may also be required.

Planning for Change

Planning for change includes deciding in advance about:

- When to bring change.
- Who will bring change and
- How to bring change, etc.

In the libraries and information centres change is usually required in the structure, technology, staff and services. Careful planning for bringing change in these elements is essential because "Planning looks at how the librarians and information scientists can develop the means to locate the resources which are most relevant to the need of users community, integrate these resources into their infrastructure, adopt the necessary technology and finally to anticipate the future trends in changing circumstances".

Accessing Change Forces

Various internal and external forces enable us to bring change. To manage the change effectively, it becomes necessary to ensure the co-operation of the people to create an environment in which change will be accepted by all. Change force, both internal and external, is an important consideration to anticipate and respond properly for the problems in the existing system.

Success in managing the change is possible only when we assess change forces and their impact on the efficiency and effectiveness of the existing system. If the effect of these change forces can be accessed, it becomes possible to take necessary actions for change.

Actions for Change

A distinguished social psychologist, Kurt Lewin, developed what he called 'Action Research' which happens to be a more motivational approach and a more evolutionary one.

According to him 'since most change efforts flounder because carefully expected plans are ignored or sabotaged', this first step is critical:

- Seek change when the people who are going to have to effect the changing are distressed and feel they have a problem.

The next step involves getting them to accept some procedure for exploring how the problem can be solved.

The manager . . . gets the department to establish a study or mini research project on the problem:

- What kind of information is needed?
- Who will collect it?

- Who should analyse it and how; what is secret and what can be openly discussed?

The manager may have to help to get the project underway. It may require some outside technical aid, a survey, a review of old records, interviews with people in the departments.

This step means the manager must:

- Get consensus on what kinds of data and what method of collection and assessment the group will accept as valid for evolving a solution to its problem.
- Make feedback then, the critical element; it becomes a catalyst to the people who will have to change, emphasising the discrepancy between what they believed and the reality of the situation.
- Aid people in coping, skill transfer, experimenting with new methods.
- Then the cycle is repeated.

Usually, the initial efforts won't be roaring successes; there will still be unresolved problems, and some innovations won't work as planned or hoped.

So the group which is the focus of change is encouraged to continue:

- Research/study the work flow problems – by collecting data.
- Evaluate and feedback.
- Consider further innovations.
- Get help in implementing these.
- Then check how these are working.

The manager's role is one of felicitato, so that the individuals will be motivated to change, in contrast to being told to change; Further, the process is, or ought to be, a continuing one'. The Lewin model has suggested that every change requires three steps – "the first step is unfreezing - individuals who will be affected by the impending change must be laid to recognise why the change is necessary. Next, the change itself is implemented. Finally, refreesing involves reinforcing and supporting the change so that it becomes a part of the system.

These steps can also be effectively applied in library and information centres to manage the change. At first step, the library staff as well as the reader community have to be informed about why change is essential to improve efficiency of services. At second step, they have to be made aware about new methods of working, new procedures adopted, their expected roles in changed environment, etc. We have to conceive them to recognise the basic purpose of change and ensure that they fit into the new organisational change for the benefit of all. At third step, integrating change into actual practice, the staff as well as readers has to adapt to the new environment with improved performance. They have to be protected from reverting back to the old and traditional behaviour.

Feedback

Feedback is essential to ensure that changed pattern is going to achieve the objectives with minimum time, money and energy and determine whether follow-up action is essential to ensure success of change in management. The impact of change is to be measured in terms of attainment of objectives, improvement of services, readers' increased satisfaction, employee motivation and increased level of efficiency and effectiveness of each activity, product and service.

3

Contemporary Approaches to Information Systems

INTRODUCTION

Without proper information, library managers will always face some difficulty in decision making. The application of management information, in particular that derived from automated systems, has a potentially important role in relation to current problems faced by libraries. Management information has been available to librarians for a long time, based on manually compiled records, but libraries have not always had access to computer generated information. Consequently, the potential of Management Information Systems has lain hidden. By the late 1980s, however, most academic libraries in the United Kingdom had computerised the main library operations.

The first part of this chapter considers the growing importance of a formal planning process in library management. Next it discusses the relationship of the library planning process and Management Information Systems, and describes how computer systems can be used as a tool to produce management information. It then goes on to review the development of automated library systems. The final part of the chapter reports on a small survey, conducted in late 1991, of selected academic libraries in Britain: four university libraries, three Polytechnics, and one Scottish Central Institution.

This survey investigated:

- The use of information in decision making.
- Whether libraries' automated systems are currently being used as Management Information Systems.
- The barriers within organisations that hinder the implementation of Management Information Systems.
- Perceptions of the future of Management Information Systems in academic libraries.

ACMADEMIC LIBRARIES AND THEIR MANAGEMENT

The higher education sector in Britain comprises universities established over the last seven hundred years, including a number designated during the last phase of expansion in the mid-1960s, and those institutions which were mostly redesignated as universities in 1992 - the Polytechnics and their Scottish equivalents, the Central Institutions, as well as certain Colleges of Higher Education. The expansionary momentum of the 1960s and 1970s was followed by pressure for efficiency and economies. The 1980s was not a period in which academic libraries prospered. The political and economic situation became difficult for all higher education institutions. The University of Sussex, for instance, and its funding reduced by 20 per cent between 1981 and 1984, and is now facing a further reduction by 1990. This was usually followed by a reduction in financial support for their libraries. Nonetheless, some found this environment a beneficial challenge. Mackenzie observed that: 'it may be that a measure of austerity is beneficial in that it encourages creative thought and more effective management.' In particular, academic library managers needed to use a more formal planning process to focus their services on meeting users' needs.

Researcher illustrated the planning process as:

- Establishing overall objectives.
- Allocating library resources to programmes.
- Evaluating attainment of objectives.

A detailed rationale for the planning process:

- In the times of economic difficulties for many academic libraries, the need for a planning process takes on significant importance in six general areas.
- First, planning provides for a rational response to uncertainty and change. Although the organisation cannot control its environment, it may be able to manipulate it - assuming there is an objective to be accomplished.
- Second, planning focuses attention on goals and objectives. Does your organisation have a written set of goals and objectives? If not, dysfunctions, departmental competition, and ineffective resource allocation are likely.
- Third, planning is important as an aid to resource allocation by establishing priorities for funding. Which services can be provided at the least cost and for the most benefit?
- Fourth, planning also serves as a basis for determining individual, departmental, organisational, or programme accountability.
- Fifth, planning facilitates control of organisational operations by collecting information to evaluate the various programmes or services.
- Finally, planning orients the organisation to a futuristic stance. Instead of always reacting to problem situations, the organisation attempts to foresee and mitigate against future problems before they become crises.
- Precise and consistent objectives provide guidance and direction for managers to develop plans . . . for allocating resources in line with objectives and . . . for monitoring and controlling these resources.

At the institutional level, all academic library managers must negotiate the library's resource requirements through various supervisory committees. To support their claims, academic librarians clearly need information which can be presented to these committees about how effectively the libraries contribute to the objectives of the parent institutions.

For example:

- 'Libraries are required now to develop services which can be targeted at different groups based on their own needs. The changing demography of higher education argues for a careful and continuing monitoring of such factors as the profile of the student population, measurement of library use by identified subgroups and experimentation with new services and assessment of their impact.'

The latest approach to higher education funding in Britain places more emphasis on requiring institutions to show how effectively their money was spent. The concept of 'cost centres' was introduced by the government's *Department of Education and Science* (DES) through its semi-autonomous funding agencies for higher education, the Universities Funding Council (UFC) and the Polytechnic and Colleges Funding Council (PCFC).

A cost centre is:

- 'a location or items or equipment in respect of which cost may be ascertained and related to cost units for control purposes.'

Subsequently, the DES encouraged higher education institutions in England and Wales to make use of performance indicators, and as a follow up, in 1990, the DES surveyed the use of performance indicators. The survey showed that, in the PCFC institutions, 43 had used performance indicators, including indicators of performance in their libraries. The two most common performance indicators applied to libraries were: Seats per-full-time equivalent (FTE) student; and number of loans per reader.

ORGANISATIONAL STRUCTURES AND INFORMATION FLOWS

An organisational structure is a means to incorporate various functions in order to pursue some predetermined objectives. Organisational structures also provide the lines along which information flows. Researchers have described two ways to organise libraries. They are:

1. Specialisation; and
2. Coordination and integration.

Coordination and integration simply means bringing together all individual efforts to achieve particular objectives. Specialisation, however, can be interpreted in two approaches: departmentalisation and hierarchy. Departmentalisation means the organisation is structured horizontally by identifying and grouping similar or related required activities or tasks into departments, for example, function, activities, geography, subjects, form of material, etc.

There are two main approaches to departmentalisation within academic libraries, function and subject, and they are matters of continual debate. The first approach is a structure dominated by administrative function. The subject divisional library is the alternative approach to the strictly functional. The staff are split by subject, with services and processing entirely subordinate.

- The introduction of computers into academic libraries is a major reason why the debate between functionalism and subject organisation has been by-passed.

One consequence of automation has been that:

- Technology has reduced the time necessary to carry out one of the most tedious part's of librarian's work, record creation and manipulation.

The second method of specialisation in organisations is the creation of a vertical hierarchy, with the individuals located on the top of organisation having more authority than those at successively lower levels.

- 'Such structures are often also represented diagrammatically as a family-tree, depicting line management responsibilities above and below. And any given structure can be either functional or subject-orientated.'

The merits of a hierarchical structure have been questioned by researcher; he points out several problems, such as:

- 'reporting lines tends to be long, and the responsibility of any individual very limited. Many staff rarely come into contact with staff more than one or two grades higher, with the result that communication is often poor and it is hard for staff below a senior level to have any sense of involvement in the organisation.'

In place of a hierarchical structure, researcher proposed a 'flat' structure as one possibility for libraries in the near future. In examining the rapid change and different climate that are being encountered by libraries, The 'flat' management structure as having:

- fewer middle managers, and more reliance on the two extremes—the senior administrators and lower level staff—to make decisions.

It could be speculated that the implications for the development of Management Information Systems (MIS) in libraries with 'flat' management structures may be comparable to the general problems of introducing MIS in small organisations:

- Larger organisations have found greater success with MIS use than smaller ones. Libraries, even the largest, are relatively small organisations and much planning is required to initiate and gain acceptance of MIS. There will be more resistance in small organisations than in very large ones since the likelihood of a lesser degree of bureaucratisation and traditional line and staff authority divisions are in place in such operations. The perception of the MIS as crystallising these divisions may offset their initial acceptance.

DECISION-MAKING, ORGANISATIONAL STRUCTURES, AND INFORMATION NEEDS

Whether organisations are large or small, there is managerial stratification. The tasks of top management are development of the organisation's domain, management of the interface with external environments and establishment of the organisation's administrative climate; middle management develop rules, procedures and policies for day-to-day operations; and technical management sees that services are rendered and policies carried out.

In a conference on Management Information Systems, researcher identified the library staff with each of these management levels as follows:

- Senior/top managers (*e.g.*, deputies and chiefs).
- Middle managers (*e.g.*, heads of major divisions).
- Line/technical managers (*e.g.*, service desk superintendents).
- 'some individuals will straddle more than one category. Deputies, for example, will be concerned with middle management and senior management. Furthermore the model is generalised, and it is true that in smaller libraries such stratification may break down since everyone is doing a bit of everything!'

Decision-making has been defined as:

- the formulation of alternative courses of action to meet the situation under consideration and in the choice between these alternatives after an evaluation of the effectiveness in achieving the decision maker's objectives. One of the most important factors is information from which an appreciation of the decision can be made.

There are three stages in decision making:

- Intelligence;
- Design, and
- Choice.

The intelligence stage encompasses collection, classification, processing, and presentation of the data necessary for the later stages of the decision making process. During the design stage, the decision maker outlines alternative solutions, each of which involves a set of actions to be taken. He usually uses quantitative techniques and design tools such as are common in management sciences and system analysis. The data gathered in the previous stage is now examined in statistical and other models to forecast possible outcomes for each alternative. In the choice stage, the decision maker is faced with various alternatives. One alternative must be selected, which becomes the formal decision and consequently generates actions to be taken.

This may seem deceptively easy, but in reality there are many difficulties that usually make choice a complex stage. It becomes clear that decision making is the conversion of information into action. The intended actions are planning, organising, directing and controlling of activities to achieve objectives.

However, decision-making at different managerial levels is not necessarily an identical process, and there are clear implications for the type of management information required.

- The degree of structure is dependent on the degree of predictability of the variables involved in a given decision. Unstructured decisions have few predictable variables; structured ones have many . . . Unstructured decisions are usually made at the strategic planning level and semi-structured decisions at the operational management level. The most structured decisions are reached at the operational control level.

Library managers might, therefore, be supposed to need access to the information which is appropriate to their level of decision making.

The relationship between the needs for information in all three levels of library management is:

- These levels and their various concerns obviously overlap, and in some cases may be undertaken by the same person, especially in smaller libraries. Nevertheless, the distinction remains a generally valid one, in terms of information need. At operational and some middle levels, formal information, systematically provided in short time comparisons, forms the bulk of what is required. Higher up the pyramid, unstructured information, much of it external, is a more significant consideration; also the more senior librarians will only want snapshot or selective sets of data derived, for example, from operational systems and the university budget.
- There are two kinds of management information, the formal and the informal. Both of them derived from external and internal sources to the academic library

but informal management information are mostly found externally such as from the users and the administrators who govern budgets.

INFORMATION NEEDS AND PERFORMANCE MEASUREMENT

Information which is reliable, accurate, timely and well presented will always help library managers to make decisions. Moreover:

- Systematic procedures are needed for allocating resources in line with objectives and ways must be found for monitoring and controlling these resources.

Performance assessment is the systematic measurement of the extent to which a library has achieved its objectives in a certain period of time. Performance assessment can be applied in libraries, in the contemporary British terminology, to: service input cost measures, service output measures, service effectiveness measures, and service domain measures. Internally, performance assessment is concerned with making the library work efficiently and effectively. Externally, it can be used by library managers to justify the budget to the parent body. Without performance assessment it is difficult to determine how well the library is progressing. The term 'performance assessment' encompasses both performance indicator and performance measure. Performance indicators:

- provide objective data on the extensiveness and effectiveness of library services. They quantify library performance in terms of goals achieved and services delivered... but to guide resource allocation.

Four types of performance indicators have been defined. They are: (i) operational performance indicators, (ii) effectiveness indicators, (iii) cost-effectiveness indicators and (iv) impact indicators. Researcher also observed that performance indicators are intended to improve decision making and service performance, aid public accountability and help define and evaluate policies. If performance indicators are seriously used and real consequences follow from the judgements based on them, then all concerned should be aware that the chosen performance indicators will come to be taken by the staff to be representative of the objectives of the library.

The relationship between performance measures and performance indicators is that they: 'can not be interpreted in the same way. Though the indicators are calculated from direct measures, there are some important factors, such as higher order effects, the particular aims of the library, or certain attributes of what is being measured, which can not be brought into the calculation. Therefore, however carefully it is arrived at, a performance indicator can not be seen as an absolute measure of performance, but as guide which needs to be considered in relation to local conditions and other indicators.'

MANAGEMENT INFORMATION SYSTEMS

Researcher has defined a Management Information System as:

- the process and structure used by an organisation to identify, collect, evaluate, transfer, and utilise information in order to fulfil its objectives. It is a system that provides management with information to make decisions, evaluate alternatives, measure performance, and detect situations requiring corrective action.

The implementation of performance assessment in academic libraries is an essential part of good management practice. Although she had reservations about the current Management Information Systems in university libraries because, for example, few academic libraries had produced a statement of their objectives, she still believed that Management Information Systems could contribute to effective management of library activities.

The four main objectives for Management Information systems have been defined as:

1. To facilitate the decision making process in the library by providing the managers with accurate, timely, and selective information that assists them in determining a specific course of action.
2. To provide for the objective performance

measurement and assessment of selected relevant areas of the library. The areas are to be determined during strategic planning.

3. To provide pertinent information about the library's internal and external environments.
4. To provide information on alternative strategies and contingency plans.

The purposes can only be implemented if people look upon Management Information Systems as an integral part of the framework of management in the academic library and not as a peripheral system which has been installed for the benefit of an individual or a single department.

- There may be subsystems within the larger system, which may be branch libraries, or departmental divisions such as cataloguing, acquisitions or circulation, but they must still be seen as integrated parts of the whole, and must function as such. In the systems approach, however, the library organisation must be seen as an organic whole, with information as its lifeblood and in which each part of the system is integrated by the flow of information throughout.

An integrated Management Information System is very important because it can be used to provide supporting information to determine:

- *Efficiency*: is the library doing things right.
- *Effectiveness*: is the library doing the right things.
- *Competitiveness*: is the library heading in a direction which is consistent with the environment.

Any discussion of the Management Information System must lead to consideration of the inputs data, processing data and the outputs data. Inputs to the management information system consist of both internally and externally generated library data. External information covers factors such as legislation, politics, trends in society, changes in technology, user demand, and comparative statistics for other, similar institutions. Internal data is that derived from administrative routines and transactional information. Administrative routines include those related to personnel, finance, acquisition, cataloguing, processing of materials, binding, building services, maintenance services, etc.

Output measures will include data of circulation, general user satisfaction, etc. All service points will need to be monitored so that internal performance comparisons can be made and the contribution of each service point are the overall objectives of the organisation assessed. In term of library managers' needs, a variety of inputs is evidently needed. It may be necessary to process information in different ways for different levels of decision-making needs, and different types of output reports will be needed to meet those different needs.

Selection of appropriate data elements for inclusion in a Management Information System assumes that:

- Clear goals and measurable objectives have been developed for the library,
- For each data element there is rationale for how it will be used or in what combinations with other data elements it can be used to determine success towards the accomplishment of objectives, overall library effectiveness, or performance measures for specific library services/operations, and
- The library can, in fact, collect reliable and valid data for a particular data element.'

The data in a management information system also needs to be processed to turn it into meaningful information for library management. For this reason, management information systems require an appropriate data processing system. Data processing is the capture, storage and processing of data for the purpose of transforming it into information useful for decision making.

In recent years, data processing for management information systems in business and industry has increasingly been undertaken by computers:

- A modem MIS will always rely to some extent on computer technology, although a computer is not a requirement. The reality of the 1980's would indicate that a computer is a necessity for the most sophisticated systems.

In libraries, in contrast, the development of the use of computer has been:

- Modular, in the sense that it is based on a single library operation such as acquisitions, serials, control or cataloguing. The more general applications of management information lay hidden, as it is often seen only as a departmental resource.

This need not necessarily have been so. An early prediction of the advantages of information produced by computers was made in 1979 by Tague, who suggested that computers should produce information for control at both macro and micro level in libraries.

However, in 1986, Brophy, having analysed eight large computer systems used in British libraries, noted that:

- Automated library systems seem to be primarily about control at the micro level. Moreover, they produced management information which was relatively crude, highly structured and very much a system by-product.

The needs of individual managers tended to be overlooked, especially when the design of MIS was in the hands of computer personnel.

- Too often, management information has been produced as an afterthought following computerisation. Most computerised issue systems, for example, were never designed to produce management information although librarians have often struggled over the data generated by these systems in an attempt to derive some meaningful information about issue patterns.

Technological changes have helped to ease this problem. As opposed to the use of mainframe and mini-computers, 'the advent of the microcomputer now provides an alternative to the dependence on large-scale centralised computer systems. Computer power can now be deployed cheaply to different parts of an organisation to allow for local processing of data.'

Computers should be easily able to provide four types of report: periodic reports, exception reports, on demand reports, and predictive reports. Periodic reports provide routine, statistical information in detailed or summarised form. Exception reports highlight areas requiring managerial attention and would focus on those that have been overlooked. On demand reports provide a response to a particular non-standard question. Predictive reports give forecasts and provide comparisons based on statistical manipulation of data.

The principal requirement of the outputs of academic library management information systems is that they should be of interest to:

- The relevant committee - the members wish to know how the library service is performing and whether the institution, is getting value for money.
- The chief financial officer - his role is primarily custodial, and he wants to be assured that there is no overspending and that money is used for the purpose intended.
- The chief librarian - who wants to know how services under his control are performing in accordance with plans, targets and budgets.
- The managers of individual sections or services—who want to have data on the operations and performance with plans, targets and budgets.
- Outside organisations requesting library performance data on a regular basis.

In these ways, the outputs of management information systems become information for decision making.

In general, management information is:

- 'The right information in the right form at the right time, so enabling the manager effectively and efficiently to do his/her job.'

The value or quality of management information is determined by three factors. They are:

1. The content of information: Information is the substance of communication, but to be information rather than data or noise, it must be meaningful, relevant and new to the receiver.
2. The form or presentation of the information: Information should be presented in a style and

format readily understandable by the manager. This means that the producer of information must be aware of the recipient's knowledge of technical terms, numeracy/literacy levels, his individual characteristics, the characteristics of the group with which he works and so on. These and other factors help the information producer to form an idea of the perception level of the manager and increase the likelihood of producing understandable information capable of being used which, it will be recalled, is the only way information can create value.

3. The timing of its presentation: Information which is produced must be communicated to the manager in time to be used. Delays in data gathering, processing or communication can transform potentially vital information into worthless waste paper.

In the planning process, information should support the decision making process. Since one of the major problems facing academic libraries is the impact of changes in available financial support, the Colleges of Further and Higher Education Group (CoFHE) of the Library Association has been considering the categories of management information required for making decisions concerning the budget.

They concluded that these are:

- Information about the institutional identity of the library.
- Information about the target group.
- Information about the collection resources.
- Information about the financial resources.
- Information about library personnel.
- Information about facilities and equipment.
- Information about various programmes and functions.

CoFHE also considered the requirements for collecting management information, and suggested the following guidelines:

- The information sought must be worth the costs of

collecting it - direct and indirect.

- Consider sources of information already available within the institution before setting up mechanisms to collect it.
- Keep the collection of information relevant, i.e., remember the purpose - 'to support the budget request.'
- Remember to consider qualitative and quantitative data as both can be relevant.

MANAGEMENT INFORMATION SYSTEM VS. DECISION SUPPORT SYSTEM

Researcher identified four major problem areas of management information systems. They are:

1. Output is undiscriminating.
2. The information is not analysed for a purpose.
3. The system is not user-friendly.
4. The information which is given by MIS may not be acceptable.

Decision support systems can be seen as an extension of the idea of management information systems to provide a wide range of information in a more flexible and interactive way. They are designed to support decision making needs of management rather than act a useful by-product of transaction processing systems.

The special feature of a decision support system is that it solves a major problem of management information systems, *i.e.*, the poor communication between the system and the users, library managers. Decision support systems have interface outputs which are more live than those of management information systems.

The main interfaces in decision support systems are:

- Regular reports which provide information on parts of the system, which are predetermined by the system's users.
- Event-centred reports in which a report is generated only when a predetermined event has occurred. This will usually be the result of an exceptional condition,

which is signalled by the system.

- *Ad hoc* reports which are generated in response to a stimulus by the system user to report on a condition which is not normally monitored.
- A query language which enables the user to interface directly with the system and to test changes in conditions experimentally. This is usually performed with 'goal-seeking' and 'what if techniques.

Beside the interface output, a decision support system also provides the report formats which may be required by the system's user, ranging from simple one-off designs to sophisticated presentations for senior managers. They are:

- *Standard reports* containing details prompted by the system user but in a format determined by standard software.
- *Tailored reports* containing information determined by the user and in a format designed by the user.
- *Tabulations* enabling the user to examine a range of statistical data rapidly, in either a standard or tailored format.
- *Spreadsheet format* allowing the user to transfer data from the system into a separate format which can be manipulated in a statistical layout.
- *Graphic presentations* providing a method of transmitting a trend analysis rapidly, and in a user-friendly manner.

Like management information systems, the data input into decision support systems can be external or internal data concerning the library. The three levels of influence on decision making can be isolated:

- Information from the library's operations.
- Information from the parent organisation.
- Information at the national and regional level.

The differences between a management information system and a decision support system lie not only their features, but also in their users. Management information systems tend to be used by lower and middle management because of their ability to assist in making structured decisions.

In contrast, decision support systems tend to be more useful to top management because they can help with decisions on unstructured issues. Where they exist, decision support systems appear to be mainly used at the strategic management level.

LIBRARY AUTOMATION

Early opinions of the potential uses of computers in libraries varied.

One university librarian observed that:

- '. . . computers can be used in library operations. It does not prove that they should.'

Despite such ambiguous attitudes, decreasing library budgets have been a significant factor in persuading the management of many academic libraries of the benefits of computerising library activities.

Many librarians have found over the last ten years or so that they have been unable to recruit more staff but their work loads have increased, perhaps by an increase in student number in an academic library, or by acquiring more books, or by the library and its services being used more. In order to cope with such situation many librarians have decided to use computer systems.

Librarians have been very careful in selecting, acquiring and installing an automated system. Moreover the setting up of library cooperatives, such as BLCMP, SWALCAP and SCOLCAP, contributed greatly to the development of library automation through a sharing of expertise and requirements. The limited abilities of the early automated systems have in many ways been overcome in the integrated, turnkey systems developed by the cooperatives and the commercial system vendors.

The decision to introduce library automation was usually based on a re-appraisal of the objectives of the library, for example:

- To make the most of effective use of existing library manpower and resources for the benefit of library users.
- To allow for integration of all aspects of information

management relevant to the library's work now and in the future

- To create a user-friendly environment in which the information handling and information processing needs of both library staff and library users, as an integral part of the learning process, are addressed
- To facilitate vertical integration of the library's current microcomputer-based systems.

In the early phase of automation, it was common that many academic libraries used their parent institution's computer facilities. Few had their own because of the then relatively high cost. Since computer prices have fallen, many academic libraries have acquired their own computers for library operations.

In the university context:

- 'libraries became less dependent upon their parent institutions for central computing facilities, and most now have their own hardware.'

Current technology may integrate the system in the library with that in its parent institutions, or stand alone.

Although IT systems may be stand-alone:

- 'The complex task of senior management in any field is not necessarily best served by the use of individual software packages. The growth of networks, the provision of information by MIS; and the ability of decision support systems to model decisions and analyse possible effects—these are likely in the long term to prove more useful tools for senior managers. The next few years will probably see a gradual increase in utilisation of these integrated management support systems in academic libraries.'

The advantages of integration are, for senior library managers, enhanced by micro-computers and intelligent terminals:

- 'The importance of these devices for the management information systems lies in their ability to acquire data from the organisation's main computer and to process it, using their own software, within the device itself. Not only is there a saving in processing load on the main machine, but the manager can be assured of a very fast response and of confidentiality and can have the software tailored to his own specifications without affecting other users. In addition many intelligent terminals provide flexible control over the information which is displayed, so that not only text but graphics can be produced and manipulated. This can be a major advantage where complex statistical data has to be presented.'

LIBRARY PLANNING AND OBJECTIVES

All the libraries had produced a statement of their mission, medium-term plans, and specific objectives or targets. One library operated on a planning cycle of three years, and the others on five years. Thus, this was a common management activity, with the potential for providing guidelines for resources allocation, and a basis for management information systems.

FINANCE

As the result of financial pressures, the libraries visited had mostly changed their approach to financial management. Cost centres and budget centres are more commonly used than in earlier years since they provide a means of allocating finance in a way more relevant to the evaluation of the library plans. The libraries which are using budget centres or cost centres have been employing a scientific/quantitative approach to resource allocation. Only three libraries still use their traditional budgetary structures and allocate resources on a historical basis. Despite differences in the schemes used for resources allocation, all the libraries had produced and continue to produce some kind of statistical data. The reasons for producing statistical data vary: in general, the data is intended to contribute information to the institution's finance system, and annual reports, or to meet requests from SCONUL or, formerly, COPOL. A requirement to produce general statistical data about the library for managerial use by its parent institution is not common; it was found in only one library.

BUILDINGS UTILISATION

The librarians were, of course, aware of the self renewing concept promoted in the Atkinson report in an attempt by government to restrict the demand for new university library buildings to accommodate ceaselessly growing collections. Attempts to apply the concept had been tried but then put aside. The reasons were clear. There have been important changes in the institutions, as the government has permitted and encouraged growth in student numbers. The introduction of new courses and an increased number of students represent different and urgent problems for academic library services, and have rendered the self renewing concept redundant—at least for the moment. Consequently, libraries had less need of information to assist decision making on what to do with their collection in order to save space. They have more need of information to assess the adequacy of their collections, study places, and usable space to meet the growing demands on them. Nonetheless, in only one polytechnic and one university did the librarians have information on shelf space available for new materials.

THE STATE OF AUTOMATION

Automated systems were mostly established in the early 1980s. Now, all librarians were concerned with the cost of maintenance, but recognised that it is offset by improved productivity in the libraries' operations. Microcomputers had been gradually introduced, but two chief librarians did not yet have them in their own offices, allegedly because they were considered too expensive. Nonetheless, in one Scottish university it was planned to introduce the use of microcomputers and spreadsheets for financial data systems. This development was being promoted by the chief librarian even though he did not have a microcomputer in his own office to use that spreadsheet. There were some indications that the librarians were willing to introduce automated management information systems. Progress had been slow, however, and finance was a major barrier.

PARTICIPATION IN COOPERATIVE ACTIVITIES

The libraries were generally members of some cooperative scheme, particularly SCONUL and COPOL, both of which compile and disseminate comparative information on library performance. Thus, to some extent, these organisations are already contributing to the development of management information systems.

ACQUISITIONS AND COLLECTION MANAGEMENT

All the libraries were suffering from reduced purchasing power. They could acquire fewer books and serials despite increases in their budgets. Overspending on periodical subscriptions was also a problem in some libraries, and had become the main issue, generally, in senior staff meetings. Most libraries had information on numbers of books borrowed, but similar data on the use of periodicals is not commonly collected, so although the librarians are aware of the reduced power of periodicals budgets, decisions on which periodicals subscriptions to retain could not easily be made. It was believed to be a very critical area that needed to be managed more carefully, and it was hoped that automated management information systems could be established to do this.

READER SERVICES

Two points were made which relate to the need for management information about reader services. First, there is a need to monitor utilisation and opening hours. Clear information on the number of users who come to the libraries in the evening, for example, must be compared against the cost of staff. Second, online services had already been introduced in all academic libraries, since they can be expensive services, charges had been introduced in most libraries. CD-ROMs are increasingly widely available free of charge; as a consequence, the number of inter-library loans has increased. Information is needed by library management on all these areas to enable the most cost-efficient and sustainable solution to be implemented.

STAFFING

All but one of the libraries had increased their expenditure on library staff as a proportion of the total budget. They all currently faced the problem of managing a workload arising from increased numbers of students with a reduced staff. There appeared to be a readiness among library staff to establish automated management information systems to monitor the workload and to simplify some reporting tasks.

EVALUATION PROCESSES

Formal and comprehensive evaluation processes might be supposed to be in place in all the libraries since all the librarians were aware of the need for quantitative and qualitative data about their libraries, but there was only one university library which claimed that it had a formal and comprehensive system for library evaluation. Most libraries claimed to have an informal system and to be trying to introduce formal ones. They were aware of the existence of performance measures and performance indicators which would help them to evaluate their libraries, but only two libraries had experimented with performance measurement, and only one had fully implemented a formal system through the development of an experimental decision support system.

Two of the eight libraries had no immediate plans to introduce the use of performance indicators. Neither the chief librarians nor senior librarians were promoting their introduction. The other five libraries were moving to introduce the use of performance indicators. This was being promoted by chief librarians because of a perceived need for quantitative and qualitative data. There appeared to be little suggestion that it was being done simply because it was fashionable. Three of the five libraries are using mostly paper-based management information systems.

Two others are using microcomputer networks. Of the rest, two libraries had discontinued collecting internal information, and one has never collected information for use as performance indicators. In terms of the use of performance indicators in decision making, the one library which uses performance indicators stated that they had a considerable impact on decision making; most of the others suggested that performance indicators had little impact on decision making. Despite the lack of formal performance measurement in some libraries, all had a financial data system. Current reports from the financial data system are said to be adequate for decision making, and for the libraries' annual, reports, as well as meeting the needs of the institutions' own finance departments.

USE OF EXTERNAL INFORMATION FOR LIBRARY PLANNING

The library plans and objectives in the libraries visited showed that they were aware of current external trends. Their parent institutions' plans were the principal source of information about future developments. In addition, they took account of information from outside institutions such as government departments and, in particular, the higher education funding councils. Other information sources which were mentioned consisted of other libraries' annual reports. *Information UK 2000,* users' comments on the library services, publishing trends, etc. To obtain comparative data about their libraries' performance, they made heavy use of SCONUL and COPOL data. Most external information is acquired in printed form. Some information sources are kept in the chief librarians' offices, others in the senior librarians': no one had a comprehensive collection of the external information in their own offices. Two libraries had recorded some external information, e.g., information on price inflation, in their microcomputers. Although there are serious problems in data processing, the range of external information held shows that there was the potential to establish a comprehensive management information system. The external information would, however, have to be tailored with other information in order to be used in decision making.

THE AVAILABILITY AND USE OF MANAGEMENT INFORMATION SYSTEMS

Three libraries claimed that they had management information systems in their institutions and libraries. One library had a partial system in both the institution and the library, and was trying to develop a comprehensive one in library. One had a partial system in the library, and was attempting to have a comprehensive one, even though there was no management information system in its institution. Of those who did not have management information systems in their libraries, three librarians offered the explanation that this was because there was no management information system in the institution. One commented that its attention was concentrated on selecting and introducing a reliable turnkey automated system. All librarians mentioned that user friendliness and inexpensiveness are priorities in establishing their management information systems.

Apart from the library which has decision support systems, current automated library systems are not fully used for formal management information systems, even though these could perhaps provide enhanced information for performance measurement and could contribute to the establishment of a more comprehensive evaluation of the achievement of the libraries' objectives. In terms of the ability of their automated system to support a management information system, all the libraries stated that existing systems were generally helpful in data processing. However, they produced output data which is crude and which has to be further manipulated before it can be interpreted.

Seven of the libraries' computer systems produce quite complete operational data such as statistics of cataloguing, circulation, etc., but no system provides statistical data on reference services. One university library struggled to collect even crude data since its turnkey system has limited capabilities. It produces only data on circulation and stocks, and lacks compatibility with any other automated system in the library or the institution. Therefore, in order to have data in usable form and when needed, all libraries must at present manipulate them.

Two libraries, however, had microcomputers which had no downloading facilities: they first had to print out the data from larger computers and manipulate it manually before inputting it into a microcomputer to be used with other information. Others did have microcomputers with downloading facilities, and could use them to process the crude data into usable outputs. All the libraries thus employ workable methods of producing management information, but they lack immediacy, and are expensive to operate. The forms of output vary. Those libraries which had formal management information systems had facilities to examine them online, but mostly data is presented in hard copy. Libraries which had informal and/or partial management information systems tended to rely on on-demand reporting. Although most libraries stated that the outputs are easily read, analysing the outputs of the system depends mostly on the abilities of the users to interpret them.

Outputs provide information for junior, senior and chief librarians. Graphical presentations were available to make numerical data understandable in a very short time. Apart from the information provided for junior management, the outputs of management information systems are generally discussed in senior staff meetings on a weekly or monthly basis. With regard to decision making in the areas of library planning and evaluation, in particular budgeting and resources allocation, two chief librarians stated that management information systems had made a great impact in the sense that all decisions were made based on the information from their systems. This is due to the comprehensiveness of the information made available. Their systems can provide only crude data, but it can be interpreted easily so that it assists in answering very specific questions.

MANAGEMENT INFORMATION SYSTEMS AND THE STAFF STRUCTURE

Seven of the eight libraries claimed that they already

had a 'flat' management structure, and are trying to avoid a more hierarchical staff structure. However, the current structure was said to be uninfluenced by the existence of a management information system. Rather, it was due to the need to establish a structure which was customer oriented, which provided a clear definition of the responsibilities of staff, and which facilitated the flow of instructions or information. One university librarian also stated that the hierarchy that had been retained was intended to facilitate staff promotion.

OPINIONS ON DECISION SUPPORT SYSTEMS

Libraries which had formal management information systems found that the management information produced by their system needed to be carefully interpreted; moreover, the management information systems were not pro-active. Therefore, their aim was the introduction of decision support systems in the near future. Those libraries which had only informal management information systems saw that they had the choice of establishing either a formal management information system or a decision support system. They indicated that they were more likely to favour decision support systems.

All of the librarians interviewed were aware of the nature and potential of decision support systems, and saw them as particularly helpful in utilising performance indicators and developing quality assurance processes in the library. One library was already experimenting with a decision support system and performance indicators, and three were aiming to have one. One librarian, however, had no intention to have a decision support system, as he felt that it could assume too much control, as well as being very difficult to establish. However, all were agreed that decision support systems are more reliable than management information systems. Nevertheless, in terms of infrastructure for decision support systems, little progress was evident. Only one library had a microcomputer based network, and one other was preparing to have one.

INFORMATION SYSTEMS AND EFFECTS ON DECISION-MAKING

All of the libraries visited already employed automated systems. However, formal and relatively fully automated management information systems existed in only two of the eight libraries visited. They had been established because of the existence of management information systems in the institutions as a whole. In the other libraries, the use of cost centres for resources allocation caused the libraries to have some formal management information. Libraries generally are not fully utilising the capability of their automated systems since some external information remains in printed form, and manual data processing is still a significant element in their analysis of the data available. Those librarians who had 'informal' or 'partial' management information systems had concluded that a management information system would be not helpful for decision making in budgeting and resource allocation, but they still faced a requirement to produce reports for their institutions, particularly for their finance departments, which incorporate management data.

They also produce summary information for various purposes, profiling their parent institution, finance, staff, users, facilities and equipment, programmes and functions. Those libraries which had management information systems possessed information which was deeper in substance and more readily available, so it was easier for them to make appropriate decisions.

BARRIERS TO THE DEVELOPMENT OF MANAGEMENT INFORMATION SYSTEMS

There were several reasons why many of the libraries visited lacked management information systems.

The criteria of an ideal management information system are that:

- They must be inexpensive to operate.
- They must not interfere with existing services.
- They must provide reproducible results.

The fact that some libraries claimed to have only 'informal' or 'partial' management information systems or to have no management information systems does not mean that they had no collection of external and internal data. They do collect and use information for establishing library objectives and priorities or for resources allocation, but they have not formalised their management information systems, typically because their institutions had not required them to do so. Other factors which had inhibited development are mainly technical and concern the libraries' infrastructures. The limited capabilities of their computers had resulted in misinterpretation of the output data, and faulty analysis by senior library staff.

This was compounded by a lack of staff training in analysing data. The emphasis on purchasing microcomputers for library users was also a drain on scarce resources which might otherwise have been used to set up automated management information systems. Incompatibility of computer systems also caused problems; for example, in the workload involved in inputting common data such as the identity of students as compared with simply capturing it from a central database. Although they had enough potential to support formal management information systems, less use is made of existing automated library systems than might be possible given some development of their software. Even in the two libraries which had management information systems, there is one evident weakness; neither library has identified a comprehensive range of performance measures.

CONCLUSIONS

The contemporary approach casts academic librarians as managers within the higher education system. Planning and controlling development is clearly an important aspect of that role. Academic libraries' objectives have become clearer than in the past, but British academic libraries' attempts to achieve those objectives have been threatened by government financial policies which, in effect, require academic libraries to provide more and better services with less money. Consequently, every aspect of academic libraries' operations has to be reviewed so that they can be managed more effectively and efficiently. It is not easy to achieve this because academic libraries are complex organisations. What academic librarians need, now much more than ever before, is the information which will allow them to plan properly, to know whether or not the library service is meeting the needs of the academic community and to be able to demonstrate that to the internal and external authorities responsible for funding.

Performance measures are also necessary in order to reveal libraries' strengths and weaknesses when compared with internal and external targets, norms and averages. From the survey, it is clear that most library managers are very concerned with the need for management information about their libraries. Libraries have generally established objectives and forward plans; there are still differences in how they allocate resources to fulfil those plans, and clear divergences of opinion on what information is required for library planning and resources allocation. Changing circumstances may call for any aspect of libraries' resources and services to be reviewed, or for them to be considered from a different perspective, often pro-actively or at fairly short notice, and the advantages of a comprehensive management information system should be self-evident.

Similarly, although at present there is much data collection, formal evaluation processes are not common. Performance measures which can compare internal and external information have not been widely utilised and have made little impact in decision making, perhaps because there is no agreement on what constitutes appropriate measures of achievement. Structured management information systems could help library managers in collecting and processing data into a useful form to assist in decision making. Most libraries appear to collect the same data, but only two of the eight selected libraries had established comprehensive management information systems for their librarians' purposes, in particular to support the planning process.

Although they had not fully automated data processing and reporting, and the information from their systems needs to be carefully interpreted, these librarians are making decisions based on outputs from their management information systems. The introduction of computers into academic libraries was largely a response to the problem of dealing with increased workloads with fewer staff, and they are now able easily to handle most of the routine and repetitive work of the library staff.

In addition, they have the capability to enhance the provision of management information, since automated data processing is able to present reports more accurately and much faster than manual systems. A limited range of data processing for management information is currently supported by the computer systems, including microcomputers, available in academic libraries, but there are still significant weaknesses in library automation systems in respect of the production of management information. For example, much remains to be done in monitoring high cost areas such as serials management and staff deployment in reader services.

Consequently, apart from the one library visited which has a decision support system, current library automation systems are not fully used for formal management information systems. It has to be said that most librarians still consider the continuous costs of automation as a worrying expense, and that the development of management information systems is not seen as a high priority compared with the introduction or upgrading of new automation systems for handling routine operations. Nonetheless, most librarians claim that they would now like to install decision support systems, even though they see the expense as a problem. The likelihood of increasing requirements for information to be provided at institutional level to meet government demands that institutions should be accountable may change priorities and foster developments.

While waiting for these developments, and for this new technology to be proved, attempts must be made to find out whether there will be support for the establishment of management information systems or decision support systems, and in particular, whether there will be support from the parent institutions and the library staff. The introduction of automated management information systems seems unlikely to pose a threat to staff in academic libraries, as most already have a 'flat' management structure, but a priority must be training programmes on the use of information in management. Support from parent institutions is also essential since the technology required for decision support systems could be expensive, particularly if they are seen as separate from the replacement of the libraries' existing automated systems.

It will, therefore, be important to convince the vendors who produce turnkey library automation systems to develop new systems which provide more of the management information that meets widely recognised needs in terms of both contents and format. There is a bewildering array of information available from a variety of external and internal sources, and, in addition to the costs of collection and collation, it generally needs tailoring to meet libraries' needs for comparable data. Cooperative groups such as SCONUL have a role to play here in developing guidelines on the information needed, and the format(s) in which it should be presented for comparative purposes. Present outputs from library automation systems are crude, but the work currently being undertaken to develop both performance measures which have wide applicability and credibility, and more effective management information modules as part of library automation systems should eventually resolve that problem.

4

Information Economy and Geospatial Information

INTRODUCTION

The recent socioeconomic trends, convergence of telecommunication technologies and the emergence of information as an integral component of the contemporary economy, have had significant effects on individuals and on wider social groups in the population. The current information node infrastructure of the telecommunications industry, which has facilitated that convergence of the telecommunications technology, is comprised of a variety of links. These links include data clearinghouses, data providers, and data warehouses, which themselves combine to form complex information networks as well as individual links, or single participants.

All of these links affect how information flows across the network. Libraries, as participants in the information network infrastructure, are well suited to affect the nature of data processes in the current information economy. Although the framework of the information economy may have been built by technological innovations and capital investments, there are cultural and political factors about the social milieu in which information is processed that affect how individuals participate in the economy. The composition of the information networks creates a variety of challenges to the successful searching, discovery, and mining of data for users in a variety of situations. Libraries can facilitate the interactions of individuals with different types of information that are integral to successful participation in the information economy. A key informational component of the information economy is how libraries can facilitate participation of their users with geospatial information.

This chapter will explore different socio-economic aspects of the information economy and the role of libraries. The development of geographic information systems, the importance of 'value added' services and an examination of how information is being increasingly commoditised is also included. Public aspects of geospatial information, such as government-produced GIS, will be discussed. How libraries can play a role in facilitating some of the social aspects of the distribution of the information economy, such as the digital divide, will also be examined.

ROLE OF INFORMATION IN CONTEMPORARY ECONOMY

In the information economy, many private sector firms and government agencies have become consolidated around a framework of telecommunication networks and related information technologies. However, integrating communications and information technologies into their organisations have affected organisational processes, including production, distribution, and administration of products and services.

Researchers have noted that organisational processes in both the public and private sectors have become characterised by applications, such as electronic data exchange, distributed databases, computer-based communication, and client server computing. Other researchers have indicated that geographic concepts, such as space and location, are significant factors in the distribution of data as it flows between individuals and organisations across communication networks, therefore, the use of geographic information systems in the facilitating and analysis of data has also increased greatly. The development and integration of geospatial information in a variety of administrative, production, and service functions within organisations in both the public and private sectors can have an effect on the role that libraries play in the information economy. The geospatial information that is used by individuals and organisations in the information economy is often produced by a mix of private developers and government agencies.

The data used by geographers and geographic information systems analysts in their operations is diverse and distributed across a wide network of server locations, over a complex series of information nodes. Libraries can provide a unique entry point to this multitude of sources. Economic activities during the past few decades have increasingly been characterised by different functional uses of information. The establishment and growth of diverse information industries, such as statistical bureaus, marketing associations, trade journals, and consulting agencies, have integrated information in their operations. The development builds on early studies of how information not only impacted, but helped define, different economic processes.

During the decades following World War II, individuals in the banking and accounting sectors began defining information as having value and affecting production. Statements, such as the 'Statement of Basic Accounting Theory,' asserted that accounting systems could be conceptualised as an "application of general theories of information to the problem of efficient economic operations". The National Science Foundation began to fund research about the economics of information. Other organisations, such as the Organisation for Economic Co-operation and Development (OECD) and the United Nations Economic, Scientific, and Cultural Organisation (UNESCO), were also debating policy issues about the economics of information.

However, to develop an information policy, one must first understand that policy is "the generic name of any formulation, simple or complex, vague or exact, general or special, discretionary or detailed, of guidance for action in the face of circumstances which, lying necessarily in the future, can be approached only by conjecture and imagination". The first bibliography of information economics was published in 1971. By the mid 1970s, developments in the literature illustrated how the general theories of information were being investigated by economists and other researchers in the sciences and social sciences.

The existence of learning processes and likely variation in policy criteria in a business organisation imply that the decision-making unit is undergoing continual change". Further, "those responsible for shaping information policy must determine the appropriate mix of information inputs to achieve social objectives, while at the same time they must have regard for equity considerations. By 1976, the American Economic Association officially recognised information as an economic topic and incorporated it into core ideas. By the 1980s, research into this area was generating much debate among researchers about what comprised information economics.

Among the ideas being debated was the emergent issue of how to incorporate information into modes of production and thereby study its effects in different sectors of the economy. Early economists described three factors of production that included land, labour, and capital. The competing theories on defining just how these three factors relate, especially capital, in a system is contentious and open to debate.

Economists differ on how to define capital. It can be described concretely as something of value as in money or more abstractly as an association with labour and consumption. In examining the value of transformative functions of an economic activity, the definition of capital can be more broadly interpreted, in some cases to include information. For example, the definition of human capital is the "sum total of skills embodied within an individual: education, intelligence, charisma, creativity, work experience, entrepreneurial vigour, it is what you would be left with if someone stripped away all of your assets-your job, your money, your possessions". A number of articles and other publications that were produced in the 1990s discussed different forms of intangible capital including information, cultural capital, linguistic capital, and social capital. Social capital would involve "networks of communication and communication-based institutions and their rules, norms of social practice, and relationships of trust".

Networks themselves would be considered as facilitating a sum of knowledge that would have value as a factor in production. Another perspective on integrating information into economic theory was in examining how change in the economy is affected by information. Researcher suggests that "the production of knowledge and its transformation into technologies and other applied mechanisms such as competition can alter the order of different sectors of the economy and thus its equilibrium".

More fundamentally, it changes the role, the function, and the perception of economic measurement data. Because information is its key resource and output, the intangible economy is highly data-sensitive and intrinsically self reflective". However, as researcher suggests, the effects of the applications of information and technology are only apparent over a period of time when it is possible to perform analysis with systematic data.

Recent studies have focused on defining the role of technology in causing economic growth. Some researchers consider economic change as being influenced by aspects of the innovation process, aspects that are characterised as being 'information intense" or more developed technologically than what had currently existed. There has been much speculation on the correlation between technological development and economic growth and the social consequences of economic activities. In Marshallian neo-classical economics, externalities refer to by-products of activities that affect the well-being of people, where those impacts are not reflected in market prices; the costs associated with externalities do not enter standard cost accounting schemes. The backbone of the information economy is in the linkages that combine to form a network.

If the network is a combination of technology and human activities that processes information as they traverse the network, then the uneven flow of information across the network can cause externalities to manifest themselves. These externalities can be caused by incomplete information that can result in the fluctuating prices of a commodity. The effect of content of information on the economy is up to debate. Are the contextual aspects of information processed in the economy irrelevant or do the contextual aspects of information in the economy have distinct sociopolitical value? For those who argue the latter, the contextual aspects of information do shape the perception and understanding of economic processes themselves. The cultural variability of information creates difficulties in determining the locational aspects of data. Data may be associated with a physical carrier, but it is not bound by the location of that carrier.

This aspect of information has created challenges to economists who have attempted to illustrate Braman's concept that would "distinguish between the costs of information at different stages of an information production chain". Further, the value of the information chain hinges upon relevance that "is a subjective question of mapping an utterance on the conceptual map of a given user seeking information for a particular purpose defined by that individual" and the "utility of a piece of information will depend on a combined valuation of its credibility and relevance". Most of the economic models that attempt to illustrate an information production chain have the elements of information creating, processing, flows, and use incorporated into their structure. A number of organisations have created models that have the elements of information acquisition, production, assembly, storage, monitoring, interpretation, and exchange. United States federal documents describe an information cycle that includes information creation, collection, processing, and distribution as do international organisations. Creators, or individuals who are involved in the innovation of new concepts and new industries, are highly valued.

However, the idea of an information sector is not new. In 1962, over 50 industries were identified that comprised an information sector. Other economists preferred to identify information sector industries by using existing industry classifications, as identified by Standard Industrial Classification (SIC) codes. However, critics of the approach questioned the validity of defining information on so specific a criteria, fearing that existing industrial classifications "ignore a major part of the processes of investment in information in the economy" and that "most significant information activities do not produce goods in tangible form and thus not included in the SIC system". The debate over how to classify industries in the information sector illustrates the variability of trying to define information for econometric purposes.

The debate is further magnified when trying to define the economic aspects of information in an international sense. Cultural context is a factor in defining what comprises the information sector, with definitions varying between countries and methods that describe material and information related production.

Even though legal negotiations about the nature of information and production between countries, such as with the General Agreements on Tariffs and Trade (GATT), have attempted to arrive at some definitional parameters for information, the process of trying to understand how information works in an international trade environment is problematic due to the great variability production across different countries. For example, the North American Industry Classification System (NAICS) was adopted in 1997, replacing the old Standard Industrial Classification (SIC) system. Developed jointly by the U.S., Canada, and Mexico to provide new comparability in statistics about business activity across North America, the NAICS also better distinguishes between manufacturing and information sectors. Although imperfect, the NAICS is an essential tool to determine service and product providers in the information sector, to remain current on industry analyses, statistics, and leading companies.

The international economic environment is indeed a complex one, and in defining how information operates within economic systems, one can examine the redefining of economic components such as the agent, the firm, and the market. As discussed in classical economic theory, agents tend to act in ways that put themselves in a better position than previously held. Braman questions the decision-making processes of economic agents as they improve their position according to economic theory. Processes including "rationality, perfect information, and individualistic independence" are subject to myriad influences and the amount of information available. Further, there are limits to the amount of information that an individual agent can have access to or even process in order to maximize his position.

Research in the fields of psychology, that is, cognitive miserliness, has indicated that there are cognitive and neurological limitations that affect how information is perceived and understood. Technology limitations can also affect the capture, recording, and transmission of information, thereby, affecting its cognition by an agent or organisation. The cultural context of information, as well, can have an affect on how information is understood.

The social organisation of society can have an significant impact on the flow of information creating barriers that can slow or impede the finding of information by individual agents. The concept of social organisation and community is also important in understanding how information is processed in regards to economic function. In classical economic theory, economic agents act purposively. Since they have an end in mind and find means to attain those ends, the actions of individual agents bear a causal relationship to overall market outcomes. Further, an economic agent uses information in order to "obtain satisfaction or benefits gained from consuming a particular good or service according to a hierarchical ranking of preferences". The social context of how information can be pursued and utilised also affects the actions of an individual economic agent.

An individual may use information and acquire goods and services beyond what is necessary for the maximizing of their position and thus, may not make the best use of information in a classical economic sense. Cultural processes can affect preferences for a particular commodity adding or detracting from its value. The decision-making process is interconnected among various individuals in society, which can affect the utility factor in economic activities. Societies and communities can be conceptualised as components of a larger structure or market in which economic activities are performed. The larger structure can operate as an "informational mechanism" with different types of information arrayed spatially across it. How economic agents operate within markets is subject to much debate as economists advocate different operational models about the functioning of markets. One model centers on the prices of commodities and services that are distributed across a market. Economic agents enter the market with a certain knowledge level and assumptions about prices that influence their interaction with the market.

The search for further price information for an eventual outcome process frames their activities in the market. Social aspects and cultural ties that are part of the market structure affect how information interacts with markets. The distribution of information across markets has an impact on the economic decision process of the firm as well as the individual. If a market is a social arrangement that allows buyers and sellers to discover information and carry out a voluntary exchange of goods or services, the firm is an alternative system of allocation to the market that exists to organise production in a non-price environment. Although there is a distinction between a market and a firm, most economists admit that the two shade into each other. A business model describes the elements and relationships that express the business logic of a firm.

Just as NAICS classes businesses into sectors, firms are often classed into 'internally consistent sets of firms,' referred to as strategic groups or configurations, allowing typologies and taxonomies to explore the determinants of performance. Early studies of information flow within existing business entities usually focused on individual managers. In a market environment in which reliable information was at a premium, business managers made decisions based on an individualised perspective that made use of personal social networks as well as market information. The growth of larger business enterprises with extensive production and distribution linkages increased the need for accurate market information, which led to the eventual progression towards extensive record keeping overseen by professional managers. The availability of accurate market information and information on other firms in related enterprises began to affect business decisions.

An increased efficiency in record management usually decreases what some economists have labeled transaction costs, or the searching for information needed for a particular type of economic activity. Early studies in the nature of transaction costs within business processes determined that firms usually invested in those transaction costs that were more expensive, while leaving the more inexpensive transaction costs to the marketplace. The application of advanced telecommunication technology by firms has encouraged commercial enterprises to distribute their transaction costs on an even wider basis for more efficiency. Contemporary studies in the nature of firms and different economic sectors have expanded the focus of study beyond the single firm to a hierarchy of firms or even larger social constructs, such as networks. Research into the role of information and economic theory bridges the mathematical boundaries of idealised econometric models to account for information sector variability and the irrationality of human behaviour.

Research in the social dynamics of industries that comprise the information sector should take a wider, holistic approach. Studies on the information sector should integrate concepts and analytical methods from other disciplines. One such discipline is political science, which has often focused on the effect of uneven flows of information and of the impact of imperfect information on decisions. In expanding their descriptive scope of the components of the information sector, economists expanded their idea of the firm and the market by including variables with wider spatial structures. Such structures include telecommunication networks and social communication networks. It is with the physical network of the telecommunications sector that some researchers, especially in the field of geography, have sought to combine spatial concepts of space, place, and landscape to provide a rigourous and quantifiable platform in which to measure the complex socioeconomic phenomena that comprises the information sector.

GEOGRAPHIES OF THE INTERNET

The study of contemporary geographic spaces and technology inevitably focuses on the ubiquitous telecommunications networks that comprise the Internet. The complex interlocking nodes of the Internet create a variety of physical spaces bounded by technology such as computer hardware, fibre optics, and communication software. Upon the network of the Internet, geographers have identified a great many physical and virtual places as well. Geographers view the concept of space as more of an abstract expression, but the concept of place is bounded in the social milieu of a given location and can evolve as the local society that identified the space changes, and as new technologies alter the unique expression of the location. Places can be a unique experience of an individual person, but more often, they are the social constructs of many people with shared experiences.

What is unique about places on the Internet is they can alter the bounded physical locations of places as identified by society and encourage the defining of new concepts of place that use elements of technology combined with historical notions of place, or "cyberspaces coexist with geographic spaces, providing a new layer of virtual sites superimposed over geographic spaces". Using such logic, geographers identify places on the Internet with a variety of parameters, including socioeconomic, political, and cultural factors. In defining their research about the geographic nature of telecommunications and of the Internet, geographers tend to focus on two broad aspects of research.

On one hand, geographers are interested in the technological aspect of telecommunications and the Internet and how society and interacts with the technology. Research by geographers on the Internet "developed lines of research focused on the technology and infrastructure of the Internet and how the use of this technology has blended with existing cultural, political, and economic structures manifest in physical places". Geographers intent on researching the technical aspects of the Internet tend to focus on analysing locationally referenced Internet infrastructure data, essentially, the locations of nodes, communications networks. Factors in locating the infrastructure across the landscape include: "amounts of bandwidth coming from a populated area, Internet fibre backbone, and points of presence (POPs) or broadband development". Many of the studies in the locational aspects of the Internet infrastructure depict an uneven distribution of its composition.

The most densely developed Internet hubs are located in larger urbanised areas, while less densely developed rural areas lack high bandwidth rates. The distribution of the Internet has a significant effect on how information flows across the Internet and how the information is used by people. The physical distribution of the Internet is especially relevant to the delivery of library information and resources. In the dynamic environment of the information sector, the library can be an important cornerstone in facilitating information flow between individuals and organisations. The stable presence of the publicly funded institutions can offer access to information as well as guidance in interpreting information for users. Libraries can also offer other services such as archival functions in an environment wherein information durability can be problematic.

CONVERGENCE OF COMMUNICATION TECHNOLOGIES

Telecommunication convergence in the information economy has had a significant effect on the delivery of library information resources and services. Convergence promises a 'clean slate' approach, where things are re-engineered to provide better, more flexible service to the user. Convergence, according to Fowler can be defined in four major categories of the telecommunications industry that correspond to layers, or sets of layers, in the Open Systems Interconnect (OSI) network model.

The categories are transport (comprising the *physical.* layer), switching, and applications:

- *Transport:* The same physical pipes and transport technology carry multiple services, usually of different customers, for example, multipleT1 or T3 links. Convergence at this level is primarily used by carriers to provision their infrastructure; it is largely transparent to users as they continue to see and pay for separate services.
- *Switching:* The same cable plant carries different types of traffic and does appropriate switching. Content and presentation to the user is unchanged, with the possible exception of new features. Historically, this has been the layer about which most discussion has centered. The distinction between services becomes less distinct or disappears entirely under network layer convergence; at the present time, Internet protocol (IP), a switching technology, is envisioned as the common medium for all types of telecommunications traffic, especially voice and Internet traffic.
- *Application (Content):* The same end-user device or type of device and network handles and delivers all content; the user does not have separate network interface devices
- *Telecommunications/IT:* There is also a fourth meaning of convergence, which will be considered here, that refers to blurring of the distinction between telecommunications and information processing. Examples are use of Applications Service Providers (ASPs) and network computing.

With convergence, traditionally separate functions are now available through one source or channel, such as an ISP or through a single vendor. Of particular interest to libraries is the technological convergence at the application level.

Multiple resources in varying formats, including text, data, images, graphics, audiovisual media, streaming media, games and simulations, and so forth, are now available over one transmission network, through the same user equipment, and through standard, ubiquitous software applications.

Previous channels would have included, and perhaps required, delivery via postal mail service or broadcast media, carrying a variety of formats and media. Enterprise systems, interactive video-on-demand, and telecalls/teleconferencing are becoming the norm. What will limit the rapid expansion of these applications will be intellectual property rights issues. As the United States continues to build infrastructure and to recreate how the infrastructure is policed, broadband will undergo a number of changes. However, increased broadband access will continue to build convergence. The United States Congress has been urged to recognise and "encourage the convergence of voice, data, image and video information into bit streams" to "[e]nsure the greatest possible regulatory flexibility, to allow for unpredictable future service needs, market developments and technological innovation". Congress has also been urged to reduce barriers to competition, restructure the market in the public interest, and increase spectrum efficiency with both licensed and unlicensed models of spectrum use.

Convergence is seen as an evolutionary, rather than a revolutionary process. Initiatives to ensure broadband to the majority of homes in the United States by 2010, if realised, may speed up these trends. Initiatives include the UTOPIA (Utah Telecommunication Open Infrastructure Agency), the National LambdaRail Network, the NorthEast Education and Research Network (NEREN), the Third Frontier Network (TFN), and the hundreds of other fibre communities in the United States. Integrated media systems that seamlessly combine video, audio, computer animation, text, and graphics into a common digital display medium were noted as a new area of convergence. Further, Mihram and Mihram predicted that infrastructure installation, product creation, and commercialisation relating to integrated media systems would become areas of research and development for both the public and private sectors.

Today, geographic information systems are seen as the next pivotal technology in this convergence, again due to the advances in interoperability and data standards. Again, we see infrastructure installation, product creation, and commercialisation in GIS becoming areas of research for the public and private sectors. Standards development, in particular, is a crucial area for GIS convergence. Many organisations work collaboratively to promote the advancement of open geospatial standards and specifications, especially as the market expands into domains associated with Internet and telecommunications communications technologies.

These organisations include the Open Geospatial Consortium, W3C, and OASIS, as well as national and international standards associations. Since much of the data in the contemporary information economy have geospatial or geotemporal components, no applications, systems, or technologies are unaffected. Further, it is through the efficient use of GIS/geospatial technologies that we are able to understand and leverage the value of spatial/location based information and processes in the broader context of ICT and enterprise information systems. Convergence continues through business processes and architectures. Business architectures are the starting point from which to develop related and integrated functional, information, process, and application architectures.

These architectures are aided by the rapid development and deployment of open, standards-based service-oriented architectures. Examples include the development of XML and XML Schema; SOAP; WSDL; and XQuery. In addition, more Web service tiers are integrated with business logic and workflow. There is increased deployment of mobile devices, communications, and services with even newer new micromobility management schema and technologies. There are also smarter and richer client tools with more robust and flexible secure information exchange solutions. Certainly, enterprise systems will serve as a 'unifying' element through their capacity to manage and utilise geospatial content, capabilities and services in enterprise environments.

As the landscape of information technology changes through the convergence in the industry, the public sector, including libraries, is affected as well. As academic disciplines transition to newer forms of working and educational environment, the situation necessitates a commitment that encompasses several objectives: to change basic educational tools, to retrofit installations of school- and campus-wide data networks, and to create affordable networks that would link schools, homes, and communities. The development of new media technologies tends to be spatially uneven, often concentrating in one sector of society while marginalising other sectors. The process of being marginalised by technology can often be through cultural, socioeconomic, geographic, technological and political means. The uneven distribution of technology, computer networks, and of the information they transmit, has been characterised as contributing to a 'digital divide' between those who do have access to the Internet and those who do not.

THE SOCIAL STRUCTURE OF THE INFORMATION ECONOMY

The digital divide has been described by researchers in a variety of dichotomies in both contemporary American and international settings. In contemporary American society, researchers apply econometrics to socioeconomic data to portray how particular income groups have sufficient capital to purchase computer hardware and software for Internet access, while others do not. Researchers also look at factors such as race, ethnicity, and educational attainment to further illustrate differences in technology access. Different technological standards are identified, within contemporary American society, that can contribute to uneven access to information technologies.

In international settings, the literature on the digital divide includes many of the factors described in articles about technology and information access in America, though other factors are emphasised, for example, political ones. Many research and policy papers that examine different aspects of the digital divide identify minority ethnic groups, indigenous peoples, and specific groups of people as being disadvantaged in participating in the information economy. Factors include low incomes, few educational qualifications, low literacy levels, unemployment, age or disabled status, and single parent households. Diverse minority groups often live in large urban centers that have complex telecommunication networks, unlike persons living in rural and frontier areas. However, both rural and urban areas may have older telecommunication infrastructures, affecting access.

In every income bracket, at every level of education, in every age group, for people of every race and among people of Hispanic origin, among both men and women, many more people use computers and the Internet now than did so in the recent past. Some people are still more likely to be Internet users than others are Individuals living in low-income households or having little education, still trail the national average. However, broad measures of Internet use in the United States suggest that over time Internet use has become more equitable.

However, there still exists a significant gap in the number of computers in low-income schools and communities. Researcher also did not find that language was a statistically significant factor in Internet access, though many research reports indicate that English language ability is an important factor in participation in the information economy. Households with a record of higher educational attainment would be more inclined to use computers, have Internet access, and place a high value on literacy. An important factor influencing participation in the information economy is the acquisition of information and communication technology (ICT) skills. Individuals who are members of the various groups that have been marginalised from computers and of the Internet often lack the necessary skills to use ICT applications.

Researcher argues that the interaction of factors, such as cost, restricting access to equipment, low educational achievement, and cultural, age or gender-based exclusion from literacy and computing skills, counteracts against the spread of such skills in disadvantaged communities. Efforts to improve access to computers and programmes to improve ICT technology skills among marginalised groups have been incorporated in a variety of community outreach programmes by both public and private agencies. Many such programmes try to establish and create a culture that is more conducive to ICT technologies.

COMMUNITY INTERNET INITIATIVES

The combination of municipal and commercial computer networks in some large metropolitan areas has led to the creation of community information networks. Community information networks are often built around existing social networks involved in neighbourhood activities like employment and economic opportunity centers, youth and family centers, health, education, and affordable housing initiatives.

The Chicago Area Northside Neighbourhood Online Network, is an organisation that offers training and Internet access to community based entities throughout the city. Building on existing human networks in the communities, the project has successfully trained residents and staff of over 60 community organisations, creating a unique multiracial, mixed-economic, and mixed-gender pool of community users.

The NeighbourTech programme works with Chicago's inner city neighbourhoods. NeighbourTech uses a variety of methods to draw in neighbourhood residents, small businesses, and non-profit organisations located in disadvantaged neighbourhoods. The Erie Neighbourhood House, a non-profit, multiservice agency in Erie, New York, operates the Erie Technology Center. The mission of the Technology Center is to provide computer and information literacy to West Town residents with limited English proficiency and low educational attainment.

By working with other educational programmes in the area, the Technology Center integrates traditional teaching/ learning methods with current technology applications for students ranging from prekindergarten to senior citizens. Grants from federal agencies, such as the U.S., Department of Commerce, are also used to build community information networks outside of urban areas in rural locations.

The ItascaNet network, established in the town of Grand Rapids in north central Minnesota, is mostly rural, with a shrinking population base. Local community leaders used the grant funds to build an online network to increase the community's access to, and use of, the national information infrastructure, reduce disparities in access levels among community residents, increase information available to community members, and facilitate the sharing of data and information among partner organisations. The ItaskaNet network involved five partner agencies that oversaw the purchasing of a server and cable for connections between the agencies.

A significant member agency of the partnership was the public library. Internet-linked computers were made available to students in the public schools and to citizens in the public library, and free computer training classes were offered to the community. Researchers have identified libraries as an important cultural resource in contemporary American society. They can be an important node in the contemporary computer network and provide computer access and information service to the user community.

THE ROLE OF LIBRARIES IN THE INFORMATION ECONOMY

The emergence of the new information economy comprised of computer networks that link users to one another or to larger organisations is creating a class of singular information users. To aid users in participating in the information economy, libraries designed a virtual presence to deliver information services, usually in the form of a 'digital library.' Digital libraries can offer a more varied informational experience to the community of online users. Libraries, with their traditional strengths of information collection, description, organisation, and dissemination, can provide a more holistic learning experience for these new user communities. In commenting on the structure and environment of digital libraries, the DLF (Digital Library Federation) has offered the following definition:

- "Digital libraries are organisations that provide the resources, including specialised staff, to select, structure, offer intellectual access to, distribute, interpret, preserve the integrity of, and ensure the persistence over time of collections of digital works".

In elaborating on the concept, Hanani and Frank define six major characteristics that should be integral to digital libraries:

1. *Collection of data objects:* A library holds together a collection of data objects, items and resources. The items can be books, journals and documents, multimedia objects. The library objects can be available locally, or indirectly, by using a network to access them.
2. *Collection of metadata structures:* A library contains a collection of metadata structures, such as catalogs, guides, dictionaries, thesauri, indices, summaries, annotations, glossaries, and so forth.
3. *Collection of services:* A library provides a collection of services, such as various access methods for as well as consultation for. different users; management of the library; logging/statistics and performance measurement evaluation (PME); selective dissemination of information (SDI) or push mode, as it is called on the Internet.
4. *Domain focus:* A library has a domain focus and its collection has a domain focus; purpose. For example, art, science, or literature. Also, it is usually created to serve a community of users and therefore, is finely grained.

5. *Quality control:* A library uses quality control in the sense that all its material is verified and consistent with the profile of the library. The material is filtered and its metadata is usually enriched.
6. *Preservation:* The purpose of preservation is to ensure protection of information of enduring value for access by present and future generations. Preservation includes the allocation of resources for preservation, preventive measures, and remedial measures to restore the usability of selected materials."

As librarians compile digital collections of materials, the networked environment of which they are a part offers access to many more information resources. In describing libraries and the new online environment in which they operate, libraries are placing lesser emphasis on the materials they collect and house, and more emphasis on the kind of material they are able to obtain in response to user requests. The trend includes libraries forming partnerships to deliver material from elsewhere in time to answer a user's information needs.

The shift to on-demand delivery of material from elsewhere is an effect of recent growth in digital networking in an environment where standards for description were established and refined over the past 35 years. Librarians are also moving primarily away from being caretakers of physical collections to people who identify resources that exist. The earlier survey of the information economy has illustrated a variety of information sector industries and organisations that utilise information, such as geographic data, in their varied production and distribution functions.

The flexibility of spatially referenced information, and its applicability to a variety of research techniques and spatially referenced applications, create a powerful tool in which librarians can raise the profile of their institution's involvement in the information sector. In defining the parameters of geographic information librarianship, the varied applications of geographic information in government functions, community initiatives, and private sector development can offer strategies in dealing with the social effects of trends like the digital divide and information marginalisation. The following part provides an overview of the development of geographic information systems and related applications.

DEVELOPMENT OF GEOGRAPHIC INFORMATION SYSTEMS (GIS)

During the 1960s and 1970s, geographers and cartographers began adapting computer analytical methods to capturing graphical data portrayed on maps. Previously, the emphasis of cartographic research was based on the idea of storing graphical features that were displayed on maps in computer files. Only with the later use of mathematical models and structures based on theory in topology were researchers able to apply logically consistent two dimensional data representations.

By the 1980s, the ability to create stable and consistent representations of map data was integral to research and development in geographic information systems. Kainz describes the impact of the micro- and personal computer in the development of powerful desktop software packages in word processing, database management, and statistical analysis and the development of desktop mapping software that could integrate visualisations of map data with corresponding data in other databases.

He further describes the rapid progression of research on spatial data structures, indexing methods, and spatial databases. A workspace in a GIS software package could contain graphic representations of a spatial dataset, integrate data from relational databases, and have other corresponding information in text formats or numeric formats. The convergence of computer hardware innovations with research into mathematical spatial modeling, and mapping software during the 1980s clearly contributed to better-defined geographic information systems.

A geographic information system (GIS) can be defined as "a computer-based technology and methodology for collecting, managing, analysing, modeling, and presenting geographic data for a wide range of applications". A GIS essentially combines five components, people, data, hardware, software, and methods, for the purpose of finding solutions to issues that have a spatial context.

The fundamental operations of a GIS application are capturing, storing, querying, analysing, displaying, and outputting data. The nature of geographic data can be best understood by three major concepts: *feature.geometry, attributes,* and *topology*.

- *Feature.geometry,* represents features, such as houses, roads, or property boundaries, and establishes where these features are located in the real world. All features are symbolised by points, lines, or polygons.
- *Attributes,* provide a description of the features and are stored in an associated table that is linked to the features. An attribute field can contain an address, street name, or land-use code, and so forth.
- *Topology,* the most abstract concept of geographic data, defines either the behaviour or the spatial relationships that exist between features.

For example, a GIS layer representing a transportation network requires topology rules to accurately depict one-way streets, overpasses, and right of way scenarios. Without topology, data integrity associated with sound editing, display, or analysis is not maintained. Geographic knowledge is represented in five data formats: *maps* and *globes, geographic. datasets, data.models, processing and workflow models,* and. *metadata.* Interactive *digital.maps.and. globes* can query information and present it to the user.

Since digital maps and globes have limited analytical functionality, they are generally used to resolve location and directional questions. *Geographic.datasets* contain feature geometry, attributes, and topology. *Data.models* are templates with defined topology schemas, and are used in the data creation process to ensure data standardisation and integrity are maintained. *Processing and workflow models* are necessary when managing GIS projects to visually depict and duplicate the geoprocessing procedures associated with the spatial analysis.

Metadata documents the four previous data formats, and is the key to organising, discovering, and evaluating GIS data resources. With the proliferation of desktop computing and numerous GIS mapping applications, geospatial data has become an important part of various socioeconomic processes, political activities, and academic research that comprise the information economy. The following discussion outlines some applications of spatial data and geographic information systems in the information economy.

APPLICATIONS OF SPATIAL DATA AND GIS

The literature of the information economy is rich with descriptions of how computer technology and the Internet are altering socioeconomic processes within organisations and throughout political and commercial networks in which they are integrated. Some researchers assert that the use of information communication technologies can facilitate closer contact between members of management and other employees of an organisation, thus rearranging lines of command for long-distance interactions, resulting in a direct savings on transportation costs, and improving the decision-making process in the organisational structure. Other scholars have discussed how the integration of information systems into government organisations' infrastructure have affected resource management, such as the decentralisation of decision making.

As part of extensive commercial and political networks, organisations exchange information through complex optical and cable networks that comprise the Internet. In summarising research about the information economy, Grubesic and Murray describe the Internet as "a complex mesh of interconnected computers, fibre optic cables, routers and human users". They further describe the Internet as "a series of smaller networks linked together by hardware, software, and many peering agreements between Internet Service Providers.

The distribution of smaller networks across the United States alone amounts to over 166 million users, 7,000 Internet Service Providers, and a large grouping interlinked cable and telephone companies that offer information services". The reliance of organisations upon a telecommunications network infrastructure to transmit different forms of electronic information adds a spatial component to the data. Grubesic and Murray note that a "unique element of many datasets is the geographical or spatial entities they represent.

The geographic component of the data could correspond to a location of a point of presence, central office, or the path a fibre optic cable traverses". Geographic information systems can analyse, store, and process the spatial data associated with an organisation's datasets. Since a GIS is often used to visually organise geographic data in order to facilitate different types of analysis for the data, geographic information systems are described as a "computer programme for acquiring, storing, interpreting, and displaying spatially organised information". Besides recording the locational aspects of a particular data set such as neighbourhood, street, or country, GIS data may have additional information characteristics, such as temperature, cost, colour, or even detailed demographic information or public health data.

The uses of GIS in the information economy are many, and often GIS databases are built with data from different types of sources in both the public and private sector, such as from ESRI, Inc., the U.S., Census Bureau, and even the Centers for Disease Control and Prevention. Definitions of geospatial data vary within the research literature in geography. Some researchers define spatial data as being "anything dealing with the concept of space, in the geographic context, primarily dealing with the distribution of things on the surface of the earth "while other researchers define spatial data as 'data that occupies geographic space".

There are many types and characteristics of geospatial data. However, most spatial or geographic data have specific location according to a global geographic referencing system, and may be illustrated by other characteristics, such as size and shape of a particular dataset. Davis further elaborates that the size would be calculated by the amount of area, and shape would be defined by the position of the shape points of the dataset, for example, an administrative zone or economic zone. Geospatial data collected by government agencies across different areas can include topographic data, hydrographic data, earth science data, and soil and forest survey inventories. Other types of information that can be geospatially referenced include social and economic data.

An important aspect of geospatial data is its potential for multiple applications. GIS technology facilitates the integration and comparison of different data sets, which allows for greater statistical analysis of the data content. It was suggested that the annual federal spending on geospatial data activities in the United States was over $4.4 billion. Since the 1960s, digital spatial data has been produced in a variety of formats and in a number of carriers. Digital spatial data can include information digitised and recorded by a single researcher, or be in the form of large-scale geographic coverages processed and packaged by private firms. Much digital spatial data is also generated by government agencies at the city, state, and federal level, and is issued in a variety of formats like on CD-ROMs with computer files with accompanying attribute data in relational databases.

The proliferation of spatial data and the rapidly evolving technological environment in which spatial data is being used in all manner of research has led some researchers to speculate on the nature of future applications of GIS. Future development in GIS will be in areas such as geocomputation, social informatics, information ecology, and a spatially integrated social science. Sui notes that the 'diffusion of spatial analytical tools" and their integration with 'visualisation tools' will lead to the use of geographic metaphors important in describing political- economic activities across contemporary social and cultural regions.

One research area involving digital geospatial data has been the electronic space of the Internet, or cyberspace. Recent trends involving spatial data and geographic research have focused on defining epistemologies and methodologies using GIS to better explain sociogeographic phenomena across different environments. Longan argues that geographers have only begun to explore social, cultural, and political aspects of cyberspace. In his examination of the community networking environment across the United States, he attempts to define a sense of place in the online environments that different neighbourhoods and towns are setting up in their areas.

Other researchers examine the Internet and the effects of telecommunications between communities and social classes and the distribution of wealth, arguing that Internet community networks may help disadvantaged groups overcome the problems of distance by using cyber communications to access needed resources or find that access to telecommunications has positive effects on a community's sense of identity Still others have used GIS and spatial data in examining urban cultural and political spaces or to study economic production and social consumption. Still other researchers envision continued development of representation of real world data using computer languages.

MAP LIBRARIES IN TRANSITION

In attempting to put some order to the many types of geospatial data produced by government agencies, private firms, and other organisations, librarians can turn to map librarianship for guidelines and best practices in designing procedures for processing spatial data. Map libraries, especially in the United States, have benefited from lengthy depository programmes wherein maps produced by the United States Geological Survey, Army Map Service, and Inter-American Geodetic Survey were deposited across many libraries. The experiences of processing the cartographic collections in libraries are beneficial in learning about the scope of map collections in libraries as well as to understand cataloging and classification schemes for maps and cartographic materials.

The rapid migration to digitally produced cartographic materials in a variety of formats presents librarians with new challenges in processing spatial data. The same technological changes that have transformed the production of cartographic materials have affected the functioning of library services and collections as well. The advent of the Internet has provided an opportunity for the traditional academic library to evolve its services and reposition its collection to take advantage of the communication possibilities that the World Wide Web presents.

Applications of GIS technology and geographic information can also provide libraries with tools that can be used to overcome technological and social barriers that have come about due to the digital divide. The public aspect of GIS, especially in terms of government produced and facilitated data, create more of a sense of urgency in providing access to the information. The discussion that follows examines the convergence of communication technologies in the contemporary information economy and its effect on various segments of the private and public sector including libraries.

5

Describing Geospatial Information

INTRODUCTION

To be optimally useful, geospatial resources must be described. This description is referred to as metadata. Metadata tells 'who, what, where, when, why, and how' about every facet of a piece of data or service. When properly done, metadata answers a wide range of questions about geospatial resources, such as what geospatial data is available, how to evaluate its quality and suitability for use, and how to access it, transfer it, and process it. To ensure consistency for access and retrieval, metadata can be standardised to provide a common set of terms, definitions, and organisation. In the desire to adequately and accurately describe geospatial resources, cataloging codes and practices have been established to accommodate these new resources to provide networked access to these resources, and to respond more effectively to an increasingly broad range of user expectations and information needs.

Issues surrounding the quality and relevance of metadata become more critical in online venues, especially with geospatial data. What kind of bibliographic records or metadata will be required to meet the different uses of geospatial information and user needs? How should these bibliographic data or metadata be organised and structured for intellectual and physical access to the works? This chapter will provide an overview of current academic cataloging principles, issues in handling evolving formats, and challenges for academic catalogs. It will also discuss the development of a MARC geospatial information record and the issues involved in adequately describing these works.

DESCRIPTIVE STANDARDS IN LIBRARIES

In libraries, the use of metadata, MARC, or any other knowledge organisational tool is based upon some form of Cutter's principles of organisation.

The *Objects.* were to:

- Enable a person to find a book for which either the author, title, or subject is known;
- Show what the library has by a given author, on a given subject, or in a given kind of literature, and
- Assist in the choice of a book, as to its edition or to its character.

It *Means*, or method of doing so, provides numerous access points, including author-entry with necessary references; title-entry or title-reference; subject-entry, cross-references, and classed subject-table; form-entry; edition; and imprint, with notes when necessary. Today, increasing numbers of library patrons see libraries more as remote resources, rather than as walk-in facilities. To meet this need, libraries must have sustainable systems of access and databases and durable objects that fulfill the three R's: reliability, redundancy, and replication of results. These 'three R's' can be seen in the development of the functional requirements for the bibliographic record (FRBR) entity relationship model for works, expressions, manifestations, and items.

An international analysis of user needs determined that there are four generic information tasks users perform:

1. Finding materials that correspond to the user's stated search criteria;
2. Using the data retrieved to identify an entity;
3. Using the data to select an entity that is appropriate to the user's needs;
4. Using the data in order to acquire or obtain access to the entity described."

These principles are still the foundation of best cataloging practice, including the notion of specificity, the consideration of the user as the principal basis for subject heading decisions, the practice of standardising terminology, the use of cross-references to show preferred terms and hierarchical relationships, and solving the problem of the order of elements. They organise the information in such a way that allows the user to eliminate irrelevancies or false cognates and to focus on specifics, thereby reducing cognitive overload. To organise information, libraries use a variety of standards to describe data, including structural frameworks, cataloging rules and interpretations, class schedules, and subject access.

MARC

The structural framework most commonly used in libraries is MARC, a communications format developed in the 1960s by the Library of Congress (LC). This format was created to represent and communicate LC's bibliographic and related information in computer-stable form. A MARC record is comprised of three elements: the record structure, the content designation, and the data content of the record. A set of codes and content designators define how the records will be encoded for the five types of data: bibliographic, holdings, authority, classification, and community information. The MARC record has evolved with networking advances. Its uniform data structure was enhanced with the development of the Z39.50 standard for the electronic sharing of data and with its XML format.

Within the United States, an American Library Association (ALA) committee, the ALCTS/LITA/RUSA Machine-Readable Bibliographic Information Committee (MARBI), is responsible for developing official positions on standards for the representation in machine-readable form of bibliographic information. For the international library community, the International Federation of Library Associations and Institutions (IFLA) works with national cataloging and standardisation committees, multinational organisations, ISO (International Standards Organisation) committees "to promote the development of an international cataloguing code for bibliographic description and access". In today's 'metadata' terminology, MARC is a schema supplemented by syntax rules with a set of constraints. Schemas typically restrict element and attribute names and their allowable containment hierarchies.

The constraints in a schema may also include data type assignments that affect how information is formatted and processed. For example, date elements would be formatted in a specific way, such as MM/DD/YYYY or MM/DD/YY. MARC is based upon ISO 2709:1996, Format for Information Exchange (INEX). USMARC is based on ANSI Z39.2, American National Standard for Bibliographic Information Interchange.

The MARC schema has three structural frameworks:

1. Bibliographic,
2. Holdings, and
3. Authority.

BIBLIOGRAPHIC STRUCTURE

The MARC bibliographic structure uses a combination of fixed- and variable-length fields. Fixed fields contain excerpted information in predetermined length strings to allow ease in searching the datasets. Variable fields have no predetermined lengths, can contain extensive amounts of information, and are of variable length because the amount of information differs for each item. All information is entered into defined fields, designating the type of data that is then further subdivided into discrete pieces.

For example, an author can be one of three types of data: a person, an entity, or a conference. Depending upon its type, the data are delineated into its three-character field. The field is then subdivided by additional information. National standards exist for minimal, core, and full coding. If materials are permanent parts of a collection, full coding, which provides the maximum amount of information to the user of the online catalog, is preferable.

```
LDR *****nam##22*****#a#4500
001 <control number>
003 <control number identifier>
005 19920331092212.7
007 ta
008
820305 s | 1991#### n | yu#### | ###### | #001#0# e | ng##
020 ## $a0845348116 :$c$29.95 (£19.50 U.K.)
020 ## $a0845348205 (pbk.)
040 ## $a<organization code>$c<organization code>
050 14 $aPN1992.8.S4$bT47 1991
082 04 $a791.45/75/0973$219
100 1# $aTerrace, Vincent,$d1948-
245 10 $aFifty years of television :$ba guide to series and pilots, 1937-1988 /$cVincent Terrace.
246 1# $a50 years of television
260 ## $aNew York :$bCornwall Books,$cc1991.
300 ## $a864 p. ;$c24 cm.
500 ## $aIncludes index.
650 #0 $aTelevision pilot programs$zUnited States$vCatalogs.
650 #0 $aTelevision serials$zUnited States$vCatalogs.
```

Fig 6.1 MARC Bibliographic Format

HOLDINGS STRUCTURE

The holdings describe what parts of a work a library owns or can access. The holdings record defines the codes and conventions (tags, indicators, subfield codes, and coded values) that identify elements for single items, multipart sets, or serials. The holdings structure is based on the American National Standards for Holdings Statements. Holdings information is important for local and union catalogs, cooperative acquisitions and collection development, preservation programmes, and as a link in fully automated interlibrary loan and document delivery systems. The holdings records are linked to the bibliographic records; holdings format information may also be 'embedded' within bibliographic records as a 'holdings cluster.'

The CONSER Publication Patterns and Holdings Project is using the MARC holdings record as the vehicle to develop a 'universal' holdings record for serial titles. To develop a 'universal' holdings record, a pattern describes the captions and pattern of issuance of a serial or multipart item. Data elements include frequency for each bibliographic unit; its secondary or lower bibliographic units and the relationship of the lower numbering system to the higher (whether it restarts or is continuous); the calendar change point; and variations in the intervals of issuance. For maps and other geospatial information that are issued in sets or successive editions, holdings information indicates what the library owns, and in a more enhanced record, what the ideal run is.

LEVEL 1 <Location Identifier>Main
LDR *****nx###22*****1##4500
001<control number>
852 ## Sa<location identifier>Main 19870414 (0.ta.4.2.8)
LDR *****nx###22*****2##4500
001 <control number>
008 8902202p####8###4001aa###0870414
852 ##Sa<location identifier>SbMain

OPAC display

Field guide and reference manual series/
[Toronto. Ont.]: Geological association of Canada, c1985-
v.:ill., maps; 28 cm.

Description

Location: LIBRARY —Circulation Collection—QE376.F54
Holdings: no. (1985)—no. 12 (1997).

Fig 6.2 MARC Holdings Format and OPAC Display

AUTHORITY STRUCTURE

Authority control is the semantic interoperability of controlled subject terminology and classification data. Authority control allows the user to find all items on a particular topic or by an author, regardless of the many term variations, synonymous terms, or languages that might be available in the catalog. The AUTHOR and SUBJECT entries in a library catalog are controlled, recognised forms of name and subject headings.

They are established in authority records and used as access points in the bibliographic record. Unlike bibliographic records, which represent items owned by a library, authority records are tools that librarians use to achieve consistency among bibliographic records, and to provide a linking framework for related names and subjects in a catalog. An authority record includes three basic components: headings, cross references, and notes. The heading is the standardised 'authoritative' form of a name, subject, or title that is used on bibliographic records. There are two types of cross references. The first type, a *see* reference, directs a user from a variant form of a name or subject to the authoritative form. The second type is a *see also* reference.

The *see.also* reference directs the user from one authoritative form to another authoritative form because they are related to one another. The references are carried or 'traced' on the record for the authoritative heading. Notes contain general information about standardised headings or more specialised information, such as citations for a consulted source in which the librarian verified a form of name or a definition.

LDR*****nz###22*****n##4500

001 <control number>

003 <control number identifier>

005 19870121083133.6

008

870121 #	n#ac a	naa	bn ###	####	###n#	aaa## #	##u

010 ## Xaex#86114834#

040 ## SaCameron, Simon, Sd1799-1889

670 ## SaNUCMC data from NJ Hist. Soc. For Bradley, J.P. Paper, 1836-1937Sb(Simon Cameron)

670 ## SaLC data base, 1-21-87Sb(hdg.: Cameron, Simon, 1799-1889)

670 ## SaDABSb(Cameron, Simon , 1799-1889, Sen. From Pa. (Republican boss);financier, Sec. War under Lincoln; Min to Russia; S. Charles & Martha (Pfoutz) C.; newspaper editor; owner Harrisburg Repbulic; commis to settle claims of Winnebago Indians; m Margaret Brua; father of J.D. Cameron (1833-1918).

Fig 6.3 MARC Authority Format

There have also been suggested changes to fields within the authority record to accommodate for and enhance resource discovery of geographically centered items. In library catalog records for maps and other cartographic materials, field 034 and field 255 unambiguously identify the location of a coverage area with geographic coordinates. However, these fields are generally used for print items only when coordinates actually appear on the cartographic item being cataloged. Other formats of materials may not have this information easily available or apparent, reducing the richness of the record-describing data that could be used for GIS layering. Modifying field 034 in authority records for geographic coordinates associated with places would eventually form the basis for coordinates-based retrieval of all cataloged records containing geographic terms.

Since different geographic areas may exist during different periods of time or coordinates may be recorded from different sources and possibly in different formats, repeatability of the field is essential. Two other areas for consideration included coordinates for the surface of planets and for the position of stars, and further exploration of the recording source of information in the field. The first indicator and subfields $a, $b, and $c were determined not to be applicable and needed no modification. Note fields have also been a repository for geographic coordinates, such as field 670, that includes cites to authoritative sources to document the place name. Repeating geographic coordinates in field 670 in a specific data field for machine retrieval would aid in user discovery of relevant materials.

Further, since authority records establish the authoritativeness of the information or the issuing body, such as the USGS Geographic Names Information System (GNIS) record for the place or the U.S. Board on Geographic Names, which often gives lists of coordinates for places, it makes sense to place coordinates in authority records. Records for place names, geographic features, and some subject headings, such as battles, buildings, and so forth, would also be affected. Several concerns remain regarding the inclusion of geographic coordinates in field 034.

Should the decimal format of data in the 034 field remain in the decimal format or be converted to degrees, minutes, and seconds? This may require catalogers use additional tools to convert coordinates, adding another layer in the cataloging process. However, to increase resource discovery, this will be a crucial component. The Board of Geographic Names uses point coordinates, not the bounding box coordinates typically used in bibliographic records, another problem to be resolved. Should bibliographic record field 034 be added *en toto* to the authority record or only those fields directly applicable to the authority record? Repeatability is also an issue.

Since Board of Geographic Names place records often provide a list of coordinates that are centers of quadrangles that together cover the area for a place, multiple coordinate fields with an additional subfield describing the specific area may be necessary. How will the date be handled? A subfield for date might be subfield y to be consistent with subject date subfields or, perhaps the 045 'Time period of heading' field already defined for authority records may work. However, to link the 045 to the 034 would require the use of multiple 034 fields subfield 8. A subfield to document source would also be helpful, since the Board of Geographic Names does not establish all forms of name and place.

MARC XML

With the emergence of extensible mark-up languages (XML), the Library of Congress' Network Development and MARC Standards Office developed a MARC XML framework to represent a complete MARC record in XML. There are XML description schemas that correspond to MARC bibliographic and authority formats. The Metadata Object Description Schema (MODS) corresponds to MARC 21 bibliographic. The Metadata Authority Description Schema (MADS) is an authority element set that provides metadata about agents (personal authors and corporate bodies), events, and terms (*e.g.*, subject headings, geographic headings, and genre headings).

The Metadata Encoding and Transmission Standard (METS) schema is a standard for encoding descriptive, administrative, and structural metadata regarding objects within a digital library, expressed using the XML schema language. The framework has additional schemas, style sheets, and software tools. MARC XML can also be used to represent metadata for OAI harvesting, for original resource description, and for electronic resource metadata packaged with the item. Toolkits are available to convert to and from XML and MARC using Java. XML is an important new language and tool since much of the geospatial metadata is created using XML generators.

AACR2R

Cataloging rules and rule interpretations allow standardisation or, from another perspective, the intellectual collocation of works and items, which aids in retrieval. This collocation facilitates 'cognitive miserliness', which is the concept that the human mind is the most efficient in acquiring information when it has to do the least work. One way that librarians have facilitated researchers is by creating a standard record format that accepts data into predefined fields and is governed by a set of rules that determine what information goes where, thereby allowing the user to predict where relevant data will be located and to ignore the irrelevant. Further, the standardisation of data allows the user to concentrate on the decision-making process to assure relevance and precision in his or her search results.

The current guide used by librarians is the *Anglo American Cataloging Rules*. Simply, *AACR2r* provides the standard for structuring catalogs with headings and references to provide links between items with similar or related characteristics. The American Library Association's Committee on Cataloging: Description and Access serves is the body within the United States that facilitates the continued development of those standards and formulates the official ALA policy on descriptive cataloging.

A representative from the CC:DA is an *ex officio* member of the international committee responsible for updating and revising the *AACR2r*, the Joint Steering Committee for the Revision of Anglo-American Cataloguing Rules, which implements updates to the *AACR2r*. In the international community, IFLA also promotes the Functional Requirements for Bibliographic Records

(FRBR) model and develops new descriptive standards and standards for access points. As an international standard, *AACR2r* facilitates data sharing among disparate systems and frees the cataloger from having to reinvent the rules for each dataset. Another advantage is that it attempts to identify the most relevant features of the item it is describing, ensuring the capture of an accepted set of information. *AACR2r* prescribes what type of data should be captured, but allows the cataloger to determine the extent to which it is recorded.

RESOURCE DESCRIPTION AND ACCESS (RDA)

An exciting initiative of the Joint Steering Committee for Revision of AACR (JSC) is their work on a new standard, *RDA: Resource Description and Access*, scheduled for release in early 2009. The *RDA*."provides a set of guidelines and instructions on formulating descriptive data and access point control data to support resource discovery". The purpose of the RDA is to ensure metadata standards for record elements, controlled vocabularies, and the overall structures of bibliographic and authority records.

RDA Element	Corresponding FRBR entity	Corresponding FRBR attribute/relationship
Scale	expression	~
Scale of still image or three-dimensional form expression	expression	n/a
Scale of cartographic content	expression	scale (cartographic image/object)
Additional scale information [cartographic content]	expression	scale (cartographic image/object)
Variations in scale [cartographic content]	expression	scale (cartographic image/object)
Non-linear scale [cartographic content]	expression	scale (cartographic image/object)
Vertical scale [cartographic content]	expression	scale (cartographic image/object)
Projection of cartographic content	expression	coordinates (cartographic image/object)
Coordinates of cartographic content	work	coordinates (cartographic work)
Longitude and latitude	work	coordinates (cartographic work)
Strings of coordinate pairs	work	
Ascension and declination work	work	coordinates (cartographic work) / equinox (cartographic work)
Equinox work equinox	work	n/a
Epoch	work	n/a
Magnitude of cartographic content	expression n/a	~
Other details of cartographic content ~	expression	~
Other mathematical data	expression	scale / projection / coordinates / geodetic, and vertical measurements (cartographic image/object)
Other features of cartographic	expression	special characteristic (remote sensing image) / +

Fig 6.4 RDA to FRBR Mapping

The point of the RDA, as with its predecessor *AACRs*, is to create a formal model, with rules and frameworks to ensure consistency in data across disparate content providers. The structure of *RDA* aligns more directly with the *FRBR* and *FRAR* (*Functional Requirements for Authority Records,* now *Functional Requirements for Authority Data*) models. One of the changes as suggested, see in the RDA is a change in how map elements are named, described, and structured. Figure provides an example of the RDA to FRBR mapping for the cartographic term, scale.

The most significant area the conversion from AACR2r to RDA will have is in the ability to better describe and embed FGDC data elements and description into the bibliographic and authority records. However, that does mean more of a challenge for professional and paraprofessional staff in cataloguing and technical services areas to fully describe the work before them. It also presents a challenge for public services staff to communicate user questions and suggestions regarding how works are named and described. This is essential, since one of the foci of the RDA is on user needs: "The descriptive data provided for in the guidelines and instructions should enable the user to: identify the resource described; select a resource that is appropriate to the user's requirements with respect to content, format, etc.

The access points provided for in the guidelines and instructions should enable the user to locate:

- All resources described in the catalogue that embody a particular work or a particular expression of that work;
- All resources described in the catalogue that embody works and expressions of works associated with a particular person, family, or corporate body;
- A specific resource described in the catalogue that is searched under a title appearing in that resource;
- Works, expressions of works, and manifestations represented in the catalogue that are related to those retrieved in response to the user's search".

As the *RDA* is finalised, the impact of increased access and description will better serve the geographic and GIS communities.

CLASSIFICATION SCHEDULES

Arranged by subject in a logical, hierarchical manner, a classification scheme divides a field of knowledge into main classes. The main classes are divided into subclasses, representing branches of the main discipline, domain, or subject area. Within each subclass, further subdivisions are made to specify form, place, time, and subject aspects. These subdivisions, from the most general to the most specific, create a hierarchical display. The more hierarchical levels, the more specificity in the classing of the item. In the United States, the USMARC Format for Classification Data defines the codes and conventions that identify the data elements in USMARC classification records.

Classification schedules contain a series of numbers, captions, instructions, and notes. Most academic libraries in the United States use the Library of Congress classification schedules. There are 21 categories, alphanumeric, from A-Z (missing I, O, W, X, and Y) with one, two, or three letters and a set of numbers denoting the class or subclass within the schedule. The Library of Congress Classification System organises material in libraries according to 21 branches of knowledge. The original organisation of the classification was based on the 'academic world of knowledge' at the beginning of the 20th century.

Each LC class schedule was developed separately, following a logical order based upon that discipline's understanding of its domain; therefore, each schedule has unique features, making it difficult to generalise about the schedules as a whole. In MARC, field 084 is designed to be the carrier for information about the classification scheme used, the classification number, captions and edition of the scheme. Authoritative classification schemes, such as the LC class schedules, Dewey Decimal class schedules, or the National Library of Medicine classification scheme, are the most commonly used. Since the classification schedules are considered a 'living' work, with new sections of classes being added or obsolete sections being deleted, the edition used in creating a class number is an important historical element. Classification numbers are used in both MARC bibliographic and authority records. Classification numbers form the basis of an item's call number.

The traditional purpose of the class number is to place an item in its respective part of a knowledge domain, that is, on the library shelf among like items. Libraries with closed stacks needed a method of uniquely identifying titles so that a page could retrieve the desired material. Libraries developed various schemes to satisfy this need. The successful scheme resulted in 'call number,' a unique extension for each item. Even libraries with open stacks understood the desirability of a unique identifying call number and adopted the practice. A patron browsing the shelves would find similar, or 'like,' materials grouped around that specific item. In an online library catalog, the class number provides the same service, allowing the user to 'virtually' browse the library's collection, whether the item is located in a physical collection or accessed off-site.

The need to 'call' for electronic titles is unnecessary, but the class number is still useful for information discovery and evaluation of the collection.. For earth sciences libraries, the U.S. Geological Survey (USGS) Library Classification System. It is also seen as a retrieval system to access materials through the subject and geographic numbers. Unlike the LC class system, the USGS class system contains seven schedules: a subject schedule, a geological survey schedule, an earth science periodical schedule, a government document periodical schedule, a general science periodical schedule, an earth science map schedule, and a geographic schedule. These schedules mirror the seven collections contained within most earth sciences libraries. The general subject collection is comprised of the earth sciences disciplines, geology, petrology, mineralogy, paleontology, and biology. Pure sciences, physics, chemistry, engineering, mathematics, and computer sciences, are included only as complements or augmentations to the earth sciences. The general subject collection consists chiefly of monographs, but may also include periodicals that are narrow in scope, international in scope, or issued by an international agency.

Also unlike the LC schedules, the USGS system segments four collections by issuance. The geological survey collection contains the monographs, periodicals, and monographic series issued by the geological surveys of the world. The earth science periodical collection contains publications issued by earth science societies, associations, and earth science departments of universities. The government documents collection contains periodicals and monographic series issued by federal, state, provincial, and local governments, nationally and internationally. The general science periodical collection contains science periodicals issued by national and international societies, associations, and universities.

USGS	LC
Title: Multivariate geostatistics / Author: H. Wackernagel, 1995.	
Class no.: 208.2	QE33.2.S82
Shelf list no.: W323	Cutter: W32
Title mark: m	
Date: 1995	Date: 1995
Call number: 208.2 W323m 1995	Call number: QE33.2.S82 W32 1995

Fig 6.5 Example of a USGS and LC Call Number

The next collection, the earth science map collection, is segmented by format. It contains earth science maps issued by national and international governments, societies, associations, and departments of universities. The last schedule, the geographic schedule, consists of numbers enclosed in parentheses that can be combined with notation from the other schedules. For example, the geographic number for the United States. This parenthetical enclosure is immediately recognisable when scanning call numbers. Once the class number has been established, to create a call number in the USGS system, the first element, an uppercase letter, is taken from the first letter of the first word of the main entry. The second element, a three-digit number, is taken from Library of Congress shelf listing tables.

The final element is the title mark taken from the first letter in the title. For the USGS, the general class is '208 Geological techniques." A unique identifier is then added, created by using the first letter of the author's surname, a number from a Cutter table, and a work mark from the first significant word in the title – W323m. In the LC system, QE places the item in Geology, 33.2 A-Z is 'special topics' and, within that, S82 is 'statistical methods.' This classification number is 'cuttered' by taking the first letter from the author's last name and appending a numeric value that will represent the second letter so that the names will fall in alphabetical order on the shelf. Finally, the year of publication is added. The LC subject is 'Geology— Statistical methods."

SUBJECT ACCESS

Researchers who are serious about retrieving the most targeted materials on a topic use subject access as opposed to keyword searching. The cataloger can use a universal thesaurus, such as the *Library of Congress Subject Headings,* one that covers a broad subject area, such as the Medical Subject Headings (MeSH), a discipline-based controlled vocabulary, such as the *Thesaurus of Psychological Index Terms,* depending upon the needs and focus of the library and its patrons.. Typically, thesauri come in three display formats: 'explicitly hierarchical' displays; alphabetical displays, showing references between related terms or references from unused synonym terms to the 'postable' or preferred term; or rotated displays, in which each word in every natural language term is used as an index term to indicate the several phrases in which it appears.

A well-developed thesaurus uses a hierarchical structure (or a set of structures) in which clusters of concepts that share common characteristics are organised in facets, and represented by natural language terms useful in the context in which the thesaurus will be used. For example, Alabama, Georgia, New York, Rhode Island, and Oregon all share the common characteristic of being STATES, in addition to whatever other characteristics some of them may share, such as History. The terms constitute the beginnings of a STATES facet. Sometimes the terms in a facet can be divided into sub-facets by secondary characteristics: Within the STATES facet, Alabama and Georgia are SOUTHEASTERN STATES; New York and Rhode Island are NORTHEASTERN STATES. Georgia is also part of a larger regional facet, APPALACHIAN REGION, SOUTHERN. Facets and sub-facets are then arranged as simple hierarchies of terms, from general to specific.

There are several benefits to a faceted approach. By reviewing a small, related group, the user can see naming consistency, order, hierarchical relationships, relationships to other groups (broader or narrower concepts), and current or superseded terms. Since a faceted approach is extensible, there is greater flexibility in adding new terms or establishing new relationships among existing terms without disturbing the rest of the thesaurus. From a psychological perspective, faceted approaches also embrace the concept of cognitive miserliness. Clearly, it is much easier for an indexer or user to understand a set of hierarchically organised facets as a conceptual map, which shows the precise level and set of associations of a term, than to negotiate a long list of alphabetised terms. To provide the most effective subject approaches to traditional and networked resources, librarians must account for the different patron strategies and models currently used in information retrieval.

The Boolean model, which uses exact match across inclusive and exclusive groupings (AND, OR, NOT), tends to provide more precision in one's search. Ranking algorithms, vector, and probabilistic models compensate for their loss of precision to a certain degree by methods of statistical ranking and computational linguistics, based on term occurrences, term frequency, word proximity, and term weighting. Controlled vocabulary offers the benefits of consistency and accuracy with better recall through synonym control and term relationships and greater precision through homograph control. Although controlled vocabulary will not replace the apparent 'ease' of keyword searching, it supplements and complements keyword searching to enhance retrieval results.

The use of controlled vocabulary in the description of metadata places the burden on the indexer rather than the user and, as further observed, "There is a burden of effort in information storage and retrieval that may be shifted from shoulder to shoulder, from author, to indexer, to index language designer, to searcher, to user. It may even be shared in different proportions. But it will not go away". Experiments conducted on subject access systems in WebPACs and metadata-processed systems demonstrate the potential benefit of structured approaches to the description and organisation of Web resources.

This would involve the use of established subject heading schemes and thesauri at a general level, recognising that more local or specific schemes may also be necessary to provide more detailed indexing. However, the success of this endeavor will depend on trained catalogers for their proper application according to current, and often complex, policies and procedures, the cost of maintenance, and their incompatibility with most tools now used on the Web.

FINDING GEOGRAPHIC INFORMATION IN LIBRARIES

Even though maps have been used throughout the centuries as essential tools for analysing current and historical conditions, the history of map librarianship in the United States really begins at the end of the Second World War. Prior to 1945, only 30 or so libraries employed full-time map librarians. Initially, there was little research concerning the management of this material. In 1945, the *Classification and Cataloging of Maps and Atlases* was published and referenced the 1941 ALA cataloging rules. The authors stressed the order of importance for entry in this order: first, area, second, subject, third, date of situation of the map, fourth, author, and, lastly, title. From 1945 to the 1960s, cartographic collections become part of mainstream library collections and services for academic and larger public libraries. With the advent of geographic information systems (GIS) and the digitisation of data, maps and other geospatial data formats have become critical elements in libraries. Librarians are generally not cartographic experts. Nevertheless, to be effective in cataloging maps, it is useful to know some key considerations about maps and in map making.

WHAT IS THE PURPOSE OF THE MAP

MAPS ARE USED TO PERFORM THREE DISTINCT FUNCTIONS:

1. Reference,
2. Analysis, and
3. Persuasion.

As reference tools, maps display 'geographically referenced' information, such as cadastral maps or topographic maps. They also provide information on the location and the spatial relationships of the features displayed on the map. Reference maps typically incorporate a lot of information about the features they describe, for example, most roadmaps show cities, counties, county seats, interstate highways, local roads, state routes, and historical or geographic landmarks. As analytical tools, maps explore the spatial dimensions of, and interrelationships between, phenomena and activities located in space and time.

Unlike reference maps, an analytic map is a working document and is used to examine different data sets and explore spatial relationships. For example, the Annie E. Casey Foundation's mapmaker on social indicators is used to generate the maps that cover time, space or place, and specific datasets on economic, social, or health issues, using data at the county level, city level, metropolitan statistical area, or congressional district. Geographic information systems (GIS) are also used as an analytical tool. Persuasive, or thematic maps, are often used dramatically to illustrate a specific point of view or an argument in print and media publications or in public presentations. Thematic maps are created to make a specific point and are often used to persuade or influence a person's decision. For this reason, the ability of the mapmaker to design an effective image is critical to a thematic map's success. Examples of thematic maps are those that chart earnings, projections of an activity, or demographics.

ISSUES REGARDING SCALE

A mapmaker may take a section of a map and magnify or 'zoom in' to look at this section at a larger scale. This does not change the accuracy of the map; it simply changes the scale of the map, that is, the relationship between the distances shown on the map and distances on the Earth's surface. The importance of scale issues has led researchers to propose a 'science of scale' that would study which measures or properties are invariant with respect to scale, methods to change scale, measures of the impact of scale change, scale as a parameter in process models, and implementation of multi-scale approaches.

Two terms that are critical to cartographers (and users of maps) when reviewing scale are *spatial accuracy* and *spatial precision*. Spatial accuracy measures how close a recorded location is to its true position on the Earth.

It is determined by two factors:

1. The care used in conducting the initial land survey and
2. Establishing the original map scale.

Spatial precision measures how exactly a location is depicted on a map; therefore, the precision of a map is limited by the width of the smallest line that can be displayed at a given scale. If the finest line on a 1:24,000 quad sheet is 0.5 mm wide, the smallest distance that can be recorded true to scale is 39 feet. At that scale, 1 inch represents 2,000 feet. Zooming in by a factor of 10 changes the scale to 1 inch representing 200 feet, making it theoretically possible to locate features with a precision of 4 feet. However, this precision is misleading, because features cannot be located any more accurately than they were recorded on the original map, that is, with an accuracy of 39 feet.

MAKING THE MAP

The process of compiling statistical or thematic data should be largely the same as for preparing a base map. The mapmaker consults existing maps and data sources, assesses their reliability and applicability, selects the most useful and dependable information, and presents it on the completed map. Unfortunately, the process of map compilation is not always as rigourous as it should be. Remember, a map is no better than the spatial and attribute data it contains. Librarians may not have the time or expertise to evaluate the reliability and accuracy of the information incorporated in maps. Fortunately, the federal government has established standards requiring that data distributors provide metadata or 'data about data' describing the content, quality, source, and other characteristics of their spatial and non-spatial data. Librarians should become familiar with these efforts, support them, and do their part by preparing metadata for the data they distribute. In addition, they should be sure that the sources for all cartographic and statistical data are clearly identified on their maps.

BIBLIOGRAPHIC ISSUES FOR MAPS

Map cataloging requires knowledge of maps. Maps combine characteristics of both books and pictures, making their bibliographic description more difficult and time consuming to create. Since the utility of each map is directly affected by the quality of the descriptive cataloging, the consequences of sloppy cataloging practices can be significant. The principles of current descriptive cataloging codes, developed during the first half of the 1900s, were authored with the book format in mind. The few librarians who championed map cataloging called for the development of specialised map bibliographic records. The map cataloging practices they preferred were those of Boggs and Lewis, published in 1945 by the American Geographical Society.

Neither the *Rules for Descriptive Cataloging* nor the *Anglo-American Cataloging Rules* adequately met the needs of librarians for maps or for standard map reference resources, such as gazetteers or atlases.

Since the most important consideration is that all maps should be able to stand alone, a map should always contain five basic elements:

1. A short, concisely worded title that indicates the map's subject, geographical location, and time frame.
2. A legend or key delineating the meaning of all point symbols, line symbols, and/or area fills used on the map.
3. A map scale to relate distances on the map to distances on the Earth's surface.
4. A locational identifier that places the mapped area in its appropriate spatial context.
5. A source citation identifying the source for the spatial and thematic data portrayed on the map, the organisation that produced the map, and the date on which it was produced.

If the mapped area is not a closed shape, it should also include a border that provides a frame for the map image.

BIBLIOGRAPHIC DESCRIPTION AND ACCESS POINTS

As we look at a MARC record, the first point of access for descriptive information about geographic information appears in the fixed field area, in the 008 field. The 008 field is a fixed field data element that contains 40 character positions. Useful for retrieval and data management purposes, these character positions provide coded information about:

- The record as a whole and
- Special bibliographic aspects of the item.

Character positions 18-21 are used to describe relief maps, 22-23 describe projections, 25 describes the type of cartographic material, 28 describes government publications, 29 describes form of item, 31 indicates if the item or accompanying material has a location index or gazetteer, and 33-34 indicates if there is any special format characteristics of the map. Character positions 24, 26-27, 30, and 32 are undefined. In bibliographic records, geographic coordinates also appear in field 034 and field 255.

The data in the 034 field is formatted and may be given as decimal degrees, or as degrees, minutes, and seconds, with the presence of the decimal indicating which is used. Four subfields define a bounding box. These are generally adequate for expressing the westernmost, easternmost, northernmost, and southernmost extent of coverage of a map. The west, east, north, and south hemispheres are indicated either with the first letter of the direction or by a plus or minus symbol. Subfields |s and |t describe G-ring latitude and longitude. The rest of the information included in field 034 applies to the manifestation.

The data in the 255 field is in a textual form in subfield |c. A cataloger transcribes the coordinates as they are written on the map being catalogued into field 255 subfield |c. He or she then codes the same data into the 034 field of the same record. In addition, in the 255 field, there are symbols for degrees, minutes, and seconds that do not appear in the 034 field.

Field 084 defines the classification system used. Most academic libraries use the Library of Congress classification scheme, although there are map libraries that retain the USGS classification system. Generally, the most significant access point for a map is the *geographic area* of coverage. However, the cataloging codes consider the geography of a map to fall under SUBJECT. Therefore, like books, the most significant access points for maps in most library catalogs tend to be authors (1xx) and titles (130, 24x).

AUTHOR AS MAIN ENTRY

For maps, author vs. area as the principle access point or 'main entry' was a major discussion point in the *AACR*. There were, and are, arguments against and for the use of author main entry for maps. Supporting area main entry is the contention that "recognition of the differences between maps and books and the need for separate rules for cataloging of maps is long overdue'. Arguments supporting author main entry for maps were based on historicity: "For an historical library, it is important to establish responsibility for the map. Thus the identification of the 'author,' or cartographer, the individual or the institution, government agency or publisher responsible for the map, is an important responsibility of the cataloger". Early map cataloging codes either considered the author and publisher to be separate entities or grouped them into one category. Prior to the 1988 revision of *AACR2,* cataloging rules stated explicitly 'cartographers are the authors of their maps.' *AACR2r* added a section on corporate authorship. This shift to allow corporate authorship of maps was an important step in the recognition of the format-specific needs of map users and catalogers. The cartographer, publisher, or government agency responsible for producing the map could end up as the 'author' of a map. The cartographer's name, publisher's name, and government agency are all valid access points in the catalog record.

TITLE

Map titles are often non-distinctive, such as 'Map of the Known Universe.' The map title, which might be prominent on the map's face, may be different on the map panel. All of these various titles are given access points in the catalog record, so that the map can be retrieved regardless of which title is used. If no title is available, the cataloger is directed on how to establish a title for the map.

MATHEMATICAL DATA AREA

Immediately after the title and edition statements is the *mathematical data area,* which includes *scale, projection,* and *coordinates.* Scale, defined as the ratio of distances on a map, globe, relief model, or section to the actual distances on the ground they represent, is generally represented with a bar scale, a written scale (1 inch = 100 miles), or a fractional scale (1: 10,000). Scale is extremely important in reference service, because it relates to the level of detail and area covered by a specific map. A large-scale map will cover a smaller geographic area with more detail than a small-scale map. The scale may be stated textually (*e.g.*, 1 mile to the inch), but must also be converted to a representative fraction in the catalog record. If no scale is given, it must be computed. In addition to its analytical functions, scale also affects map display, which may be a critical point for the user.

The smaller a map's scale, the more generalised the map's features are. A road that is very curvy in physical space may be represented by a fairly straight line on a map, or if on a very small scale-map, be dropped altogether. *Projection* is an equally important but more complex concept. The projection is the type of distortion that occurs when a curved surface is forced onto a flat surface. Converting information from the curved surface of a globe (latitude and longitude) to a flat one (x,y coordinates) of a map involves a mathematical formula called a map projection, which uses a projected coordinate system.

However, this flattening process causes distortions in one or more of the following spatial properties: distance, area, shape, and direction. No projection can preserve all these properties, and as a result, all flat maps are distorted to some degree. However, the type of projection can assist in the choice of the map. *Equal Area* projections preserve area and are used in the making of many thematic maps, for example, maps of the United States commonly use the Albers Equal Area Conic projection.

Conformal projections preserve shape and area. Although shape is preserved for small areas, large area shapes, such as a continent, will be significantly distorted. Conformal projections are often used for navigational charts, weather maps, and Mercator maps. *Equidistant* projections preserve distance true from one point (or a few points) to all other points or along all meridians or parallels.

Equidistant map projections are often used to find geographic or man-made features that are within a certain distance of other features. *Azimuthal* projections preserve direction from one point to all other points. Azimuthal projections can be combined with equal area, conformal, and equidistant projections. When available, information about coordinates is also given in the mathematical data area.

BIBLIOGRAPHIC NOTES

Bibliographic notes for maps serve a dual purpose: to explain elements of the bibliographic record and to provide information about the map's contents. Although map catalogers are instructed to favour bibliographic over content notes, limit the total number of notes, and simplify contents notes, these restrictions can have a negative impact on OPAC searching by limiting what can be retrieved using a keyword search.

The bibliographic notes area of a map record follows a set order, outlined in AACR2r. Notes contain information on any accompanying material (typically text or charts), the map's publishing history, its overall scope, additional geographic area covered, cartographic details (such as the type of map), or other helpful information (*e.g.*, insets, indexes, and legends). All of these notes greatly enrich the catalog user's knowledge of the content of each map and allow patrons to decide if the map is potentially useful to them or not.

DATES

Librarians need to be aware of the meaning and complexity of map dates. The date of publication is the printing date. This might not be the same as the date of situation, defined as the date of the information displayed on the map. Furthermore, a map can have many dates of situation; there might be a different date for each type of information displayed, for example, the date of field check, date of survey, and so forth.

For research purposes, the date of situation is generally the most important. However, maps can lack a publication date. Descriptive cataloging rules emphasise the publication date, placing the date of situation to the notes area. AACR2r does not specifically mention the date of situation in the notes section of cartographic materials, though an example of the date of situation is included. The reader is invited to review additional manuals developed to assist to catalogers in understanding the intricacies of map information.

PRIMARY ACCESS POINTS: GEOGRAPHIC AREA, SUBJECT ANALYSIS, AND CLASSIFICATION

The primary access points for maps are geographic area, subject analysis, and classification. How do you ask for a map? What terms do you use to get at the subject or content of a map? Geographic area headings are a challenge to the cataloger, particularly in determining the name of a geographic area.

SUBJECT HEADINGS: GEOGRAPHIC AREA AND GEOGRAPHIC PLACE NAMES

Jurisdictional names are based upon political jurisdictions, for example, a country, state, or city, such as France, Louisiana, or Apopka. Maps with jurisdictional boundaries are important in the location of events and individuals. Many governmental records, including genealogical records, are created and stored by jurisdictional entities that may not be the actual place where the event occurred or the individual resided. Noting jurisdictional boundaries also allows the user to locate a historical location that is now divided between two or more modern locations.

Jurisdictional names are constructed following rules in *AACR2r*. *Non-jurisdictional names* are based on geographic features. These include named rivers, lakes, or mountains, such as the Seine (France), Okeechobee, Lake (Florida), and McKinley, Mount (Alaska), or named places (*e.g.*, battlefields, national parks, or forests, such as Gettysburg National Military Park, Pa., Ocala State Forest (Florida), and Yellowstone National Park. Inverted forms of the name are used when the natural feature begins with a generic term, such as Mount or Lake, except when it is an integral part of the name, for example, Mount Baker National Forest (Wash.). Non-jurisdictional names are constructed using the *Library of Congress Subject Cataloging Manual*. State names are abbreviated when used as a qualifier to a place, but are not abbreviated when used as a subject subdivision. Therefore, both the abbreviated version of the state name (as specified in *AACR2r*) and full name must be used to find all appropriate geographic items.

For example, when searching for maps of Ocala, Florida, a general map will be found under the subject heading OCALA (FLA.)—MAPS, while a thematic map may receive a subject heading formulated as PARKS—FLORIDA—OCALA—MAPS. The most difficult factor in determining map subject headings is determining the area covered by the map. Geographic areas are not tidy plots of land clearly defined by straight lines. Often a map of one area will include a nearby area. Sometimes these nearby areas are mentioned in the title or notes. Catalogers use their judgement as to when these nearby places should receive subject headings.

There are similar problems with boundary maps that do not typically incorporate the whole of a political or geographic area. Name changes of the geographic area shown on the map are also problematic. Currently, catalogers assign subject headings under the latest name of political jurisdiction, regardless of when the map was made. This has implications not just for bibliographic control but also for authority control, both of which affect searchers. For example, with the fall of the Soviet Union, new subject headings were created for each distinct geographical entity. The old heading, Soviet Union, was no longer an accurate subject heading. Another example is Siam, which is modern day Thailand.

SUBJECT HEADINGS: ANALYTICAL/TOPICAL

For libraries using Library of Congress classification and subject headings, the first heading will be the one that most nearly represents the predominant topic of the work. Thematic maps use the topical heading to which the geographic location is attached as the first subject heading (*e.g.*, SPIRIT CENTERS—UNITED STATES—MAPS). A single map can contain a variety of information requiring several subject headings. The range of topics in a map collection is very wide as well. Two examples of Library of Congress subject headings are ELECTION DISTRICTS—UNITED STATES—MAPS, and MIDDLE EARTH (IMAGINARY PLACE)—MAPS, which refer to the titles

The.Almanac.of.State.Legislatures:.Changing.Patterns.1990-1997 and *A Map of Middle-Earth*, respectively. Another example is topographic quadrangles. At a minimum, these maps receive a general heading, STATE—MAPS, TOPOGRAPHIC. In large collections, individually cataloged quadrangles would be augmented with more specific subject headings for better retrieval. Specificity, again, is critical in the cataloging of geographic material.

CLASSIFICATION

The classification of a map is seemingly straightforward. Contrasted to books, which are classified by topic and then by place, the map is classified first by place and then by topic. Although classification reflects the geographical area depicted, complications arise when the map contains two or more areas. With two areas, catalogers are instructed to class the map under the first one named in the title. For maps that contain three or more areas, catalogers are instructed to use the next higher administrative or regional class number that includes them all.

SET OR SEPARATE DECISION

Most cartographic collections include a category of multipart items traditionally stored together and controlled by one catalog record. Maps are often distributed as part of a set or a series. The map series or set is printed on a number of sheets. Some are published at one time, some over many years, with no predictable seriality. The series has repeated and connective information on each sheet enables the sheets to be used singly or in conjunction with all or part of the remaining sheets. Among the common map series are the topographic maps from the U.S. Geological Survey. These are not the same as a *multi-sheet single map,* which is usually published all at one time and contains fewer sheets, all intended to be thought of as a single map and used together. Some map sets include thousands of sheets, each with unique sheet level data elements.

Libraries can choose to catalog each component on a separate record or put them together on one record, depending on their local needs. This decision affects access on many levels. For instance, a map set that is cataloged as a set will receive one bibliographic record and contain general subject headings for the whole. The titles of each individual sheet will be accessed only through a contents note, and the item will be filed together. When each part is cataloged on its own record, the same map set will receive more specific subject headings and title access for the individual sheet. The set title will remain accessible as a series title, and each unit may possibly be filed in different areas.

Sheet level data elements may include some or all of the following types of elements: sheet titles, sheet number, coordinates, edition or version, issuing body, ISBN, stock or publisher number, date, supplements/separate indexes, or grid structure/number. Caveats in cataloguing sheet maps include multiple languages or scripts used in the sheet title, number, supplement, or index; sheets may or may not be textually enumerated or be an alphanumeric system relating to the grid structure of the set; edition or version of a map set may include updates during the span of the set edition; and sheets in the same set may be issued by differing entities. Another area of concern is how to address holdings.

MARC Discussion Paper No. 2006-DP07 proposes several possible ways of recording information for multipart cartographic materials data using MARC 21 Bibliographic and/ or Holdings Formats. However, the discussion paper does not provide a clear solution that can satisfy the needs for enhanced records or address the realisation that there is increasingly a diminished amount of time spent on cataloging full records, even by large academic/ research institutions. The Task Force recommendations ranged from creating a full level record for each sheet, giving all data and access points, even if they are already on the record for the set, to creating a record for each set plus brief records for each sheet, with links to the set bibliographic record through 773 fields.

However, both of these approaches present difficulty in the display of collective and individual data in an understandable format to the user. Another suggested approach was the use of the 505 notes field, again problematic in the sense that one cannot parse out discrete subfields for searching and for displaying results. The use of the 774 fields (Constituent unit entry) in the bibliographic record for the set as a whole was also suggested, allowing the parsing of data elements into separate subfields. The use of holdings fields 844, 853, and 863 was another alternative. Field 034 could be added to the holdings format, since coordinates will be needed at the sheet map level.

However, that presented several problems, such as separate holdings records for each sheet map, linking multiple 844s to the appropriate 85X/86X pair, and the change of the 844 field $a (Name of Unit) to a repeatable subfield to handle parallel or variant titles. Disadvantages to the use of this approach included the inability to generate accurate institutional holdings based on the data in multiple separate holdings records, resistance to adding bibliographic information to the holdings format, and search issues at a systems level. Similar to print maps, geospatial data also comes in single-type collections or multiple-type collections.

A single type collection is an aggregate collection of multiple data units collected in similar conditions with equivalent semantic content. Each unit can stand on its own as a geographic information item and does not require additional processing to generate it. These would be classed as a spatial collection (spatial division), a temporal collection (time-series or periodicity), or a spatio-temporal collection that has both spatial distribution and periodicity. A multiple-type collection would have data layers or components from two or more different datasets that require compilation to generate a product based on user queries. Creating nested collections, or sets/series, would aid in resource discovery and guide users to layered, hierarchical items more easily. To date, there has been little exploitation of MARC to create 'intellectually related' collections.

A minimal record will not provide the richness or completeness of information to guide the user to a specific item with any ease. Aggregate collections require both the aggregate information, as well as the single item information, to be updated whenever there is an addition or removal of an item to the collection or when an item is modified. An advantage is that much of the base information, or description, for the item and the collection level record is similar, or 'inheritable.' This creates the possibility of generating new content from existing records more easily, a feature that catalog developers should consider when creating new library management systems.

Another important component of spatial-temporal data to consider is that spatial-temporal values of the descriptive elements may themselves be aggregated or averaged over the values of the items within the collection. Collection level display in a catalog should be different from the item level display, providing the user the possibility of reviewing an aggregated view of search results, grouped by scenes/data/time series.

CONCLUSION

In 1967, it was estimated that the annual cartographic output ranged from 60 to 100 thousand sheets, including new and revised editions, with American university and public libraries adding an estimated 15 thousand sheets per year. Over the past 50 years, an exponential amount of geographic information was created, produced, and distributed in digital form, particularly by the United States government. There are map-based graphical interfaces to perform geographical queries. The Web-based catalogs, hyperlinked with the MARC 856 field, allow patrons merely to click on the index to the map set in order to determine which map a library actually houses. In many libraries, maps are being digitised for online use.

In the midst of this abundance of raw data, "skills that assure consistency, predictability, and repeatability of access are as needed as ever" in order to ensure that users can find relevant materials. However, there are still a number of challenges that must be dealt with, such as legacy data, regularising OPAC displays of bibliographic information for geographic data, and the possibility of incorporating thesauri data. Nogueras-Iso, Muro-Medrano, and Zarazaga-Soria suggest there are additional problems that also hinder the correct use of metadata for geographic and geospatial resources. The sheer amount of geographic resources that has been created without associated documentation makes it difficult to identify groups of related resources.

Hierarchical identification of collections and sub-collections by the use of the series field in MARC, a mechanism frequently used in print collections, should be used in the cataloging of these related resources, facilitating resource discovery, and creation of metadata. The diversity and heterogeneity of metadata standards is also problematic. Legacy data and different software applications require interoperability and crosswalks to ensure transferability and, again, resource discovery. The use of a summary view of the data using MARC and specific geographic metadata, such as ISO 19115, ensures access by the general public and discovery agents.

Finally, heterogeneity of metadata content makes it difficult to identify the values given to metadata element in two different records that mean the same, conceptually, but use different terms. Authority records, a common feature of library catalogs, can address this problem. However, it will require a commitment on the part of library administration to see the value of enhancing both bibliographic and authority records. At the 1997 International Conference on the Principles and Future Development of AACR, the charge was to review the underlying principles of AACR, and take into account present and future trends in information resources and information management.

Among the recommendations was to advance the discussion on the primacy of intellectual content over physical format. IFLA's FRBR requirements emphasise the importance of ensuring access based on user behaviours while not forgetting the primary function of the librarian is to best organise and make accessible the items held within its collections, physical and digital. In 1999, the ALCTS Subcommittee on Metadata and Subject Analysis recommended the use of a combination of keywords and controlled vocabulary in metadata records for Web resources. The focus on integration for the user has led the library community to standardise the data exchange format (MARC) and the content description (*AACR2, LCSH,* and other subject authority lists, internationally accepted classification schemes). The adaptation of *LCSH*'s rich vocabulary, syntax, and application rules to a Web-based environment would create a system "relatively easy to apply and maintain–and easier and more effective on the searching end as well", particularly using a faceted, post coordinate approach.

User query analysis could be used as a means to develop or link existing terms to user-centered terms in authority files. This would move online catalogs away from data information retrieval to information retrieval strategies. Another area that will be equally important to consider is the capability to use seamless languages. If English is assumed to be the primary language, then titles and subject areas will need to be enhanced with translations, particularly for transliteration for non-Latinate languages.

Variant or translated titles/abstracts, and so forth, for non-English materials will need to be created to provide access to those items. Finally, a link to a translation engine to create some sort of translation of the item and vice-versa may also be required. Differing formats and hardware/software necessary to view content will require notes to inform the user that to view this data one would need X software/plug-in application(s), Y amount of space on their drive to install and run said plug-in, and so forth. Plug-ins may be critically important to visually display or load updated geographic or spatial data.

Search languages, that is, the language of the catalogue, will need to ensure consistency, accuracy, precision, and negotiation power between the remote parties as well as to accommodate whatever communication languages will be needed for disadvantaged users. There is a need to establish naming conventions for geographic/GIS access points to enhance precision and relevance in one's retrieval when searching. In fact, the literature attests to user frustration when trying to find a relevant something and then having to sift through hits that are contextually irrelevant, although their term(s) might be somewhere in the record. Thesauri and ontologies that can create the hierarchical, attribute, entity, and bibliographical relationships among content and context of items are critical.

Catalogers attempt to create listings of various depths and degrees of detail to record the existence of research materials. Researchers then search for answers to their questions and to make the best possible use of recorded knowledge. As Smiraglia states "That is, they seek to exploit what is already known, so as to create new knowledge." The content richness of the MARC database makes it desirable to maintain and add MARC records as the digital environment evolves. Increasing the interoperability of MARC with XML to integrate with other types of metadata records is a considerable return on the enormous investments that have gone into and go into preparing MARC records.

This will allow libraries to improve the interoperable capabilities of existing bibliographic data assets and to advance integration of bibliographic systems in a manner that is sensible and best practice in the cataloging of geographic and spatial data. In 1994, it was suggested that "[t]he twenty-first century will see geographic information transported from remote nodes using computer networks to support decision making throughout the nation.... Timely use of these data would be difficult due to ill-defined format, quality, and accuracy.

National or regional decision making would be severely impaired because most data sets are not adequately characterised." We posit that the use of library best practices can successfully address the description, querying, and discovery of geospatial information. All libraries containing digital collections of geospatial data would become geo-libraries, allowing searches by geographic location, returning any item in any format, from maps, images, books, reports, photographs, music, art, archaeology, and so forth, identified with a particular location.

6

Spatial Databases and Data Infrastructure

INTRODUCTION

The emergence, in recent years, of digital libraries and of Internet-based communication applications have led some researchers to propose that the emerging data infrastructure of the Internet and the capabilities of digital libraries can be used to organise and ease data-mining digital geospatial data across the Internet. Digital geospatial data interoperability, the target of major efforts by standardisation bodies and the research community since the 1990s, "has been seen as a solution for sharing and integrating geospatial data, more specifically to solve the syntactic, schematic, and semantic as well as the spatial and temporal heterogeneities between various real world phenomena".

Some researchers point to the problem that many GIS systems are singular in nature, are generally isolated, and lack interoperability, due in part to the computer architecture upon which they are based. This chapter will discuss the emergence of a national spatial digital infrastructure vis-à-vis the development of a national telecommunications infrastructure. Federal policies, standards, and procedures will be reviewed that assist in the management and production of geospatial data. Several examples of current geospatial libraries will be examined. The chapter will conclude with a short implications section on what are necessary next steps and future trends.

CHARACTERISTICS OF SPATIAL DATA

Geographic data is comprised of variables that represent real-world phenomena. These can be natural such as climate regions, topographic features, vegetation zones, and other natural processes. They can also refer to entities and objects that represent manmade activities such as buildings, roads, bridges, cable networks. In representing real-world phenomena, researchers use various abstract models that can represent some or many characteristics of the phenomena under consideration. Having been recorded by the individual researcher or captured by mechanical means, the data representing different aspects of the phenomena are often arranged in layers.

The layering of information is representative of the cognitive process. Individuals tend to perceive information about the particular space they occupy by mentally processing inputs from a variety of senses, thereby building up a mental image or map of the area. The layering or thematic ordering of a particular place is thus rendered. Other attributes of real-world phenomena are its spatial characteristics and its temporal characteristics. The definition of space is integrated with not only the cognitive processes associated with human perception, but also of cultural values as well. Culture affects the value and rendering of a conceptual map of particular place.

Other factors helping to define space are found in various classical and contemporary concepts in mathematics, such as Euclidian notions of geometry and measurement. Contemporary ideas of quantum mechanics further add to the concepts of space in the environment by blurring the boundaries of Euclidean geometries. The concept of space in models representing real-world phenomena are also conceptualisations of the space of data features. It has been noted that "spatial information is always related to geographic space, that is, large-scale space.

This is the space beyond the human body, space that represents the surrounding geographic world. Within such space, we constantly move around, we navigate in it, and we conceptualise it in different ways". The most common form of model used for representation of real-world phenomena is the map. Maps are two-dimensional depictions of a particular aspect usually rendered on paper or other print media. Maps can be general, thematic, and even topographic in nature. Statically depicted phenomena are bound within the parameters of scale and accuracy of the data captured or recorded for depiction.

Map scale determines the spatial resolution of the information. Determining the correct scale for a particular rendering of spatial data or map generalisation is part of the processes associated with cartography. Cartographic concepts of data representation and of the graphical layering of data form essential parts of digital geographic databases and geographic information systems. Creating digital representations of real-world phenomena in a database form are discussed next.

CONCEPTUALISING SPATIAL DATABASES

Much like maps, spatial databases store representations of phenomena in the real world. Geographic information systems use spatial databases, aka GIS databases. Spatial databases comprise a system, or hierarchy, of data models. The representations of the data and its potential applications across a network area drive its definition. The data model closest to the level of the end user is referred to as a conceptual data model. To design an effective database, the developer must know how the spatial data will be used and what the intended product will be.

The definition at this level will identify what possible applications the spatial data will have, such as flood zone analysis, voting district redistribution, or library user analysis. The "commonly used conceptual data model is the entity-relationship (ER) model; it uses primitives like entity type to describe independently existing entities, relationship type to define relationships between entities, and attributes to describe characteristic values of entities and relationships". A conceptual database schema is the definition for the entire hierarchy of data models. A central assumption for the design of a spatial database schema is that spatial phenomena in a real-world setting exist in Euclidean space. Complex relationships exist between all the phenomena in the real world.

These relationships have a variety of characteristics that give them specific spatial and temporal attributes. The real-world phenomena depicted can also be classified thematically. The thematic classification of data in layers can depend on the purposes for the data depicted. The data can thus relate to items such as economic zones, library service areas, hydrographic areas, or physical features. Researcher suggests that "the representations of spatial phenomena are stored in a scale-less and seamless manner. Scale less means that all coordinates are world coordinates given in units that are normally used to reference features in the real world. From there, calculations can be easily performed and any scale can be chosen for visualisation."

As in print maps, the accuracy of the data being recorded or captured is significant in the composition of a spatial database. Information derived from direct observation of phenomena should have the geographic coordinates defined. The accuracy of spatial database attributes is also affected if the data was derived from a secondary source of cartographic information such as a map. The scale of the data from the map would shape the feature coordinates in the database. An advantage of digital spatial databases is that a database does not depict boundaries between spatial phenomena, such as in map sheet boundaries or other partitions of the geographic space, other than imposed by the spatial features themselves.

Spatial databases are real-world models in "that they are scale-less, potentially three-dimensional, dynamic, and seamless. It is easy to query a database, and to combine data from different layers. Spatiotemporal databases consider not only the spatial and thematic but also the temporal extent of the features they represent". However, the basic elements of a spatial database schema provide a structure in which to design a system for spatial querying and retrieval of information.

ELEMENTS OF DATABASE DESIGN

As discussed earlier, spatial data are representations of real-world phenomena. The digital representation of the real world is often referred to as a digital landscape model (DLM). With the flexibility to represent different characteristics of the features of data at different levels of scale, the DLM is a central component in the processing of spatial data and for analysis. Model generalisation, or conceptual generalisation, refers to the process that uses a geometric component in the model. Generalisation means the reduction in the complexity of information. Unlike in cartography, which means suppressing unnecessary detail, in database development, generalisation means information abstraction, or the suppression of detail in order to widen the meaning of the information. Utilising the digital landscape model, the user can derive graphic representations of different aspects of spatial data in either digital form or traditional cartographic processes. A common model is the ANSI/SPARC layered model of database architecture.

Three schema, a physical schema, a conceptual schema, and user views, comprise this model. For example, using this model in the building of a spatial database provides organisation to a data set. A schema adds order to the variables in a database. An overall framework is identified and defined as the physical schema. Database variables are mapped and their attribute relationships identified. Concepts can be mapped as well and their relationships are also identified. The first step in organising a spatial database is defining a logical schema for a set of variables.

This initial step recognises data categories that outline the parameters of groups of data. The framework allows for inserting attribute information, which further describes the attributes of the variables. Populating data categories creates a DLM. Since the DLM is an object-orientated topographic database, its data structure facilitates spatial analysis and linkage of geographic objects to external data. A DLM uses the vector as its primary geometric form, and often contains explicit or implicit topological information.

The objects, their attributes, and the relations between the objects are referred to in terms of real-world entities. Entities are comprised of type classification, attributes, and relationships. An entity may have one or more attributes, such as a building's attributes may be its characterising material, such as block, brick, or frame. Attributes describe quantitative data ranked by three levels of accuracy: ordinal, interval, and ratio. Ordinal may rank an entity from "worst to bad to good to better to best," interval may address an entity's age or income, and ratio may address the length or area of an entity.

Table 5.1 ANSI/SPARC Architecture Data Models and Schemas

Schemas	Models
Schema	Model used to drive the schema
External views	Based on different in use Perspectives, a spatial model is created by defining and describing a subset of the real world.
Conceptual schema	External views synthesized to create conceptual schema using semantic data modelling techniques, for example, the entity-relationship approach.
Logical schema	Conceptual schema transformed into a logical schema using the relational model. Emphasis is on redundancy removal.
Physical Schema	Logical schema mapped into data structures and algorithms. A 'Hidden' process not accessible or seen by user.

Another aspect of designing a database is in evaluating user perceptions of the data. Since a database generally serves multiple users or user groups, users may have very different perceptions of the attribute data collected. Each user receives his or her external view of the database to create a personalised conceptual database schema. Database designers then merge the external views of the data into a single conceptual schema of the database. In designing a database, a conceptual schema is not determined by the parameters of a measurement tool, technique, or paradigm, but by its flexibility, which allows it to deal with the vagueness and uncertainty of defining different aspects of humancentered phenomena in the real world. After the phenomena types are defined, the conceptual schema is transformed into a logical schema using one of the logical data models, such as a relational data model. Since each fact should be stored only once in a database, the logical schema allows the development of a redundancy-free dataset. A physical schema is the result of the implementation of the logical schema with particular database management software.

Table 5.2 Data Modelling

Physical Reality	Real World Model	Data Model	Database	Language
Phenomena	Entity	Object	Object	Symbols
Properties	Type	Type	Type	Lines
Connections	Attributes	Attributes	Attributes	Text
	Relationship	Relationship	Relationship	Images
		Geometry	Geometry	Tables
		Quality	Quality	Charts

The structure of spatial databases provides a method for libraries with digital geospatial data collections and services to create a system for the discovery and querying of geographic information across the online environment of the Internet. Many of the sources of digital geospatial data, such as private corporations and government agencies, reside in locations across the United States and the globe. Besides spatial databases, building a digital geospatial collection in an online environment will use a variety of software applications and hardware tools that will assist in the administration of information as it passes from host to user. Next is a brief discussion of the development of some of the applications and protocols utilised in data transfer in the online environment of the Internet.

EMERGENCE OF A TELECOMMUNICATIONS NETWORK

The contemporary information economy emerged as industries in established economic sectors, such as manufacturing and production services, incorporated computer technologies to their daily operations. The concentration of industrial, technological, and social capital of such industries in urban areas enabled the building of advanced telecommunication services. Firms were able to take advantage of existing telephone lines and exchanges to build new information networks that were quickly using new communication software applications. In 1961, a researcher at RAND for the U.S., Department of Defence, working on how the U.S., telecommunications infrastructure could survive a "first strike, published a proposed digital data communications system based on a distributed network concept".

He introduced the concept of redundancy and the use of message-block networks with no single outage point as a method of building communications systems to withstand outages. This became the underlying data communications technology for the Internet. The development of ARPANET, created by the Advanced Projects Agency of the U.S., Department of Defence in 1969, was an early catalyst in the integration of computer and telephone technologies, and enabled the exchange of information related to scientific study occurring in advanced computing centers.

Table 5.3 TCP/IP Protocol

Layer	Function	Protocols Used
Process (Application) Layer	'Higher level' protocols, such as SMTP, FTP, SSH, HTTP, and so Forth operate in this layer.	SMTP, FTP, SSH, HTTP, DHCP, IMAPA, IRC, MIME, POP3, SIP, SNMP, TELNET, TLS/SSL, RPC, RTP, SDP, SOAP
Host to Host (Transport) level	Flow control and connection Protocols live here, Opens And Maintains connections. Ensures packets are actually received.	TCP, UDP, RSVP, DCCP, SCTP
Internet (Internetworking) layer	Defines IP addresses and routing Schemes for navigation packets From one IP address to another. Performs network routing, flow Control, network segmentation/desegmentation, and error control functions.	IP, ARP, BGP, ICMP, IGMP, IGP, RARP
Data link layer	Responsible for node to node (hop to hop) packet delivery.	ATM, Bluetooth (PANs), DTM, Ethernet, FDDI, Frame Relay, GPRS. Modems, PPP, Wi-FI
Physical layer	Describes the physical equipment Necessary for communications, Such as twisted pair cables, the Signaling used on level protocols Using that signaling.	Bluetooth RF, Ethernet physical Layer, ISDN, Modems, RS232, SONET/SDH, USB, Wi-Fi, power Line communication

In the beginning, ARPANET's architecture consisted of 4 nodes located at the University of California at Los Angeles, the University of California at Santa Barbara, the University of Utah, and Stanford Research Institute. Early experimentation with the system resulted in the creation of Telnet, an openly accessible public packet data service that allowed a computer operator at a terminal or PC to log onto a remote computer, run a programme, and initiate FTP, an early file transfer protocol (FTP). The CCITT (International Consultative Committee on Telephony and Telegraphy) approved the first guidelines for X.25, a network protocol using virtual circuits that became the backbone of the TCP/IP (Transmission control protocol/Internet protocol) protocol.

Why is a communication protocol important? Communication between computers means sending messages from one machine to another. There are three types of communication. Simplex communication is message travel in only one direction. Half-duplex communication is asynchronous message travel in both directions. Halfduplex communication is not simultaneous, for example, much like using ham radio, the first person must say 'over' at the end of his communication so the person at the other end knows that it is his turn to talk.

Full-duplex communication is simultaneously sending and receiving messages in both directions simultaneously, with no lags or gaps in the transmission or receipt. Obviously, addressing mechanisms that allow unique identification of senders and receivers are very important. Other critical mechanisms are rules on how data travels, error-detection and error-correction, disassembling and reassembling long messages, avoiding data overflow due to fast transmitters and slow receivers, and routing of messages.

Table 5.4 The 14 Fields that Comprise an IP Packet

<table>
<tr><th colspan="5">32 Bits</th></tr>
<tr><th>Version</th><th>IHL</th><th>Type-of-service</th><th colspan="2">Total Length</th></tr>
<tr><td colspan="3">Identification</td><td>Flags</td><td>Fragment offset</td></tr>
<tr><td colspan="2">Time-to-live</td><td>Protocols</td><td colspan="2">Header Checksum</td></tr>
<tr><td colspan="5">Source address</td></tr>
<tr><td colspan="5">Destination address</td></tr>
<tr><td colspan="5">Options (+ padding)</td></tr>
<tr><td colspan="5">Data (variable)</td></tr>
</table>

TCP/IP is the basic communication language, or protocol, of the Internet and for private networks. TCP/IP communication is primarily a point-to-point protocol (PPP), meaning each communication is from one point in the network to another point. There are five layers to the TCP/IP protocol. The higher layer, the transmission control protocol, disassembles a message or file into smaller packets that are transmitted over the Internet and received by a TCP layer that reassembles the packets into the original message.

The third layer, the Internet protocol, handles the address part of each packet so that it gets to the right destination. TCP/IP and the higher-level applications that use it are collectively said to be 'stateless' since every client request is considered a new request and unrelated to any previous request. Being stateless frees network paths so that everyone can use them continuously, unlike 'dedicated' lines, such as plain old telephone service (POTS) or fax lines. By the late 1980s and early 1990s, the Web was accelerating away from a dedicated mainframe environment to a distributed client-server system. This distributed system challenged the development of new protocols.

Considering the variety of personal computers, simple terminals, servers as well as platforms, and operating systems, requirements for new protocols had to be simple, cross-platform, and non-computer specific. Based upon the idea of HyperCard, Berners-Lee of the Conseil Européen pour la Recherche Nucléaire (CERN; European Council for Nuclear Research) developed hypertext transfer protocol (HTTP) and its accompanying text format, hypertext mark-up language (HTML). HTML was based on SGML (standard generalised mark-up language), an internationally agreed upon method for marking up text into structural units, such as paragraphs, headings, and so forth, that was non-machine, non-platform specific.

Two significant components of HTTP and HTML are the use of hypertext links to 'anchor' items to each other inside and outside the 'page' and the 'www' naming protocol (URL) used for addressing Web sites. A uniform resource locator

(URL) consists of three parts: the name of the protocol (http), the host name where the page resides and the name of the hypertext document. HTTP, TCP/IP, FTP, Telnet, and SMTP form a 'suite' of protocols that Internet users use as a matter of course. Building on a basic design of a document-sharing protocol, the Web eventually developed into a medium for the creation of a variety of Web sites that met myriad individual and organisational demands and needs.

Although many of the top-level domains of the net were still educational, much of the early development of the Internet occurred in the private sector, with Internet service providers (ISPs), such as America Online (AOL). From its beginning as a specialised dial-up service for Apple Macintosh users in 1989, within 6 years AOL had a million subscribers. This was a substantial inroad in an environment where there were about 20 to 30 million users. The success of these early Internet service providers triggered tremendous growth in the number of Web sites during the second half of the 1990s.

The availability of inexpensive access through local land telephone lines and relatively cheap cost of transmitting data. The number of commercial (.com or dot com) domains increased from around 1 million in 1994 to nearly 25 million at the beginning of 2000, while other categories of users (.net.mil.org, and.gov) added another 19 million domains, of which 15 million were cable-based net service providers. The development of HTTP and HTML spawned thousands of new sites and inspired new information services, such as 'browsers,' 'search engines,' and 'portals' to enable net users to find information of interest.

More specialised and powerful search engines continue to emerge, including the current leader, Google. Additional Web-based services, and continued growth depended on the established telecoms or cable TV systems and their telephone wire infrastructure. Rapid development of the Internet in the 1990s was accompanied by a simultaneous investment in construction of new telephone access lines in the United States. Investment in new lines by major carriers in the United States increased 32 per cent between 1990 and 2000 from 119.8 million to 157.6 million lines. The number of the new lines that incorporated ISDN (integrated services digital network) technology was 129.6 million, an increase of over 850 per cent from the previous number of 13.6 million. Transmitting data at speeds ranging from 128 kilobits per second to over 150 megabits per second, ISDN networks support a wide of range of simple to complex voice and non-voice services, and allow for the transmission of multiple channels of information, such as voice, data, fax, and video, over a single wire. The spatial distribution of ISDN-technology-enabled networks across the United States is uneven, with a concentration of high-speed data lines in areas that have the necessary infrastructure for its development.

Broadband, defined as 200 megabits per second of data output, is about fourtimes faster than a 56 Kbps dial-up modem and about eight-times faster than most people's actual download speeds, since many IPS's modems offer a maximum of 28.8 Kbps. Since many contemporary computer applications, for example, music clips, video clips, and streaming video, use considerable amounts of bandwidth, broadband access is growing as an essential Internet service expectation. These graphics intensive applications have many business and entertainment functions, and are not possible at lower dial up Internet connections.

Broadband Internet access is usually provided through digital subscriber line (DSL) technology. Data on the Regional Bell Operating Companies indicate that more than 56 per cent of all cities with populations above 100,000 had DSL available, but less than 5 per cent of cities with populations less than 10,000 had DSL service. A number of ISPs have been building data lines in predominately rural areas. These ISPs tend to be small businesses that fill in gaps in data line access where no larger telecommunication firms are present.

Since the costs of establishing Internet service warrant a subscriber base of at least 200 households, some small telephone exchanges are too small to sustain an ISP of that size.

The rural ISPs offer dial-up access in low bandwidth transmission formats. Most of the Internet services in rural areas tend to be related to e-mail and e-commerce transactions. If access to more services or larger bandwidth is required, costs are significantly higher for the user as well as the ISP, hence, Internet use in rural areas is held down by higher costs. The economics of fibre optics can be expensive for urban connections as well.

In situations where new trenches must be dug for the cable, installing fibre in metro areas can run in the hundreds of thousands of dollars per mile. Although installation cost can often be reduced by intensive use of existing infrastructure, it is difficult to justify the investment when existing phone lines can deliver adequate bandwidth via ADSL (Asymmetric Digital Subscriber Line) technology. ADSL is a modem technology that transforms POTS (plain old telephone service) lines into high-speed digital lines. By splitting an existing telephone line signal into two, one for voice and the other for data, ADSL technology can work at up to 8-Mbps download.

Since the baseband is occupied by POTS, should ADSL fail, POTS service is guaranteed. Similar to telephone switching centers, the Internet requires specialised host computers called servers and routers. Servers are typically clustered in so-called 'server farms' around the world, located in urban areas where most of the traffic originates. Server farm capacity is currently increasing at an annual rate of 50 per cent.

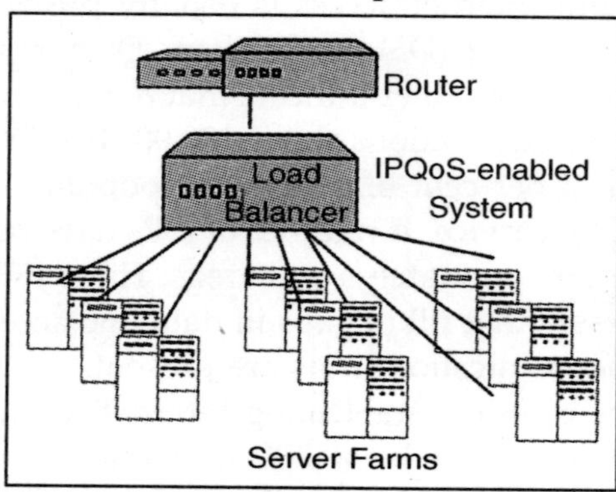

Fig 5.1 Server Farm Configuration.

One of the biggest providers is Exodus Communications, with 9 server farms in Silicon Valley alone and 35 more in big cities around the world. Think of server farms as 'wholesalers' in the Internet and the 'data caches' as retailers, located around the world near consumers of content. Technically, the function of the data caches is to recombine the individual packets of data, dispatched by the routers by different routes (because of changing conditions from moment to moment), into coherent streams designated for final customers. The leader in this field is Akamai, with 11,000 caching servers in 62 countries.

Akamai's customers are the content providers (including CNN and Yahoo!). The net result of all this investment was to create an oversupply of long-distance fibre-based carrier capacity, without a matching growth in local broadband access capacity for which the established telecoms retained their monopoly (except where cable TV was also available). As of early 2002, long-distance optical fibre channel capacity is said to be only 2 per cent–5 per cent utilised, whereas local access in many places outside the biggest cities, still dependent on copper wires, is badly congested. The limiting factor is electric power consumption, especially as the farms get larger.

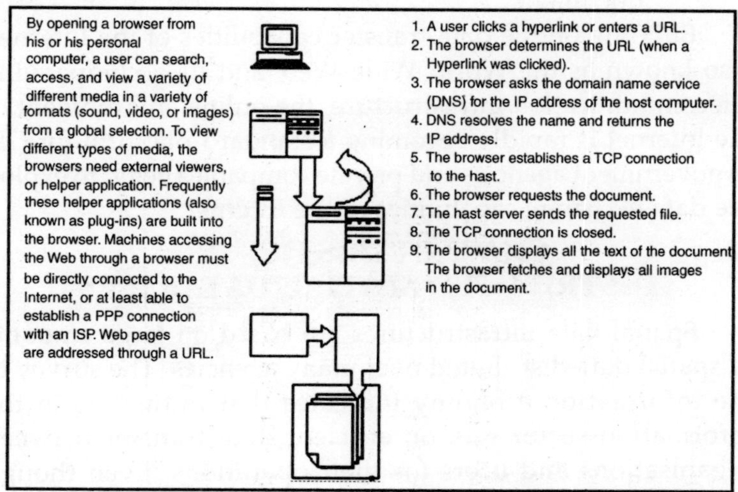

Fig 5.2 Putting it all Together: Retrieving Data from the Web

By opening a browser from his or her personal computer, a user can search, access, and view a variety of different media in a variety of formats (sound, video, or images) from a global selection. To view different types of media, the browsers need external viewers, or helper applications. Frequently these helper applications (also known as 'plug-ins') are built into the browser. Machines accessing the Web through a browser must be directly connected to the Internet, or at least able to establish a PPP connection with an ISP.

Web pages are addressed through a URL:

- A user clicks a hyperlink or enters a URL.
- The browser determines the URL (when a hyperlink was clicked).
- The browser asks the domain name service (DNS) for the IP address of the host computer.
- DNS resolves the name and returns the IP address.
- The browser establishes a TCP connection to the host.
- The browser requests the document.
- The host server sends the requested file.
- The TCP connection is closed.
- The browser displays all the text of the document. The browser fetches and displays all images in the document.

Building on the data transfer capabilities of the Internet, also known as the World Wide Web, and its accompanying telecommunication infrastructure, the online environment of the Internet is rapidly becoming a standard platform for GIS as government agencies and private companies begin to exploit the data exchange capabilities of the Internet.

CHARACTERISTICS OF DISTRIBUTED SPATIAL DATABASES

Spatial data infrastructures are based on large amounts of spatial data distributed over many agencies. The survey of the information economy indicates that industries in the information sector rely on efficient data transfer between organisations and users for their operations. Even though spatial databases may have useful socioeconomic purposes, a system linking many spatial databases would have far greater applications in the distributed environment of the information sector. What is the structure of a distributed spatial database system? First, two components, a database and a database management system, comprise a database system. The database (DB) is an organised collection of stored data; the database management system (DBMS) is software for building and maintaining a database. The strength of a database system is in its design. It contains a number of features, such as "persistency, storage management, recovery, concurrency control, *ad hoc* queries, and data security," that allow for the efficient processing of data. A persistent storage capability allows data to exist independently of the application of a programme.

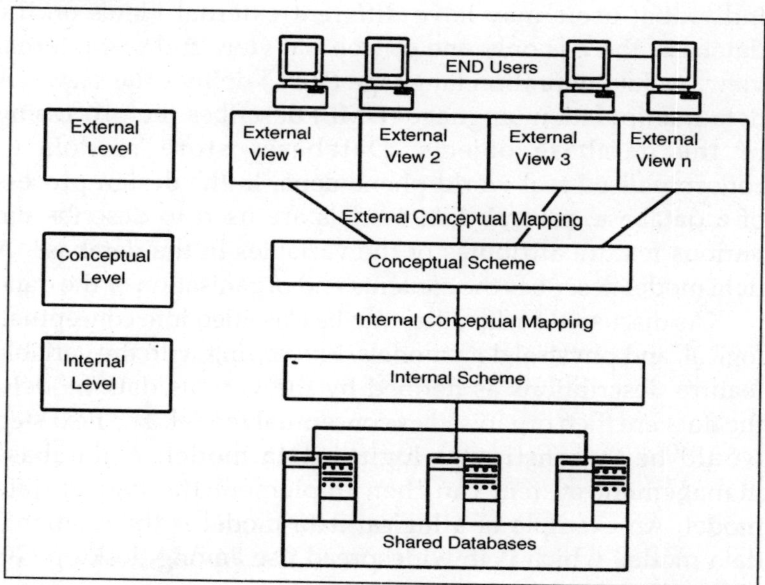

Fig 5.3 Visual Representation of the ANSI/SPARC Architecture

The ability to recover data is important in the workings of a spatial database system. If in the execution of a programme is not successful, the database management system can return the database to its former state before the attempted software application or to its former uncorrupted state. A concurrency control mechanism is also part of the normal operations of a distributed spatial database system. Its purpose is to avoid inconsistencies caused by concurrent read and write operations to the database and security access to the server on which the database is located. The ability of the database system to offer access to multiple users is also based on having data access security delineations.

The architecture of most databases is based on the standards of the ANSI/SPARC Study Group on Data Base Management Systems. These databases have three levels: internal, conceptual, and external level. The external level is closest to the user, the internal level is closest to the physical storage, and the conceptual 'exists in the middle.' Although individual users may have different external views on the database, there is only one conceptual view and one internal view. A data definition language (DDL) defines the views. A data manipulation language (DML) describes the processing of the database objects. Databases store models of conceptualised real-world phenomena. In the design process of a database, several data models are used to describe the various feature attributes of the variables in the database. A data model describes the contents and organisation of the data.

As discussed earlier, they can be classified into conceptual, logical, and physical data models. Proceeding with the variable feature descriptions as defined by the various data models, the data are then organised as conceptual model. The next step would be to construct a logical data model. A database management system can then implement the logical data model. An example of a logical data model is the relational data model, which is in widespread use among desktop GIS users using commercial software.

A relational data model is characterised by a clear distinction between the graphical and descriptive data of features representing real-world elements. Graphical elements are stored in layers of the digital map file and attribute data is stored in the form of a relational database table. Spatial features on the digital map are linked through the identifier with the record of the relational database table containing further descriptive data of the feature. A commonly used language for the relational database model is structured query language (SQL).

Supported by all major relational DBMS vendors, SQL is both a data definition and data manipulation language. In a spatial data infrastructure, many databases are distributed over many organisations across a network, and are interconnected through a communication network. Every site runs a unique database management system. Local applications operate on local hardware, while distributed or global applications can involve multiple sites on the data infrastructure. The design process for distributed databases builds on the design process for most database design, that is, it has a conceptual step, logical step, and physical design phase step. An additional design dimension is the distribution design step. The integration into a network introduces a number of design ideas to the building of distributed databases, such as distribution transparency, fragmentation, and replication.

Distribution transparency indicates that most users do not know where the data in a database is actually located. Replication, where duplicate datasets may be stored in different locations, and fragmentation, when different parts of a dataset may be stored on different servers, are frequently performed for security and practical reasons. In both cases, the user always perceives a centrally located database. Kainz notes that "there are two possible approaches to the design of distributed databases: top down and bottom up.

The top-down design is applied to new databases that are designed from scratch". Many GIS data producers and providers participate in the United States Federal Geographic Data Committee (FGDC) data infrastructure initiative. A system of distributed spatial databases that provide users with access to myriad federal, state, and local datasets, the central component of the data infrastructure is the 'clearinghouse.' Originally defined as a "system of software and institutions to facilitate the discovery, evaluation, and downloading of digital geospatial data," today the FGDC defines a clearinghouse as "a community of distributed data providers who publish collections of metadata that describe their map and data resources within their areas of responsibility, documenting data quality, characteristics, and accessibility.

The FGDC clearinghouse(s) also address the descriptive component of the data through the use of metadata. The clearinghouse computer systems integrate many inter-operating metadata servers, using a distributed, client-server architecture. On the client side, the most common software application is usually browser-based, such as Internet Explorer or Netscape Navigator. A client residing on computer X can interact with server Y, located at another location, using a set of instructions called protocols.

Since most traffic on the Internet uses the TCP/IP (transmission control protocol/Internet protocol), the TCP/IP software suite is frequently embedded in a computer's operating system (OS) software, such as in Microsoft Windows, MAC OS X, Unix, and Linux free ware. One protocol selected to provide search interoperability among different servers is the ISO 10163-1995 search and retrieve protocol. The Z39.50, initially developed for the library community, contains client and server software that establishes a connection, relays a query, returns the query result, and presents retrieved documents in various formats.

DATABASES, WEB SERVICES, AND INTERNET GIS

There are a number of advantages to a GIS that is available from the Internet including world wide accessibility, use of a standard interface, and cost-effective maintenance. The traditional model of GIS is a system that consists of a single software package, and accompanying data on a single machine. With the advent of distributed producers and consumers of digital geospatial data, this model is no longer valid. As Green and Bossomaier note "many GIS projects are often multi-agency, multi-disciplinary, multi-platform, and multi-software. Large numbers of contributors may be involved, and there may be a large pool of potential users".

Further, "a central practical issue is how to provide widespread, device-independent access to GIS for large numbers of contributors and users". The essential differences between a traditional GIS and an online GIS are the "separation of user interface, data storage, and processing". In stand-alone GIS, all of the elements are within a single machine; in an online environment, the elements are distributed across many computers.

During the 1980s, GIS was conceptualised strictly as a software application: "a computer based system that provides the following four sets of capabilities to handle georeferenced data:

1. Input;
2. Data management;
3. Manipulation and analysis; and
4. Output".

This definition is accurate when conceptualising GIS as an application; however, it does not address GIS as an interactive system where hardware, software, data, methods, and people come to create geographic knowledge for distribution. In the early 1990s, the concept of a GIS system evolved. ESRI, a privately held consulting firm, defined GIS as an "organised collection of computer hardware, software, geographic data, and personnel designed to efficiently capture, store, update, manipulate, analyse, and display all forms of geographically referenced information". The exploitation of geospatial data within diverse policy environments, allied with the increasing attention being afforded to cross-discipline social and environmental issues, has led to the demand for infrastructures to assist in the discovery, dissemination, and exploitation of geospatial data.

The authors also note that the structures are often referred to as spatial data infrastructures (SDIs). Most SDIs will integrate geospatial data and metadata, which can provide the means to access the data and also establishes the needed licensing agreements between users to make use of the data. The diverse information services of SDIs mirror information services of digital libraries, the latter defined as a collection of services and the collection of information objects that support users in dealing with the information objects and the organisation and presentation of those objects through electronic means. Three significant factors of SDIs are the provision, organisation, and presentation of information and services to a specific group of users.

By integrating with the digital library environment, the process of mining through digital geospatial data becomes more varied with additional data added to the original projection datum. In delivering digital geospatial data over the Internet, the identification, retrieval, and delivery of information in a virtual environment is described as a "URL-addressable resource that performs functions and provides answers". Web services are described as an "encapsulation of existing software functionality in a common form that allows the services it performs to be visible and accessible to other software applications". The single Web services-based application can request services from other Web services, and can expect to receive the results or responses from those requests in an expected form.

One advantage of Web services technology is its ability to interoperate in a loosely coupled manner, an 'ask and wait' approach. The user can request a certain type of service across the network, and wait for responses. Web services can also be found and used by other applications, agents, and clients on the Internet. In a digital geospatial data retrieval system, a Web service can be published inside or outside the host's firewall by providing a document describing its operation and function.

Using the Web services definition language (WSDL) markup language, the core of the document may illustrate a service when interpreted on a national grid reference responds with relevant coordinates on the host's mapping system. The document then described how the service is prompted and what the executables are. The document can also be published to a node, a clearinghouse, or other Internet site using the Universal Discovery, Description, and Integration (UDDI) registry.

Parson also notes that communication between Web services pass "XML messages wrapped in an interoperable framework to allow the messages to cross different networks, use different application architectures and systems". The widespread use of digital geospatial data by a number of different individuals and agencies in both the public and private sectors will continue to create large amounts of archived data. To make such data sets searchable across the environment of the Internet, librarians must be willing to take a varied approach in determining the appropriate metadata scheme to enable effective mining across the World Wide Web. A significant factor in the development of Web GIS services and in online services in digital libraries has been the National Spatial Data Infrastructure initiative by the Federal Geographic Data Committee.

ORGANISING A NATIONAL DATA INFRASTRUCTURE

In 1994 the Federal Geographic Data Committee (FGDC) recommended that a National Spatial Data Infrastructure (NSDI) be organised. The NSDI would be an "umbrella of policies, standards, and procedures under which organisations and technologies interact to foster more efficient use, management, and production of geospatial data". The NSDI was conceptualised as fostering more cooperation and interaction between different organisations from the public and private sector.

The recommendation was a response to alterations in the traditional flows of data across the government based on new convergences of information, computer technology, and communication. A significant component of the data being used in government transactions and commercial transactions was digital geospatial data. The FGDC considered digital geospatial data as being critical to solving many "environmental, economic, and social problems." The FGDC had also recognised that "the use of GIS technologies for the digital analysis of spatial problems had become pervasive". With the integration of GIS and increased use of geospatial data into problem-solving operations, a major goal of the NSDI was to make "an environment to respond to the current need of digital geospatial data."

The FGDC envisioned building the framework around the procedures, technology, and guidelines that enhance integration, sharing, and use of these data, and the institutional relationships and business practices that encourage the maintenance and use of data. The framework would represent the best available data for an area, and be certified, standardised, and described according to a common standard. Today, the FGDC standards provide a foundation on which organisations can build by adding their own detail and compiling other data sets.

MEETING DIGITAL GEOSPATIAL DATA NEEDS

The FGDC reported that many billions of dollars are spent by organisations on an annual basis in both the public and private sector in attempts to manage digital geospatial data. With digital geospatial data becoming a valuable asset within the business practices of many public and private sector organisations, most organisations can only afford to collect or purchase only a small portion of information they require. Often only the most basic digital geospatial data is acquired by organisations, usually a dataset that pertains to a specific geographic area or that has some unique attribute characteristics.

The datasets are often incompatible with other datasets, due to differences in software platforms. Researchers at the FGDC found that data collected by differing organisations may be similar in geographic extent use different geographic bases and standards. Hence, many of the resources organisations spend on geographic information systems (GIS) go towards duplicating other organisations' data collection efforts. The same geographic data themes for an area are collected again and again, at great expense.

A data framework would improve the ability for organisations to share data. The framework would provide a basic geographic data in a common format and an accessible environment that anyone can use and to which anyone can contribute. In this environment, users can perform cross-jurisdictional and cross-organisational analyses and operations, and organisations can funnel their resources into applications, rather than duplicating data production efforts. Researchers at the FGDC further noted in their findings that geographic data users from many disciplines have a recurring need for a few themes of basic data: geodetic control, orthoimagery, elevation, transportation, hydrography, governmental units, and cadastral information. Many organisations produce and use such data every day.

The framework provides basic information for these data themes. By attaching their own geographic data, which can cover innumerable subjects and themes, to the common data in the framework, users can build their applications more easily and at less cost. The seven data themes provide basic data that can be used in applications, a base to which users can add or attach geographic details and attributes, a reference source for accurately registering and compiling participants' own data sets, and a reference map for displaying the locations and the results of an analysis of other data. Researchers at the FGDC envision the information framework to be an evolving data resource to which geographic data producers can contribute.

Integral components of the information network incorporate procedures, guidelines, and technology to enable participants to build, integrate, maintain, distribute, and use framework data. These elements ensure that users can depend on accurate, detailed data that can be certified and integrated into the framework to create a trustworthy data source; users can update their data holdings from the framework data; and users can attach additional information to the framework. These procedures would ensure the standardisation of datasets and enable the efficient transfer of digital geospatial data across the Internet. The FGDC envisions the information framework integrating data from all types of organisations in both the public and private sector. The framework environment is designed to be responsive to the needs of the geographic data community in terms of data creation and maintenance, and provides unrestricted access to data.

A COOPERATIVE INFORMATION NETWORK

The FGDC also envisions organisations building the information framework by coordinating data development activities. Organisations can coordinate framework data along two dimensions. "The first dimension emphasises opportunities for organisations with similar needs. An example is a metropolitan area in which local governments, their customers, state and federal agencies with facilities in the area, utilities, and others require high-resolution spatial data for their operations. In this case the framework provides a starting point for sharing the commonly needed geographic base information and allows each organisation to add the unique information it requires to meet its business needs".

The second dimension emphasises opportunities for organisations needing different amounts of detail for an area. For example, a local government, a regional transportation planning organisation, and a state transportation agency may require road data for an area, but at different levels of geography. For efficient data sharing the organisations would have to share the results of their individual efforts and would benefit from using a common geographic base and generalised data created from this base.

The framework provides a starting point for a base and the data generalised from it, "providing the organisations with contemporary and consistent data for decision making and helping them avoid confusion caused by differences in the vintages, common attributes, and other characteristics of the base data". The framework is being developed by this entire community, with organisations from all areas playing roles. For some, the framework will supply the data they need to build applications.

Others will contribute data, and some may provide services to maintain and distribute data. Some organisations will play several roles in framework development, operation, and use. An essential community partner in the information network can be libraries. Librarians have the skills and experience needed to help the information network to facilitate digital geospatial data and to aid in its search and mining procedures. Some researchers have advocated the 'geolibrary' as a possible model for a library to facilitate digital geospatial data.

DIGITAL GEOLIBRARIES AND DIGITAL COLLECTIONS

One approach used by librarians in making digital geospatial data available to their users is to incorporate Web-based mapping functions with their library geospatial information holdings. Such efforts combine the locational aspects of the metadata descriptions of the geospatial data in the catalog with the mapping capabilities of GIS software. In building Web-based functions into their geospatial collections, some libraries have termed their collection a 'digital geolibrary.'

Different perspectives about geolibraries have been discussed in the scholarly geography and information science literature such as from Boxall and Goodchild. Goodchild refers to a geolibrary as being comprised of georeferenced information that can be accessed by a geographic footprint. Likewise, in his discussion of geolibraries, Boxall notes that their scope extends beyond the traditional map library if the construct of a geolibrary is based upon the idea that information has a geographic footprint. His discussion references earlier research that explains georeferenced information as including such things as photographs, videos, music, and literature that can be given a locational variable that defines a footprint. The collection areas of geolibraries extend beyond the traditional scope of map libraries and archives to include almost all information contained within libraries.

He later mentions that it can include information outside of libraries as well. This is the theoretical basis for what we now view as geolibraries. Boxall discusses that a significant focus of geolibraries is on digital information and metadata, as well as the distributed nature of the libraries and 'collections.' He adds that '...Distributed geolibraries provide a useful framework for discussion of the issues of dissemination associated with the National Spatial Data Infrastructure (NSDI)". The vision is readily extendible to a global context. Boxall feels any discussion of "Digital Earth' (DE), the 'Global Spatial Data Infrastructure' (GSDI), and 'Distributed Geolibraries' should be framed around the broadest definitions of information and infrastructures; namely to include and focus upon the people, technology and organisations which give rise to and sustain such infrastructures'.

An early significant effort at establishing a digital spatial library was the Alexandria Digital Library at the University of California Santa Barbara. The Alexandria Digital Library was one of six federally funded library projects. The U.S. National Science Foundation founded it in early 1994. The Library's collection and services focus on georeferenced information: maps, images, data sets, and other information sources with links to geographic locations. Much of the information in the collection was primarily of the University's service area, or Southern California.

A key aspect of the collection is the ability to perform data queries and retrieve results by geography location. The basic means of describing and finding information is with a geographic footprint. A footprint depicts the location on the surface of the earth associated with either an object in the collection such as a map, remote sensed image, or aerial photograph, or with a user's query. The footprint may be represented as a point or polygon, with latitude and longitude coordinates. As a user queries the collection through a user interface, the user creates a footprint or an interactive map to indicate the area of interest.

The query area is matched with the object footprints in the metadata to retrieve relevant objects about the query area. This approach to query structure allows the user to choose arbitrary query areas and is not limited to geographic areas with place names. The objects in the collection that fall within a particular query area do not have to have the names associated with them that the user enters for a text based query. By translating a user's textbased query into a footprint query for a certain geographic area, the user can retrieve all types of information about a location such as remote sensed images, data sets, aerial photographs, and textual information. The catalog for the Alexandria Digital Library is configured for searches that will retrieve objects that are either in an online format or physical location as a map.

Using the Alexandria Digital Library as a model, the Idaho Geospatial Data Center was started in 1996 by a team of geographers, geologists, and librarians. The aim of the team was the establishment of digital library of public domain geographic data for the state of Idaho. As a theoretical and practical foundation for their digital spatial collection, which they termed a 'geolibrary,' the team used a set of parameters as defined by Goodchild. Goodchild defined a geolibrary's components as including a browser or specialised software application running on the user's computer and providing access to the geolibrary through a computer network. A geolibrary also includes a 'basemap' or geographic frame of reference for the browser's queries.

A basemap would provide an image of an area corresponding to the geographical extent of geolibrary collection. The basemap would depend on the scale of the search being performed from a large geographic area, such as a state, or a smaller location, as a city block. A gazetteer or index that would link place names to a map would also be included. A large collection of collection catalogs would be maintained on distributed computer servers. The servers would be accessed over a network with the browser, using basic server-client architecture.

A geolibrary would ideally provide open access to many types of information with geographic referenced queries regardless of the storage media Using a grant from the Idaho Board of Education's Technology Incentive Programme, the team built a geographic digital data repository or the Idaho GeoSpatial Data Center (IGDC). The library contained a number of digital geospatial datasets that was searchable through a flexible browsing tool. The collection contained a number of public domain information such as Digital Line Graphs and Digital Raster Graphics from the United States Geological Survey and U.S. Bureau of the Census TIGER boundary files for the state of Idaho. The site provided an interactive visual analysis of selected demographic/economic data for Idaho counties.

The site also contained interactive links to other Idaho and national spatial data repositories. A key aspect of the IGDC's collection was the development of the GeoLibrary's browser, which was implemented using MicroSoft Visual Basic 5.0 and ESRI MapObjects technology. The interface of the browser consisted of three panels resembling the Microsoft Outlook user interface. A first panel, a map panel, would be used to explore the geographic coverage of the geolibrary and to select an area of interest.

A second panel in the interface was where the query would be performed. The final panel is where the query results would be displayed for analysis and to download spatial data. In many ways, librarians are well aware of the ideas outlined in the discussion on the concepts and components for digital data infrastructure. Library collections and services in electronic form, such as a digital library, integrate many aspects of the client-server architecture in providing access to materials in an online distributed environment. Digital libraries have in them collections of digital information objects of various formats in an ordered database defined by descriptive data standards.

Organised in a regular manner, the database is searchable using query applications via a user interface, usually through an online catalog. Information is compartmentalised in short descriptions using metadata tags to ease search and retrieval applications. The overall structure is guided by administrative oversight that takes into account the needs of the various users involved in the community. Researchers, such as Goodchild, envision an intersection of the concepts of the digital library and that of the spatial data infrastructure in a sort of 'geolibrary'.

Researcher envisions a geolibrary as a library filled with "georeferenced information that can have a geographic footprint.' Including multimedia, images, and music that could be assigned a location attribute, geolibraries would thus extend beyond the scope of a traditional map library and provide new services and resources for users to discover. The survey of the characteristics of spatial data databases and related infrastructure indicate the involvement of many different factors in assembling a data infrastructure. However, in addition to data providers, databases, metadata, data networks, technology, and institutional arrangements, there is also a significant in organisational and human resource factors.

Researchers offer six talking points that are essential to consider in building a spatial data infrastructure. These include technology, policies and standards, human resources, institutional arrangements, spatial data and metadata, and data networks. They suggest that spatial data infrastructure should not recreate the wheel in its technology development. It would be prudent to look at what information technology has accomplished to date, and then integrate that knowledge with GIS expertise, regardless of the difficulties involved. Integration of existing technology also applies to standards and policies. Standards enhance communication and development with a common language and concepts, leading to guidelines that affect architecture, processes, methods, or policies.

There should be a common consensus of minimal guidelines that can accommodate those working with geospatial data, retrieval, and discovery. User-guided development is also critical when examining the human resources side of GIS information and technology. Further, the use of qualified researchers and developers is essential. To create institutional frameworks, agreements have to be certified to establish national, regional, and global spatial data infrastructure. These spatial data infrastructures should be created over the geographic data, stored in the spatial databases, and their description in rich, descriptive metadata. Finally, open systems and ease of access is of strategic importance to ensure quality and accuracy from remote systems.

The need for data description standards for digital geospatial data is especially apparent in the proliferation of WebGis applications in the wake of spatial data distribution enabling initiatives, such as the NSDI. WebGIS (also known as Internet GIS) describes a type of geographic information system. WebGIS basically consists of client, server, and network model, wherein the client is integrated in a Web browser. While creating many opportunities for librarians in making available unique geospatial datasets, the tremendous growth in WebGIS has created many challenges for libraries in trying to incorporate digital geospatial data in their services and legal considerations in the use of distributed data.

WEB GIS AND LIBRARIES

In recent years the number and scope of WebGIS applications has grown tremendously. In their survey of WebGIS applications, Researchers discuss a wide number of interactive mapping sites available on the Internet. They note that many users of the Internet have already experienced using WebGIS software tools through interactive mapping tools available on the Internet. Such sites include: Yahoo Maps, National Map, and GoogleEarth Other WebGIS applications that are available on the Internet give access to a varying amount of specialised geospatial data.

Many local government Web sites for city and county governments across the United States offer interactive mapping sites such as the City of Albuquerque and City of Durham for users to access technical data about their municipalities. These mapping sites give access to socioeconomic, demographic, and planning data. Many government sites use ESRI software products such as ArcGIS and ArcWEB services to facilitate data searches for information.

Other WebGIS applicatiosn include environmental planning, agricultural planning wetlands management, archaeological research, health planning research, transportation planning, citizen political participation and education planning. Other developments in WebGIS include different data visualisations to offer unique perspectives on information for analytical purposes, such as three-dimensional modeling and combinations of software such as multimedia and WebGIS to offer comprehensive views of geospatial data A net effect of the increasingly popularity of WebGIS. The popularity of WebGIS applications among the public has led to unequal data distribution across the Internet, since bandwidth is constrained.

In their study of WebGIS, Yang identify two issues related to improving access to digital geospatial data on the Interent. The first issue concerns the sharing of and interoperability for heterogeneous data among different systems, different communities, and different users. The second issue is a quality of service issue, that of how to improve the system performance so data are delivered to the users within a reasonable time span. In regards to the first issue, the authors identify international organisational efforts at creating accepted conventions in data descriptive standards in regards to interoperability and data access. The strides being made by the aforementioned organisations and agreement between international geospatial data producers and providers is creating an environment wherein libraries have access to geospatial Web Services, such as ESRI's Geography Network and Geosptatial One Stop. Web service Internet sites essentially provide access to GIS data, software, educational and mapping, or related services.

For libraries, the services can give access to current and large amounts of geospatial data are usually available in a timely manner. In his study of how academic libraries can integrate digital geospatial data into their collections and services, Morris provides a good overview of the issues involved in trying to facilitate Web Service data in an academic library. Some drawbacks of attempting to integrate Web services into a library environment can include lingering technical issues like linking data resources, developing sustainable licensing models, and negotiating access rights to digital geospatial data.

CONCLUSION

The current environment of academic libraries are made complex with the addition of many technological factors such as: electronic bibliographic databases, numerous operating systems, Web browsers, HTML, and other markup languages. Increasing amounts of information like text, video, audio, and graphics are available in an online format. Many print materials are being digitised into electronic format. As a result of the changes in technology, librarians are required to learn about metadata and description for electronic data especially for GIS data. In digital collections, such as the FGDL, cataloging and data access issues are even more significant to librarians.

In comparing spatial data infrastructures and geolibraries Nogueras-Iso offer some discussion about their characteristics that are valid here:

- Spatial data infrastructures have an important political and social component. Government involvement in the creation and maintenance of spatial data has created a hierarchy of local, state, national and regional levels that can affect access to data.
- Standardisation processes in spatial data infrastructures involve not only the organisation of data, but also issues related to the capture and integration of these data. These problems are inherent to digital libraries but are aggravated in the case of geo-referenced data. The wide range of data users can have a significant effect on visualisation and manipulation of data.
- Necessity of interoperability with other digital library systems. As a consequence of the necessity for managing heterogeneous information, spatial data infrastructure services could be developed over the services provided by other digital library systems.

Traditionally, geospatial data has been produced in limited formats, either as a paper map, atlas, or as reproductions of aerial photographs. With the application of data processing capabilities, advances in graphic presentation, and production, digital spatial data presents unique problems in description and classification. The high variability of the subject content of digital spatial data elements, though, may require additional metadata structure for better access by users. Since the 1960s, digital spatial data has been produced in a variety of formats and in a number of carriers. Digital spatial data can include information digitised and recorded by a single researcher or be in the form of large-scale geographic coverage processed and packaged by firms like International Computer Works, Inc. Much digital spatial data is also generated by government agencies at the city, state, and federal level and is issued in a variety of formats like on CD-ROMs with computer files with accompanying attribute data in relational databases.

7

Reference Services

INTRODUCTION

Geographers often define the spatial parameters of different environments by integrating diverse data sets with locational coordinates to create an attribute-rich digital geospatial dataset. From these datasets, researchers can observe and record phenomena and create new geographic metaphors in describing the geographic spaces of places, physical or virtual. One challenge for librarians is to be cognizant of not only the spatial extent of geospatial data, but to have the ability to interpret the socioeconomic milieu, which characterises the attribute data and the environment in which it describes and to make it accessible for the user community. A second challenge is how to reinterpret traditional patron interactions in an increasingly online service environment and the best use of applications that must be used to 'push' information to the patron.

A third is how to market the library's GIS services and resources to our patrons, both old and new. A fourth challenge is how instruction and instructional support must be reconfigured to meet the needs of a variety of users, including librarians, with a range of skills and knowledge levels. The final challenge is instructing patrons to achieve appropriate levels of information competencies.

This chapter will examine the 'new world' that reference librarians find themselves in today, how they may approach the challenges of geospatial reference, and inculcate information competencies and lifelong learning skills in their patrons.

SPATIAL THINKING

Any discussion on reference services must begin with a definition of what it means to work with geospatial data. To work effectively with geospatial data requires the librarian and the user to understand spatial concepts, tools used to create representations of geospatial data, and the cognitive processes used to frame questions in a geospatial manner. The Geographical Committee of the National Research Council suggests, "It depends on understanding the meaning of space and using the properties of space as a vehicle for structuring problems, for finding answers, and for expressing solutions. By visualising relationships within spatial structures, we can perceive, remember, and analyse the static and, via transformations, the dynamic properties of objects and the relationships between objects.'

We can use representations in a variety of modes and media to describe, explain, and communicate about the structure, operation, and function of those objects and their relationships'. Many of the elements identified in this passage are currently activities done by reference librarians, such as 'structuring problems' are a function of the reference interview. However, for many librarians, providing reference services using geospatial data is a new, sometimes overwhelming experience. There are different levels of GIS services libraries can offer.

These range from high-level, which require a full GIS set-up, to mid-level, which utilise Web-based GIS applications and require user input, to low-level, which uses online static maps. In 1997, the Association of Research Libraries (ARL) surveyed their research library members who participated in the GIS literacy project. Of the 72 respondents, 64 reported that they provide GIS services, either at the library or at academic departments offering GIS. Among libraries that offer GIS services but do not administer them, the most common activity is offering guidance in finding appropriate data sets. For those libraries that do not have a GIS unit, GIS services are offered at the general reference desk. Librarians use a variety of hardware; platforms; and software.

The training offered by the Literacy Project was aimed primarily at documents and map librarians. Most of the respondents also had training by GIS software providers or GIS coursework. Technical support for GIS hardware or software was provided by library staff at 51 institutions. GIS patrons were primarily students and faculty/staff, although there were a number of users from community, business, and government.

A 2005 survey examined the use of GIS implementation within 168 academic libraries in institutions classed as Master's Colleges and Universities I and II. Almost a third of the respondents either currently support or plan to implement GIS services in the future. Only half of the libraries surveyed have staff devoted to GIS part time. Librarians had to have knowledge of a range of hardware, platforms, software. Further, training is variable, from no training, to training outside of the library, to on-site training that itself ranged from one-on-one instruction to the use of group or individual tutorial programmes.

Further, the collection resources ranged from Internet resources, software package data, reference databases with spatial data, archives, and institutional research. Staffing levels were widely divergent, ranging from full-time employees who assist with GIS in addition to other duties to student workers who were knowledgeable about GIS. Finally, academic patrons' interests, specialties, and areas of interest included geography, geology, natural resources, business, engineering, sociology, political science, environmental science, biology, landscape architecture, planning, history, and nursing.

The findings of these, and other surveys, touch on four of the challenges:

1. Interpreting the socioeconomic milieu, which characterises the attribute data and the environment in which it describes and making it accessible for the user community,

2. Reinterpreting the reference interview,
3. Reconfiguring instruction and instructional support, and
4. Instructing patrons to achieve appropriate levels of information competencies.

INTERPRETING THE MILIEU OF SPATIAL DATA

Traditional reference is "a mediated, one-on-one service that intervenes, and stands ready to intervene, at the information seeker's point of need. That need ... is every information seeker's universal predicament of wanting to move forward but being unable to progress until some missing information is found". Today's information seekers want and need that gap filled with as little interruption as possible, so they can continue where they left off. Further, users want support in *their use of information* instead of *their seeking of information*.

Today's users of geospatial data also require simple yet stable means of data distribution, innovative data discovery and interpretation mechanisms, and enhanced spatial content publishing, including the means to create and propagate spatial data beyond the academy while retaining local control of the data content. Multilingual support is becoming a necessity with geospatial content crossing boundaries and users forging new, global partnerships. For this new patron group, librarians need to be well versed in geospatial and geographic data discovery tools and support.

A quick review of job opportunities illustrate minimum requirements for librarians working with geospatial data: develop and manage spatial and numeric data resources and services; support teaching, research, and engagement; provide consultation to faculty and students; develop instructional modules; handle and create data documentation and research resources; and establish configurations for GIS workstations. This has implications for the traditional roles of librarians in collection development, which now has an intensive data focus; cataloging and creating metadata; current awareness and selective dissemination of information; scholarly activity

may need to be re-projected while data may need conversion. Is there information accompanying the dataset that describes if these activities need to be performed or how best to perform them? Ease of access is also a basic question, from one large download to numerous extractions of data that are then recompiled. Licensing and pricing concerns may also require examination of redistribution rights for faculty and/or researchers.

Additional questions may concern types of service, such as image, feature, or geo-coding, access protocols, and reliability and uptime. Also, for all beta or demonstration content/services, *caveat emptor*. Kinikin and Hench's survey of smaller academic libraries reported significantly different results from that of larger academic libraries. Of the 11 smaller academic libraries surveyed, 8 of the libraries indicated fewer than two users per week with only one library reporting more than five users per week. Houser describes the joint Library and GIS/Data Lab services at the University of Kansas Libraries. After the integration of the Map Library and GIS lab services, the number of data consultations with library staff increased from 82 to almost 160 interactions during 2003-2004, with the 2005 monthly averages showing an increase of 16 per cent over the previous year.

As with the Kinikin and Hench study, more granular statistics were not available. However, longitudinal study from the Yale Map Collection GIS Service indicated that the average amount of time spent per consultation with a GIS librarian is about 4 hours. The Yale statistics also indicate that faculty and doctoral students typically average about twice as much time per consultation than undergraduate or master's level students. The Yale Map Collection GIS Service staff average approximately 155 consultations a year, with faculty and students generally making four visits each, most face-to-face. However, it is not uncommon during complex, long-term projects for the librarians to have multiple consults with a single patron.

The Yale statistics show that 30 consults between one patron and a GIS librarian. Abbott and Argentati saw the provision "of access to spatial information and software tools and facilitating intellectual access to GIS concepts and applications" as a 'natural evolution and extension of existing library services and expertise". However, researchers and librarians have also warned about the complexity and technical difficulty of GIS reference.

For example, a staff person may need a minimum of at least 20 hours to complete a GIS tutorial that will allow him or her to begin working on complicated research problems. One also must be practical. Finding or processing spatial data usually takes twice as long as initially expected. Basic cartographic elements and their placements require a knowledge of map display and rudimentary statistics to insure that appropriate statistical measures are used to calculate and display information. Reference librarians also need to be aware that paper maps may themselves be essential in determining preliminary data patterns or trends, for collecting additional data, or may themselves be repurposed to digital formats.

Visualisation and analysis of digital spatial data is in itself a complex process, involving the understanding and use of legacy materials in other formats, and requiring the reference librarian to delve into new, uncharted areas or to think in new ways about content and context of information. Questions may be asked at all stages of a research process or arise serendipitously. In addition to the traditional interview, reference librarians will need to know other service parameters for their GIS users.

These include basic access questions, such as whether they have access to the necessary data or what are the rules regarding access to a GIS laboratory. Other issues include knowing the appropriate software and hardware for that researcher, if there is enough data storage capacity, and how data may be distributed. Reference librarians may have to determine if there is a need to obtain GIS assistance from campus staff or other expert users and the types and levels of training and related resources required for the project. Librarians may be asked about purchasing and licensing of GIS software, if there are campus GIS list serves, and what commonly used datasets are housed and maintained by the library.

The availability of grant sources to support GIS development and use in research projects, collection development, staff training, and new services will be a frequently asked question by doctoral students and research and teaching faculty. Traditional maps and statistical publications are static resources, with no capability for the researcher or librarian to merge, create, or modify data spontaneously. GIS adds an opportunity for librarians to become producers of information as well as enter into collegial, scholarly relationships with fellow academic researchers. However, entering into new publishing or scholarly relationships require reference librarians to understand not just the traditional reference question but also the acquisition and use of geospatial resources. A clear understanding of intellectual property, data redistribution rights, and derivative rights are critical in the reuse or manipulation of geospatial data, whether public domain, public sector, or leased proprietary data.

Opportunities and challenges presented by new information technologies redefine intellectual property issues around the world, almost on a daily basis. Since researchers have responsibilities to promulgate their research, retaining rights over how their results are used is essential, especially for long-term or multiyear studies. Intellectual property issues can influence their ability to distribute their products. Reference librarians who work with researchers need to be current to be effective.

For example, national and international projects may be affected by confidentiality clauses that may exist in software licences, use and access agreements for geospatial data, project documents, or funding arrangements. For librarians who are acquiring, supporting, or providing access to researchers, contract terms and/or license language will need to accommodate different countries or different legal jurisdictions. Longhorn suggest that "both staff and institutions should recognise their rights and responsibilities in such cases, and stated policies should be in place, including appropriate non-disclosure and confidentiality agreements and forms, both in contracts of employment and perhaps even on a project basis".

Since university policies vary, the reader is asked to consult the General Counsel's Office of their university as well as to review the policies of the corporate entity owning rights to the original datasets. Ethics also come into play. Researchers conducting research with groups of people must go under an *institutional review board* (IRB). Any study involving observation of or interaction with human subjects that originates at an academic or research setting, including course projects, reports, or research papers, must be reviewed and approved by the IRB for the protection of human subjects in research and research related activities. The IRB ensures that data about study participants are kept confidential, secure, and, if health related, that the data complies with the parameters of the federal Health Information Portability and Accountability Act. Further, in academic libraries that host human subjects datasets, researchers are responsible for obtaining approval of their research projects from the appropriate local or private IRB responsible for assuring protection of human research subjects.

For example, if a library hosts research data from a local or national study, and students need to access it as part of a class project, IRB approval may be needed before access to the system is provided. Librarians should be familiar with what requirements must be formally filed and approved, as in the IRB, for access to certain datasets or even the GIS, if bought for that project. Understanding how to operate within current intellectual property and copyright concerns is also crucial in developing resource management policies and procedures as part of a research team when working with multiple private and public sector vendors. If the reference librarian has part of his or her time assigned to a research project, he or she may be considered a research collaborator. Either as an official or unofficial member of a research project, or as a reference guide, the librarian may be held accountable should liability issues arise. As a result, librarians seek to adapt their behaviour, resources, and services to better serve their clientele and define their own roles.

EVALUATING AND ASSESSING SERVICES

Library measurement has been defined as "the collection and analysis of objective data describing library performance on which evaluation judgements can be based". It has been suggested that librarians use effectiveness, cost effectiveness, cost benefit, and performance measurement as measures for evaluation which can be related to inputs, outputs and outcomes. Inputs are system resources, such as library budgets and finances, staffing, and print and digital resources. Outputs are the activities the system provides, such as transactions, hours of access, the availability, use, and usability of resources. Although there have been numerous reinventions of the role of librarians, the quantitative and qualitative measures by which they determine how well they are performing have not changed.

Input measures, such as volumes held, serial subscriptions, expenditures, and staffing are not correlated to output measures, typically transactions. This is compounded by counting data downloads that can only measure what the library does have, not what it does not. More rigourous market analysis may be required to adequately assess use, identify shortcomings, and predict demand. When creating a new service area or services, quantitative and qualitative measures allow library management to determine the implications of a major change in order to deal with all of the elements that must be addressed.

Using quantitative indicators, such as frequencies of interactions, and qualitative indicators, such as effectiveness, libraries can "increase their visibility, restructure to meet the needs of their users, achieving their objective of remaining the pre-eminent source of information within the academy". In addition, statistics and measures are powerful planning tools that show emerging trends that require additional resources, workflow processes, training needs, staffing changes, and entrepreneurial opportunities. They also allow comparison with peer institutions and aid areas planning a new service to project staff, instructional, and technology demands. Problems with library measures are legion.

Traditional counts of productivity may underestimate the actual volume of work performed, as the actual volume of business is becoming more complex to gauge. Ways of counting are problematic. Few libraries use their reference counts to determine frequently asked questions or monitoring changes in the types and complexity of questions asked. In the interest of accumulating higher numbers, these qualitative aspects are often lost. Even if the question comes through an 'Ask-A' service, there is no systematic coding or review of the questions, recording the length of time spent on answering it, or the number of and types of resources consulted to answer a particularly exotic question.

Repurposing and measuring existing operations may provide more effective library measures. For example, Steinhart's description of the benefits of sharing data provides additional measures that could address institutional and academic support as well as outreach and partnerships. The number of inter-organisational activities and reuse of geographic data by external organisations certainly count as outreach or academic-community partnership activity. Data error correction can be counted as response to user feedback and the use of geospatial data may be counted as part of public distribution requirements. Training and education also measure professional development as well as meeting institutional or organisational competencies in the use of geospatial data.

Definition of quality of services also varies and, in the library literature, the concepts of quality and satisfaction are used interchangeably, even though the two are not necessarily the same. Further, instruments meant to measure service quality are often better measures of satisfaction. However, service quality is seen as the antecedent of satisfaction, that is, without service quality, satisfaction cannot be measured. Assessing customer satisfaction may be more critical if there are other service providers or competing resources for users than just the library's GIS services and resources.

Sometimes, the difference is never clarified on the questionnaire or survey. Take the example of the service quality measure, LibQual+™, created in 1999 as a standardised measure of library service quality by the Association of Research Libraries (ARL) in collaboration with Texas A&M University. LibQual+™, measures library users' evaluations of service quality on four dimensions: 'Affect of Service,' 'Library as Place,' 'Personal Control,' and 'Access to Information.' The structure of LibQual+™ mirrors that of SERVQUAL™, an industry- based service performance measure. Although LibQual+™ is described as a measure of service quality rather than satisfaction, users of the questionnaire frequently consider it a measure of the latter. In addition, many library measures have a problem with validity and reliability.

For example, performance-only assessment is the most valid framework for gauging customer satisfaction when using LibQual+™ or SERVQUAL™. By eliminating the difference scores in these instruments, the problems with reliability and validity are eliminated and respondents will need less time to complete them. Another suggestion is to use a shorter version of the LibQual+™ with just performance-only ratings, as in the case of the SERVPERF, the performance- only variant of SERVQUAL. Libraries may also choose to use assessment guidelines in higher education as a model for library or service assessment.

Dow describes how the University of Rochester, a Carnegie 1 research university, used the American Association of Higher Education's (AAHE) *Principles of Good Practice for Assessing Student Learning*, as part of its strategic assessment. The principles identified included effective ongoing assessment, asking questions that people cared about, attentiveness to outcomes, and gathering evidence as to how and to what degree its programmes influenced the quality of effort that students and faculty invested in learning experiences. This was a departure from traditional resource-based input and output measures to define quality and impact.

The ARL New Measures agenda examines learning outcomes, research outcomes, institutional outcomes, and personal control or electronic service quality issues. Smith examined how accreditation agencies were identifying student outcomes while tying them back into institutional objectives. He suggests that a library should understand its students, not just what their knowledge and skills are when they arrive, but also what challenges they face in the future as to learning. He also suggests that a library should understand what learning outcomes are required for student success and on which dimensions of learning it should focus its efforts on. He further suggests that a library effectively measure the extent to which outcomes are achieved as well as those that are not achieved.

After all, without understanding where problems lie, there is no opportunity to correct or change them. Finally, after correcting the problems or making identified changes, is the library meeting its defined outcome? Franklin examines the relationship between a library and sponsored research activities within university settings through a review of 20 years of KPMG reports.

Using three indicators, total research and development funding at a university; total library expenditures, and library expenditures in support of sponsored research as a percentage of total library expenditures, there was a high correlation between total R&D funding and total library expenditures. Little or no correlation was found between total library expenditures and percent of library expenditures in support of sponsored research.

Little or no correlation was also found between an institution's R&D funding and percent of library expenditures in support of sponsored research. This may be due to the fact that few libraries track expenditures other than by departmental/college codes and do not track by contract or grant codes.

RECONFIGURING INSTRUCTION, TRAINING, AND INSTRUCTIONAL SUPPORT

In 1966, four skills were considered critical for understanding GIS:

1. Literacy (text),

2. Articulacy (spoken words),
3. Numeracy (mathematical notation), and
4. Graphicacy (visual communication).

All four skills enhance one's ability to communicate effectively and understand those relationships that cannot be expressed solely with text, spoken words, mathematical notation, or visually. Text, mathematics, graphics, and discourse complement one another, and all are necessary in various contexts for the successful comprehension and exchange of ideas. Balchin and Coleman argue "neither words nor numbers nor diagrams are simpler or more complex, superior or inferior. They are only more suitable or less suitable for particular purposes". For example, users may have difficulties in conveying their information needs to learn content-based image retrieval systems or to deconstruct a map. Compounding communication is recent research that suggests only a very small percentage of the general population prefer to learn by reading. Clearly, understanding when a particular communication mode is more appropriate than another is and how to use each mode effectively become essential knowledge-sets and skill-sets for librarians.

CREATING PATTERNS: INFORMATION-SEEKING MODELS

Digital geospatial data archives and repositories are directly related to specific question- answering research, which 'reflect[s] the information needs of their creators' and "tend[s] to be tailored to the specific cultures of research communities, rather than adhering to existing blueprints for access resources". Since disciplines play an important role, especially in the influence of context and search task on information seeking, the impact of the different types of conceptual models for information seeking and retrieval will impact how librarians themselves learn and instruct others in the use of geospatial information.

Such models serve different research purposes. What kind of models are there and in what ways may they help librarians to better instruct, train, and support GIS research and reference activities? Are different types of models needed for various purposes? Differences in discipline affect faculty and student information seeking skills. Individuals in the hard sciences, such as engineering and math, use a search strategy based on a specific problem-solving process while individuals in the humanities are more likely to be based on a topical interest that is extensively researched.

Understanding diverse analytical models of task-based information seeking can contribute to the development of a research area, that is, "Conceptual models may and should map reality, guide research and systematise knowledge, for example, by integration and by proposing systems of hypotheses". One such critical model on information-seeking behaviours was developed by Ellis based on Glaser and Strauss's grounded theory for data analysis. He determined six generic information behaviours: *starting, chaining, browsing, differentiating, monitoring,* and *extracting*. Each of these activities can involve a librarian.

For example, *starting* is comprised of the initial steps to finding information, such as a review of indexing and abstracting sources or consultation with a librarian in starting a literature review. *Chaining* is following 'chains of citations' between sources identified, such as following references from an initial source or following other sources that refer to an original source. *Browsing* includes scanning of published journals and tables of contents, as well as references and abstracts of other literature reviews or bibliographies. *Differentiating* is qualifying sources of information to ensure relevance in one's information search. *Monitoring* is a current awareness activity in which one regularly examines core journals, conferences, new books, and catalogs of resources via hand searching or by using current awareness services. *Extracting* selectively identifies and acquires relevant material from resources.

Ellis notes:

- ... the detailed interrelation or interaction of the

features in any individual information seeking pattern will depend on the unique circumstances of the information seeking.activities.of.the.person. concerned.at.that.particular.point.in.time.

Similar to Kuhlthau's model in terms of the various types of activities or tasks carried out within the overall information-seeking process, Ellis's empirically based model is considered authoritative in its classification of types of information seeking behaviours.

Building on Ellis' work, four new areas have been added to his model:

1. Accessing,
2. Verifying,
3. Networking, and
4. Information managing.

With the increasing dependence on online resources, Meho and Tibbo suggest that, "Although not all of these new features are information searching or gathering activities, they are tasks that have significant roles in enhancing information retrieval and facilitating research". *Accessing* is a critical component of information seeking because without access, one may miss essential pieces of data to answer one's question. In addition, given the importance of archival materials and other forms of primary sources in geospatial data, librarians may need to investigate why access to information is denied and to intervene to obtain the items. *Verifying* are those activities that establish the accuracy and authority of the data or information.

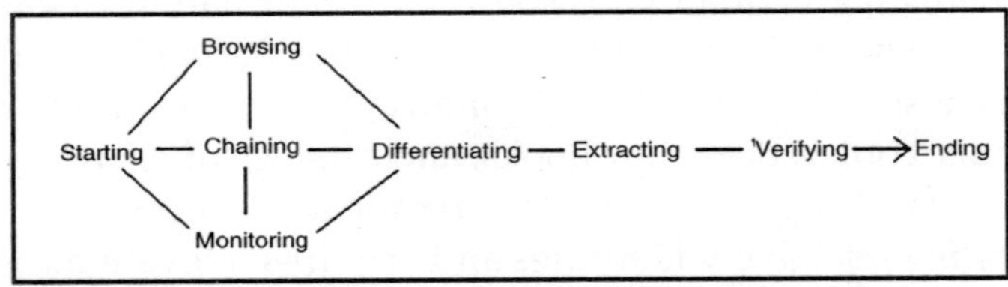

Fig 7.1 A Process Chain of Ellis's Information Seeking Activities

Librarians and researchers should consider bias and lack of reliability and accuracy in materials produced by governmental agencies as well as private sector organisations. Detailed metadata on lineage of data can alert users to discrepancies in data and in use of such information. Data comparison with other sources can also point out errors in data. *Networking* are those activities associated with communicating or maintaining relationships with fellow researchers or governmental and non-governmental organisations, or individuals who could provide access to or verify information or data. The final information-seeking activity is *information managing,* which emphasises the importance of filing, archiving, and organising the information used to facilitate one's research.

Ellis, Meho, and Tibbo conclude that the activities identified in their studies may not be entirely or always sequential. However, Meho and Tibbo suggest that the information-seeking behaviours of social scientists are divided into four interrelated stages, *searching, accessing, processing,* and *ending,* that then contain a number of activities. For example, during the *searching* stage, all of Ellis' activities and Meho and Tibbo's networking activity begin. During the *accessing* stage, decision-making to continue on to *processing* or to return to *searching* is based on acquisition of requested materials. It is the author's belief that *information managing* also begins in this stage to document acquired items.

During the *processing stage,* chaining, extracting, differentiating, verifying, and information-managing activities begin or continue as do syntheses and analyses. There will be constant motion between the searching, accessing, and/or the processing stages until the *ending* stage, when the project is completed. Ellis' existing and extended models, which examined primarily social scientists, are expanded upon by Palmer, who suggests that scientists and humanists use primarily four research activities: confirmation searching, discovery searching, collecting, and consultation. Further, there are important distinctions in source selection, decision making, and how materials are used, which can impact reference services and support to research faculty. To act as a consultant, reference staff need to increase significantly their own understanding of the different research processes and information-seeking behaviours.

In addition to activity models, reference librarians also need to be familiar with various cognitive models for information seeking. Ingwersen's cognitive model examines how the search process itself affects information retrieval. He suggests that the all facets of the information-seeking system, from the user's questions, documents, or objects retrieved, interaction with intermediaries, such as search engines, and, by extension, librarians, are the result of explicit or implicit cognitive models of the domain of interest at that particular point. Ingwersen also suggests that the user experiences various cognitive transformations from where he or she begins the information-seeking process to the point where a search is successful in identifying objects to answer the user's questions. Therefore, users usually have implicit models of their information need or work task that they can tell individuals or query systems.

These cognitive structures and their transformations need to be effectively communicated throughout the information system as identified previously, again which includes the reference librarian. What is even more crucial is the cognitive framework of the reference librarian, since his or her knowledge structures "are determined by the individual and its social/collective experiences, education, etc." The librarian and, ultimately, the user, are influenced by his or her environment "which may possess social conventions, preferences, and collective cognitive structures adhering to domains".

This extends to the transformative aspect of knowledge and the importance of effective communication, since "elements of a communicated message must be perceived or recognised, in order to allow the message to transform into a new state of knowledge. This transformation does not necessarily produce a simple accumulation of categories or concepts, but can be seen as a reconfiguration, a restructuring or a compression in part of the recipient's knowledge structures". Järvelin and Wilson expand on a cognitive model and address how user-perceived tasks must be considered. They suggest that individuals interpret the same objective task differently, particularly for what is perceived to be a complex task.

Task complexity entails a number of variables: "repetition, analysability, *a priori* determinability, the number of alternative paths of task performance, outcome novelty, number of goals and conflicting dependencies among them, uncertainties between performance and goals, number of inputs, cognitive and skill requirements, as well as the time-varying conditions of task performance". How the user perceives the task is the basis for the actual performance of the task, the interpretation of his or her information needs, and the decision making to ensure satisfaction, or successful completion of the task. Järvelin and Wilson consider five classes of tasks. These are automatic information processing tasks; normal information processing tasks; normal decision tasks; known, genuine decision tasks; and genuine decision tasks.

These range from simple computational tasks that are *a priori* completely determinable and structured to decision-making tasks, where information, result, or process is unknown, and the first task must be to create the information-seeking structure. Byström and Järvelin examined what types of information are sought through which types of channels, from what kinds of sources, in which kinds of tasks. They determined that as task complexity increases the needs for domain information and problem-solving information increases.

Complexity also increases the proportion of general-purpose sources and decreases that of problem- and fact-oriented sources. Finally, complexity decreases the success of information seeking, decreases the internality of channels, and increases the number of sources. There are a number of studies that show clear differences in student and faculty information-seeking behaviour across disciplines and in how faculty and

Conceptual models ensure the transferability of competencies across systems, and improve synthesis and evaluative thinking. Interactivity is an attribute highly valued by generation Xs and Ys. It provides active and situated learning through simulations as well as opportunity for online collaboration with other learners and instructors. Interactive mapping and direct manipulation of data to create graphic display mirrors many simulation and real-time activities with which users have grown up. Geospatial data is also very media rich, with multiple formats and output styles and indexing or descriptive metadata.

Adaptive learning systems permit a variety of presentation styles, and also allow users to index and organise data for their own use. Users will wait to the last possible moment to learn a new system for a class project or paper. Just-in-time, or point-of-need, delivery provides training at the exact time and place that it is needed for the user to complete a specific task. Adaptive instructional methods emphasise user-centric environments. In this type of environment, the learner takes responsibility for his or her own learning and the librarian is seen more as an expert guide and facilitator. However, tutorials are best seen as complementary or as supplementary instruction rather than as an effective stand-alone teaching tool. Gutierrez and Wang found that "students who regularly used the library benefited the most" from literacy instruction.

Their study reinforces the argument that research skills require practice, that is, a single, traditionally conducted library research class will not significantly improve the ability of the user to perform research. In addition to user education, librarians have important roles in curriculum development. Serving on a curriculum committee provides reference librarians a stronger voice in the planning and implementation of a curriculum's information management component and information resources by students. Librarians also become more involved as a resource person for faculty, instructional support staff, and students, ranging from basic assistance or instruction at the reference desk to resource management and utilisation to consultation with faculty and students. How librarians conceptualise government information should be changed.

Researcher suggests that librarians "teach faculty and student researchers why, not just how, to use government information rather than agency organisation and its function". This concept reduces the emphasis on government information as "a separate specialisation, based on its provenance, rather than its subject content". This approach clearly favours the range and breadth of GIS as both a subject within a discipline as well as a discipline in its own right. Understanding the user's information-seeking need, based on identification of the user's discipline and question, can create better use of government information as well as better users of that information. Users generally do not care how the information is organised as to agency, division, or department, just 'does it answer my question?' This applies not just to search skills, but also to our 'how to use the library on X' lectures, instructions, workshops, and tutorials.

Both broad exploration and specific searching have their particular benefits dependent on the stage of the research process, or a preferred way of learning, which also affect instruction. Järvelin and Wilson emphasise the use of conceptual models to "map reality, guide research and systematise knowledge, for example, by integration and by proposing systems of hypotheses". Teaching and research models developed by reference staff should focus on developing problem solving skills, critical thinking skills, and effective information-seeking behaviours. By focusing on how "... information contributes to their critical thinking within the context of a discipline", librarians will be able to create effective instructional and training materials for their users.

CONCLUSION

There are a number of issues that are still of concern in offering reference GIS services. In addition to establishing standards for GIS centers and services to reduce variance in user needs and expectations across academic libraries, reference librarians have several other key opportunities in collection development, instruction on accessing spatial information and software tools, and facilitating user knowledge of GIS concepts and applications. GIS is an example of an interdisciplinary tool that is used across colleges, departments, and academic administration. Regardless of the size of the college or university, libraries may be the point-of-access for students, faculty, and community users. Further, since GIS is data centered and makes use of many secondary and tertiary products, the library is a natural choice to establish a GIS service point.

More importantly, GIS offers libraries a new venue to create, market, and distribute specialised content. Finally, as the level of reference services using GIS data increases, so does the level of complexity and base knowledge the librarian must have to interact effectively with advanced users or participate on research teams. This has implications for continuing professional development and library education. However, the rewards of working in a more dimensional manner with students and faculty, as well as highlighting the library's support of research at the university level, are well worth the time and effort involved.

Bibliography

Aghatise, E.: *Automation and Academic Library Structure*, Maharashtra: Pune Publication, 2004.

Anderson, B.: *Library Management Styles and Structures: A Need to Rethink*, Toronto: Thomson Nelson, 2008.

Bandyopadhyay, N.: *Library Automation as a Source of Management Information*, Hyderabad: Economic and Political Weekly Press, 2005.

Bertozzi, S.: *Management Information: The Academic Library*, Maharashtra: Pune Publications, 2006.

Chattopadhyay, A.: *Principles of Information Systems for Management*, Hyderabad: Economic and Political Weekly Press, 2005.

Cockburn, A.: *Management Information Systems can Help Senior Library Managers*, New Delhi: Long Life Publication, 2006.

D'Cunha, J.: *Performance Measurement*, Toronto: Thomson Nelson, 2008.

Doezema, J.: *Measuring Academic Library Performance: A Practical Approach*, Maharashtra: Pune Publication, 2000.

Gajic-Veljanoski, O.: *Strategic Planning for Library Management*, Toronto: Thomson Nelson, 2007.

Jana, S.: *A Model of a Management Information System for Library and Information Service Managers*, New Delhi: Long Life Publication, 2003.

Jeffreys, S.: *Effective Library and Information Centre Management*, Toronto: Thomson Nelson, 2006.

Kapur, Rajesh.: *Personal Management Skills*, Maharashtra: Pune Publications, 2001.

Kempadoo, K.: *Computer Potential for Management Information,* Hyderabad: Self Publications, 2000.

Mackenzie, A.G.: *Academic Libraries in Contraction: Facts, Theories and Fancies,* USA: Aslib Proceedings, 1996.

Madhusudana, B.: *Management Information and Decision Support Systems in Libraries,* London: Weekly Press, 2002.

Nag, M.: *Management Information Gleaned from Automated Library Systems,* Hyderabad: Economic and Political Weekly Press, 2006.

Payne, P. and Willers, J.M.: *Using Management Information in a Polytechnic Library.* NJ: Journal of Librarianship, 1999.

Rodger, E.M.: *Evaluation of Library and Information Services in Times of Economic Restraint,* UK: Outlook on Research Libraries, 2000.

Sparrow, E.: *Management Information in the British Library Humanities and Social Sciences Division,* UK: Journal of Librarianship, 2002.

Index